Journalism

A Critical History

Martin Conboy

SAGE Publications
London • Thousand Oaks • New Delhi

First published 2004

SAGE Publications Ltd
1 Oliver's Yard
55 City Road
London EC1Y 1SP

SAGE Publications Inc.
2455 Teller Road
Thousand Oaks, California 91320

SAGE Publications India Pvt Ltd
B-42, Panchsheel Enclave
Post Box 4109
New Delhi 110 017

British Library Cataloguing in Publication data

A catalogue record for this book is available
from the British Library

ISBN 0-7619-4099-5
ISBN 0-7619-4100-2 (pbk)

Library of Congress Control Number available

Typeset by C&M Digitals (P) Ltd., Chennai, India
Printed in Great Britain by Cromwell Press Ltd, Trowbridge, Wiltshire

Lara Mathilda

Für-niemand-und-nichts-Stehen.
Unerkannt,
für dich
allein.
(Paul Celan)

Contents

Acknowledgements

This book is the product of a great deal of collective effort which has unselfishly and often, I suspect, unknowingly guided my reading and writing or even, quite simply, created the space necessary. Whether I have made best use of all of this assistance is the task of the reader to judge. It has been a privilege in the course of writing to be able to take the time to involve myself in the study of many specialist texts which deal with the historical aspects of journalism. These include original manuscripts, microfilm and a wide range of published work, both contemporary and out of print. I have been absorbed by the depth and range of material which there is to explore. I hope in return that I have been able to produce not just a synopsis but rather a synthesis which will enable students of journalism to develop an understanding of its historical complexity and wealth. Many cohorts of students both at Potsdam University and the Surrey Institute of Art and Design University College have played their part in contributing their enthusiasms to the long gestation of this work in their listening, questioning and participation, confirming that there can be a genuine link between research and teaching in the interests of students and the wider academic community.

As a great deal of the research for this book has taken place in libraries, I must thank the many librarians who have assisted by their support and by their meticulous attention to a variety of requests. The librarians at Colindale Newspaper Library and the British Library have been efficient and enormously co-operative. From among all the smiling faces at the library in Farnham, I must single out Gwynneth Wilkey and Lorraine Langdon who have provided a level of expertise which would be the envy of any library in the world.

A special debt of gratitude is reserved for Jim Beaman, Jane Taylor, Bob Turner and Martin Pover without whose support, in different ways, in the most trying of circumstances, this project could never have been completed. They may not be as aware as they should be of the impact they have had in enabling this book to reach the publication stage. They illustrate not only the truth of Hazlitt's comment that 'honesty is militant' but in addition that it always emerges, in institutional terms, from below. Jane Taylor, in particular, has provided inspirational leadership in ways which indicate that there is no incompatibility between managerial excellence and academic integrity, a rare feat these days and one for which she deserves more credit. The sleuth-eyed Delwyn Swingewood has earned a special thanks. The Surrey Institute of Art and Design University College Research Fund has provided support for travel, archival materials and indexing.

Thanks are also due to Jamilah Ahmed and Julia Hall at Sage whose shared enthusiasm has moved the book from concept to production and who continue to engage creatively in the emergence of this area of the British intellectual environment.

Finally, to Simone for displaying her characteristically unflinching and unconditional optimism towards this particular project and life in general. Vorwärts, und nicht vergessen…!

Introduction

Journalism: History and Discourse

This book is an attempt to provide an accessible yet challenging history of the development of journalism in England. It will concentrate on journalism as a range of communication styles in order to emphasize the diversity which journalism has always encompassed. As it is a relatively short book dealing with a potentially vast topic, it will restrict itself chiefly to a discussion of how journalism has emerged from London within an English context. In all this, the role of London was essential in the development of English journalism: 'London and the London press was crucial. Through its press, London provided the national focus for the expression of views and transmission of information' (Harris, 1996: 51).

It will not attempt to cover the journalism of the other constituent nations of the British Isles, nor will it deal with international developments other than when they have a direct influence on journalism in England. To avoid complaints of anachronism, the book acknowledges from the outset that the term 'journalism' was introduced into the English language rather late in the day, at about the halfway stage in this account, in the 1830s. However, many of the practices and traditions of this form of public communication had been well established by then. It is to clarify how they eventually come to be formally defined as journalism that this account begins with the first experiments in printed news and opinion on contemporary events from the late sixteenth century onwards. It will seek to explore what coherence journalism has displayed over time, the better to assess its contemporary configuration. It will do this by dispensing from the outset with any notion that journalism has followed a simple evolutionary path from the margins to the centre of our culture or that it has been shaped by constant opposition to the vested interests in society. This book will demonstrate that in the process of providing an intermediary between a consuming public and social and political change, journalism has been as much involved in resistance to change as a conduit for it. The book will provide an overview which will try to capture the ways in which the range of practices which have been described as journalism came into existence and how they have been defined by the ages through which they have passed as well as helping to define them. Over four centuries, journalism has moved from the printing of events, to the publishing of opinion, to the reporting of news and then to the contemporary structured ideologies of narrative and readership. Over the same period of time, journalism has charted many key aspects of broader social and political thinking. In many ways, it is both the medium and the message of that thinking, supporting the validity of the claim that: 'The journalistic text is viewed as the product of a wide variety of cultural, technological, political and economic forces, specific to a particular society at a particular time' (McNair, 1998: 3).

Journalism has over time invigorated this social activity by opening up new areas for scrutiny. As it has done so, the political and cultural forces which enabled it to begin the process in the first place gain increasing momentum among a wider public and therefore greater legitimacy with that public. This reciprocity between practice and public has been one of the key dynamics of journalism and remains an essential part of its appeal to the present day.

Many books on the history of journalism do provide a triumphant narrative. Herd's title from 1952 *The March of Journalism*, for example, speaks of this celebratory approach. Such a narrative is expressed as its most teleological, told from the viewpoint of a triumphant ending as if inevitably destined to emerge in its present form, in the mid-Victorian *History of British Journalism* by Alexander Andrews:

> From a miserable sheet of flimsy paper, blotted with coarse letter-press, describing some fabulous event, or retailing some more than doubtful story: or, now, a mass of slavish panegyric, now of violent and undiscriminating abuse, issued stealthily, read under the breath, circulated from hand to hand unseen, we all know that our modern newspaper has sprung. But the change has been the work of more than two centuries. Dependent as it was on the progress of public enlightenment, of government liberality, of general liberty and knowledge; checked by the indifference of a people or the caprices of a party; suppressed by a king, persecuted by a parliament, harassed by a licenser, burnt by a hangman, and trampled by a mob, the newspaper has been slow in climbing to its present height. It surely must be worth while to glance back at the marks it has left in its steady though gradual ascent: to review the growth of the Giant which now awes potentates, and it may scarcely be too much to say, rules the destinies of the world. (Andrews, 2000 [1847], Vol. 1: 1)

Joad Raymond has identified the narrative task for a contemporary generation in relation to newspapers: 'We stand, then, at a juncture which invites post-revisionist narratives of the newspaper combining scholarship and sensitivity to the problems of narrative history with the sustained and integrating vision the Victorians brought to bear on the subject' (1999a: 9).

This book is a modest attempt to contribute to this goal. It seeks to recapture something of the overall chronology of journalism's development while rejecting any naïve celebration of a triumph of the political freedom of our news media. The narrative is as much characterized by rupture as by continuity, by impediments to freedom of public expression as by liberation. Over time, journalism is not a linear process of the breakdown of censorship and the evolution of political freedoms. Briggs and Burke have observed more of a zigzag, 'noting particular moments in which access to information became narrower rather than wider' (2002: 74) as indicative of the more complex path of journalism's progress. Here we will extend the varieties of media and format which have come to form what we understand as journalism which have in their turn affected the discourse of newspapers themselves as part of the journalistic ecology in the early twenty-first century.

This book will argue that there is not and never has been a single unifying activity to be thought of as journalism. On the contrary, journalism has always been associated with dispute – dispute about its value, its role, its direction, even its definition – and journalism has always been constructed as a diverse and multiple set of textual strategies, differing practices attempting to champion or challenge whatever has been the dominant version. Even though in its earliest manifestation, politics was very much to the fore, journalism has always been broader than the specifically political and it has indeed needed to be to survive. Journalism is the working and revision of a combination of novelty, information and entertainment which has the topical, even the ephemeral, very much to the fore. It is formed by a combination of elements which must be negotiated, on a regular basis, as acceptable to a readership which is commercially viable. In any history of journalism it is important to banish any thought of a predetermined agenda to its evolution. There have been significant shifts in its practice and content, shifts which this book hopes to trace. For instance, it has moved from a private exchange of intelligence to the public consumption of information, as well as from a clandestine operation to an officially sanctioned activity. Yet it has achieved its official recognition at the same pace as it has accepted an internal set of restraints to set against the older external threats of censorship. From pamphlets and newsletters to the Internet and twenty-four-hour digital television news, journalism has always evolved pragmatically, according to social and technological determinants, adapting to them and surviving, changed but not necessarily improved.

Discourse as Analytical Tool

Before the historical coining of the word journalism, we can identify aspects of a news culture and a struggle over the control of the flow of public knowledge which is fundamental to any form of journalism. Over the course of four centuries, it has been characterized by a constant experimentation and has become inflected by many generic features and methods. Its formation is characterized by such variety and the recombination of communicative elements continues from the first naming of 'diurnalists' in the mid-seventeenth century to experiments with 'blogging' today. Because of the complexity and variety of journalism throughout history, as well as its integral relationship with questions of political and economic power, it may be helpful to refer to journalism as an example of a discourse. A first definition of discourse is in terms of the co-existence of text and context and the impossibility of understanding one without the other or prioritizing one as more important than the other. Both are complex, as is their interrelationship. The relevance of this to journalism is clear. It means that we must always keep in mind the multiple relationships of journalism with society, with the economy, with politics and also as a relatively autonomous cultural practice in its own right with its own traditions. Journalism can be viewed as an intersection of many conflicting interests, some of which, at some points in history, have clearer priority than others. Discourse, in the second sense, in which it is often used in contemporary debates on language and culture, is a term influenced by the writing of Michel Foucault (1974). This too has a direct relevance to journalism, as it is predominantly conducted through language and seeks to act upon the culture in which it operates as a mirror or a catalyst, drawing much of its legitimacy from these claims. This view of discourse claims that the language used about a particular practice in turn forms the objects of which it speaks. Journalism is therefore made up of the claims and counter-claims of a variety of speakers on its behalf. What journalists say about their work, what critics and political commentators say about journalism, the perceived effects of the language of journalism on society, the patterns of popularity among readers and viewers of journalism, all take their place in defining the discourse of journalism. Discourses, according to Foucault, are also intrinsically bound up with questions of power as they give expression to the meanings and values of institutions or practices and, in doing so, claim authority for themselves. The discourse of journalism defines, describes and limits what it is possible to say with respect to journalism, whether at its margins or at its institutional core. It describes the ways in which it is possible to think about and criticize the characteristic practices of journalism. One advantage of considering journalism in this way is to de-naturalize certain common-sense assumptions made about it and enable us to criticize them and question their logic. It also assists in assessing how the dominant opinions in debates over journalism's power and value have altered over time. Certainly, over time, many aspects of journalism can be regarded discursively such as the freedom of the press, the news media as a 'Fourth Estate', the objectivity of journalism, the normative political functions of journalism or what journalism should and should not do and the often obscured economic imperative of journalism – its political economy.

Another advantage of considering journalism as a discourse is that it enables us to view news production and dissemination as creating new forms of power, as well as new forms of access to representation. Journalism has never simply contested a sort of political power which lay outside its own sphere of influence. It has always been deeply involved in the creation of power structures – particularly those involved in public communication. One of the most widespread fallacies, the Whig account of journalism (see Curran and Seaton, 1993) sees journalism as the triumphant march of the political emancipation of Western societies through the news media (Siebert, 1965). Journalism has contributed itself to this account and draws upon it as a way of legitimizing its relationship with the political status quo.

Considering journalism as a discourse disrupts this account and highlights its contested nature, as well as encouraging us to see it as the variety of practices which it has incorporated over the centuries. Much of journalism's resilience and vitality comes from an ability to adapt to changes in cultural and economic imperatives. Writing specifically about newspapers, Black sees the whole of this area of journalism's history as being profoundly informed by the changes necessary within a competitive market:

> Change is therefore a central theme in newspaper history, not only because of its occurrence, and the speed of its occurrence, but also as the awareness of change creates a sense of transience and opportunity. Each period of English newspaper history can be presented as one of transformation, shifts in content, production, distribution, the nature of competition, and the social context. (2001: 1)

Contemporary historians less keen on the historical grand narratives so favoured by the Victorians, often focus on the radical and disruptive effects of printed news on culture as a whole from its development in England in the early seventeenth century (Anderson, 1986; Sherman, 1996; Sommerville, 1996). Yet although printed news and topical opinion were facilitated through the technological innovation of printing, they corresponded to and were additive to broader cultural changes already evident in social life (Burke, 1978). Even before the development of printing, Western Europe had been witnessing a shift in the ways in which social life was represented, causing a gradual reconfiguration of patterns of communication and status which would culminate in radical consequences. From the late Middle Ages to the Early Modern period, we can observe changes in cultural conventions in the transmission of imaginative knowledge from the epic to the romance, for instance, which included more subjective aspects to human experience and which emerged from the restructuring of social formations and world-views. These involved a greater emphasis on the specifics of time and place, more interaction between protagonists and the narrative and, above all, more of a sense of the importance of human agency. This re-centring on the human was an integral part of the Renaissance or Early Modern world-view and formed part of the paradigm shift which printing was able to harness as it developed journalism as a distinct material contribution to the increasing importance of individuals in the social and political concerns of the post-medieval world. Print reinforced the greater authority of the written over the spoken and took on some of the rhetoric of spoken language to better legitimize itself in terms of custom and practice (Ong, 1982). These cultural changes were to lead to greater demands from broader sections of society for access to information about political affairs and journalism would in time provide it. The Renaissance in England saw a revitalization of interest in classical rhetoric and argumentation at the same time as the Reformation was beginning to demand an increased level of literacy to enable people to cope with a vernacular Bible and religious services. Power was being transformed into an ability to control communication. This clearly had implications for the ruling classes: 'During the first half of the sixteenth century, the English gentry came to realize that its continued access to the controls of power would depend less on birth and military prowess and more on literacy and learning' (Levy, 1982: 11).

Gossip and Rumour: the Antecedents of News

Before the formalization of communication in various forms of newsbooks and newsletters, at which point we can begin to identify certain characteristics of early journalism, all levels of society had been lubricated by the more informal exchange of information known as rumour and gossip. While the elites may have been able to communicate through charters, manuscripts, treaties and proclamations, the majority of communication was oral. Unattributed and often scurrilous, gossip provided a vicarious involvement in the affairs of others, often of higher social status, and also provided a platform for discussion of a proto-democratic nature concerning the subjects of gossip and their alleged activities. Rumour lies beside the recorded facts of history and the latest reliable information of the news. Successful newspapers and magazines and other later technological variants of journalism have always been able to match the intimacy of the kind of relationship shared by exchangers and recipients of rumour. It also shares with news an intrinsic popular appeal. Neubauer claims that 'rumour' has as its siblings 'news' and 'gossip' (1999: 1) and he adds that all three continue to appear regularly in all media of information from the newspaper to the Internet.

Our earliest records of the formal transmission of news in a modern sense comes with the *Acta Romana* which have been related through the works of classical authors such as Tacitus. They seem to refer to a variety of practices which publicized events in ancient Rome, from the daily news of police courts, accidents, deaths and the range of public events which constituted Roman urban experience, to the reporting of municipal councils, courts of law and even the Senate. These reports were posted outside a variety of public buildings for the perusal of interested citizens. In the Roman Forum, beneath the rostra where the speaker stood, Neubauer speculates that people gathered who were the forerunners of modern journalists who traded in generating and disseminating rumour (ibid.: 44). Rumour and formal news might never have been that far removed from each other. Written news and broadcast news in all their forms, when they are successful, have always been able to establish a relationship with a certain orality which is linked to the rumour. Such was the cumulative historical and social potential of rumour that print was perceived by certain monarchs early in the history of printing as one way in which its corrosive effects could be restricted. The first Tudor monarch, Henry VII, realized the convenience of printed information circulated before rumour and gossip about affairs of state could be spread by more haphazard means. Henry VII may have been in regular receipt of handwritten manuscript newsletters which contained news of economic and political intelligence considered important to the stability of his reign, but he developed the use of printed proclamation to establish authorized accounts of what he considered were the important issues of the day.

In feudal times, authority needed to control and if necessary suppress information since knowledge has always constituted an important form of power. The medieval statutes referred to as *Scandalum Magnatum* had been the means through which rumours liable to damage the power or reputation of the king and the nobility had been suppressed. The purpose of this control was to maintain power over this information and furthermore to prevent the destabilization of the political status quo. As early as the fifteenth century, an increased need for a flow of reliable information for the purposes of trade meant that merchant groups were beginning to invest systematically in informants and the gathering and communication of intelligence. Capitalism, as the newly dominant economic formation, was to have a profoundly disruptive effect on feudal patterns of communication, especially as it depended on a freer and speedier exchange of information in order to move investment and commodities to best effect. War, disruption of routes of communication, disease, change of policy in foreign countries were all things which merchants needed to know about as quickly as possible. As commodity capital established itself, possession of high quality news was every bit a matter of political and economic survival as it was a mark of status. This point is underlined by Habermas in his thesis on the development of early news media in Europe: 'With the expansion of trade, merchants' market oriented calculations required more frequent and more exact information about distant events' (1992: 16). Changes in the flow of information would have profound implications for the structure of society and the role of knowledge within that structure. At this time, formal news came as private letters not as a public discourse. The most famous form of these newsletters was developed by the Augsburg banking family the Fuggers in the sixteenth century to keep their agents informed of relevant developments which might have been of concern to the commercial and political interests of their business.

News Dissemination

News, commissioned by the wealthy and by aristocrats and senior clerics, had been transmitted orally by messengers and in manuscript form before the arrival of printing in Western Europe in the fifteenth century. More informally, it had been carried by people on the move – travellers, merchants, soldiers and other adventurers. As the world of the Early Modern period began to quite literally expand, with the so-called voyages of discovery and the subsequent increase in commercial traffic, people were keen to keep in contact vicariously with a more dynamic world. Travel was the lubricant of information exchange and in places where travellers and merchants gathered such as coaching inns, commercial centres, ports and markets, news was most commonly sought and dispersed. News had a structural effect as part of that flow of information which reshaped Early Modern European societies because it allowed the recipients to imagine their place in a world which was wider than its medieval predecessor. The social imperative for news meant that there were well-established and regular networks of communication across all parts of Western Europe before the introduction of printed news. Print simply followed the trail. These networks had, by the time of the introduction of printing, become formalized in the form of manuscript newsletters. However, this distribution was not always an even affair. The weather was better in the summer and the roads, rudimentary by modern standards, more accessible. There was literally more news in late spring and summer because of the increased volume in traffic. News came slowly for periods of time and then in rushes so there was much scope for repetition, variation on themes and plagiarism. This was exploited by the generic patterns of the ballad and the pamphlet. These were circulated and sold commercially from the fifteenth century. They mixed informational content with strong narrative and entertainment values. Ballad and broadsheet, together with business and political newsletters, are ample proof that the desire for the latest information, whether amusing or informational, was well developed in Western Europe even before the advent of printed news at all levels of society.

Despite such early attempts to contain the information flow within the social and political elites, rumour remained the main source of communication which leaked from those in power, or with privileged access to power, throughout the sixteenth and seventeenth centuries and it was profitable to those who dealt in it. A market developed in the provision of such information, although its unreliable reputation was already drawing criticism as early as 1591 when a character in John Florio's *Second Fruits* cautions: 'A man must give no more credit to Exchange news and Paul's news than to fugitives' promises and players' fables' (Fox-Bourne, 1998: 2) and St Paul's Walk in London was described by Bishop John Earle in 1628 as 'the eares Brothel' (Raymond, 1999b: 115). Yet such exchanges are the earliest manifestation of the spaces between authority and the people in England which would lead to a public sphere of information.

1

The Consequences
of Printed News

Beginnings – from Culture to Controversy

The suitability of print as a technology to disseminate news was not immediately appreciated. The point must be emphasized that although printing was not journalism or even news in itself, it constituted part of the social and economic changes which would create the conditions in which printed news and early versions of journalism could emerge and then flourish. Caxton set up his Westminster Press in 1476 and printing was at first used to reproduce what could be generally considered religious and literary works such as the Bible and the works of Chaucer. The Tudor monarchs were all concerned to maintain their political authority and thereby the integrity and stability of the realm, and this meant controlling the flow of political information. Concerns about the control of this new technology and its consequences for political stability were heightened by vivid memories of the preceding anarchy of the Wars of the Roses (1455–87). It was not until the accession of Henry VIII that the social and political potential of print was beginning to be appreciated as its use spread from arts and literature to the political and religious controversies of the day. In fact, it could be claimed that the Reformation in England constituted the first widespread and sustained debate that was, through the medium of print, made into a public and even a national one because of this linguistic power shift. A few key dates will enable us to chart the development of the Tudor approach to the potential power of printing.

In 1513 the first known surviving news pamphlet was printed and disseminated concerning the Battle of Flodden, *Hereafter ensue the trewe encountre or Batayle lately done betwene Englande and Scotlande*. This pamphlet also contains a woodcut illustration of troops preparing to fight in the battle and is an astute attempt to bridge its appeal between a literate readership and those whom Watt describes as on the fringes of literacy, enabling them to become involved in the cumulative process of cultural change:

> Printed words were disseminated by word of mouth, transforming the culture of the 'illiterate', and the oral modes of communication shaped the

structure of printed works. The interesting process was not only the spread of literacy and readership, but the complex interweaving of the printed word with existing cultural practices. (Watt, 1991: 8)

This pamphlet was, of course, printed and disseminated by royal authority as much for propaganda as for informational purposes. Heretical printed books, as distinct from the previous manuscript translations, were being imported from 1520 in the wake of the Reformation in Germany, especially the work of Martin Luther which explicitly linked the flaunting of the authority of the Catholic Church in Rome to the printing and dissemination of religious texts in the local language. This use of the vernacular had enormous implications in the development of secular society as it wrested power away from the ancient language of authority, Latin, guarded by religious and political elites, and broadened discussion of religion into the language of the everyday (Anderson, 1986). This was an important moment in the break from religious literacy to political literacy. The Church in England was unable to control the flow of these texts translated from German and into English which were subverting its authority over religious language and thought and turned to the Crown who found that the fear of execution was more effective than the Church's threat of excommunication in controlling it. Despite the fact that unauthorized printing continued, albeit at a lesser rate, in 1529 the first list of prohibited books was published to reinforce the threat. Those works prohibited included: 'any book or work, printed or written, which is made, or hereafter shall be made against the faith catholic, or against the holy decrees, laws, and ordinances of holy church, or in reproach, rebuke or slander of the king, his honorable council, or his lords spiritual or temporal' (Siebert, 1965: 45).

   In 1529 and 1530 Henry VIII issued two proclamations which outlawed importing or being in possession of heretical books printed in English on the Continent and the printing of any religious book without approval from the appropriate religious authority. In addition, in 1530 and 1538 proclamations were issued which constituted the earliest attempts at systematizing the licensing of printing. To a large extent, the reactions of the Tudors were retrospective attempts to come to terms with a technology whose power was only emerging incrementally. In 1500 there were only five printers in London and their increase to 35 by 1523 was indicative of the growth of the trade in the Tudor capital. The Royal imperative to protect the stability of the country and the welfare of its people was applied with regard to print throughout the Tudor era, but it was already in conflict with the profitability of printing. Astutely aware of the potential impact of printing on authority, particularly because of events in Germany, Henry VIII's reforms throughout his reign were widely publicized in the form of printed news pamphlets by loyal supporters. By the time of the 1534 Act of Supremacy the monarch had total control of the state, church and printing and from 1546 there could be executions for the expression in print of 'erroneous opinions'. These royal proclamations, together with the short chronicles published by men like William Rastell and Richard Grafton in the early to mid-1500s, indicated that news had begun to make its way into print (Woolf, 2001: 91).

Inevitably, the dissemination of printed news was conducted in the vernacular as it formed part of this process of the widening base of people with a stake in the functioning of the economy and the polity. Eisenstein (1979) claims that it was the activity and implications of print itself which provided the impetus for the revolutionary changes such as commodity capitalism and secularism which restructured Western Europe in the Early Modern period. The impact of print in Western Europe at this particular time therefore surpassed the merely technological and had a growing influence on the changes in the structures of political and social authority. Print enabled topical information to be reproduced quickly enough to produce a profit at a time when an increasing number of readers were interested in rapidly evolving political and social events. The shift precipitated by printing was emphasized by a move from letters and literature to politics and religion as the key texts of the era. This immediately posed problems for those in authority which would remain as salient for any form of journalism to this day. In its potential to disrupt closed circles of communication among elite groups and in its ability to act as a rapid conduit for dissenting opinion, print threatened hierarchies, especially religious and monarchic ones, during a period of rapid social change and economic growth. This potential is claimed in its strongest form when Herd elides the role of journalism and the contestation of authority: 'There has never been a period in our history when authority has genuinely liked the idea of full publicity for all its activities and unchecked criticism of its conduct' (Herd, 1952: 11).

If the threat of the Reformation spreading from Germany had been the first battle for the English authorities against the onslaught of print, on the European mainland, the *Gazetta* of Venice was an indicator of the commercial and political anxieties engendered by a danger from a different source, the threat of invasion by the Turkish Empire. This first news-sheet of modern times provided the merchant and political classes of Venice with eagerly anticipated news of the perceived threat of the Turks to the whole of central Europe and the progress of the war being waged against them. They were at first handwritten from about 1536 but later, from about 1570, they made best use of print technology. Their contents were read aloud in public arenas which meant that the contents were written partially with an ear for public performance and that the culture of the written word was more efficiently disseminated through alignment with older oral traditions. In England, with less foreign trade and a more centralized monarchy, developments in print culture and, in particular, its ability to deal with news were slightly slower than elsewhere on the Continent, which would explain how regular news in print arrived in England as late as it did in the early seventeenth century.

The Strategic Incorporation of the Printers

One of the first alternatives to the plain outlawing of printed matter was the foundation by Royal Charter in 1557 of the Stationers' Company. This demonstrated a prescient awareness of the potential for a self-interested collection of printers to police their own output and thereby encourage them not to jeopardize their profitable business by falling foul of a higher authority. As with the other better established guilds of the Middle Ages, they were awarded the power to regulate the craft and output of printing from within their membership. In order to effectively self-regulate, they had the powers to grant the rights of property ownership, record and accredit apprenticeships and ensure the trade was kept free from opportunists and work of poor quality. These rights could be enforced through property searches if the members felt it justified. The Charter constituted an enormously influential set of powers over the embryonic printing trade. The political elite felt that these rights fully incorporated the printers into the existing political power structures and demonstrated this by allowing the members of the Company voting rights in London and parliamentary elections. There were not only profits to be made for stationers from their monopoly on printing, they were also quick to exploit the more punitive aspects of their authority in terms of fines for unlicensed printing or sales of printed matter. Records indicate a healthy income from 'fynes for defautes for pryntynge withoute lycense' (Clegg, 1997: 15). These violations indicate that there were still financial benefits or matters of belief significant enough for printers to be willing to provoke the wrath of the newly formed Company. The practice of printing was clearly too volatile to be entirely controlled by statute alone and too hybrid in the motivations of printers in this era of ideological turmoil and increased interest in commercial enterprise.

After the rigours of Henry VIII's pursuit of absolute control over printed matter of all kinds, books, pamphlets, ballads and other scurrilous printed material flourished in an age of religious antagonisms under the early tolerance of first Edward VI and then during the early years of Mary before many printers fled abroad under the restrictions of her later reign to countries with more liberal attitudes to printing freedom. This indicated that such was the appetite and the economic incentive for an increasingly diverse range of printed matter that whenever restrictions were relaxed, the floodgates opened and in a competitive environment the print culture diversified and flourished, developing a whole gamut of possibilities for printers, publishers and writers. Printers, non-conformists and occasional Members of Parliament all drove the increasing curiosity over current news and opinion. The dissemination of such material was located in a complex position somewhere between profit, conviction and ambition. It seems likely that no one at this time really objected to some form of control in principle, as patterns of social deference still meant that there was a broad acceptance that there must be some limitation on the trade in opinion, but most objected to somebody else having final authorization over the acceptability of their own printed output in practice. In this way, printing freedom developed pragmatically in its relationship to authority.

In 1559, the London High Commission had been founded as the principle means by which Elizabeth's regime expected to suppress opposition to her religious settlement and by now this meant printed opposition as well. It was partially because of the failure of this to adequately deal with the flow of material that the Stationers' Company was given more authority. From 23 June 1586, the first formal licensing system established by the Star Chamber decree was to be the most thorough articulation of control and laid the foundation for the subsequent regulation of printing until 1637 when it collapsed along with the crumbling authority of Charles I. Under the terms of the Decree, further restrictions were placed on the numbers of printers and apprentices. London and the Universities of Oxford and Cambridge were the only centres allowed printing presses and employment was restricted to members of the Company and their apprentices. This meant that Elizabeth's solution to the flow of unlicensed material was a return to the severity of Henry VIII's time, with the Stationers' Company more fully and formally charged with the control of the press. Enlightened self-interest backed up by the weight of the Crown epitomized the practices of the Stationers' Company. In their zeal to control the flow of unauthorized printed material and in their deployment of their increased powers of search and seizure, the Stationers' Company blended protection of their own privileges and the imposition of the expectations of the governing classes. Siebert has characterized this political delegation in the following way: 'The skillful use of the corporate organization of printers and publishers in the suppression and control of undesirable printing has long been considered a masterstroke of Elizabethan politics' (1965: 64).

Much of this pragmatism was directed by the Tudor monarchs towards the suppression of opposition to their religious reforms, as they recognized the potential of printing to stabilize their rule and the powerful incorporative effect of offering the printers a privileged position within the output of the presses. The Stationers' Company control must have been deemed more successful than the ultimate sanction of execution which the Crown reserved for itself, since this was only resorted to once in this century when the Catholic William Carter was hanged, drawn and quartered in 1584 for 'the printinge of Lewde pamphlettes'. A variety of punishments was used in addition to threats of execution or excommunication which included pillory, removal of ears, imprisonment, branding and the removal in perpetuity of writing or printing materials. In addition, printers such as Bastwick, Burton and Prynne were prosecuted for the very malleable offence of seditious libel. Yet in an expanding market, the authority of the Stationers' Company was undermined by the gradual increase in apprentice printers with no prospect of work in the trade once they had served their time. This meant that they were drawn by economic necessity to the printing of illicit material for which there was always a ready market and a good profit margin. This perspective of the trade was complemented by responses from readers. As the culture of print expanded its reach, it has been eloquently described as 'the low rumble of the demand of the people to see, hear and to know was gathering momentum' (Siebert, 1965: 87).

In the early history of printing, it was not facts or even rumour but the powerful assertion of informed political opinion which drove the production of the most incendiary materials of the age, the political pamphlets, and it was these which preceded the development of regular printed news. There were always those willing to make a point or a profit by printing such dissonant opinion. In 1579, John Stubbe wrote, and Singleton the printer produced, a pamphlet entitled: *The Discourie of a Gaping Gulf Whereinto England is like to be swallowed by another French marriage; if the Lord forbid not the banes, by letting her Maiestie see the sin and punishment thereof.* This was written in reaction to the rumour that Elizabeth I had offered herself in marriage to the Duc d'Anjou, the brother of the King of France, Henry III, in order to delay the annexation of the Netherlands by Spain. Stubb was tried and imprisoned but despite the Queen's desire that he should be executed for this 'lewde and seditious book', he was condemned to the lesser punishment of having his right hand severed.

The restrictions imposed by the Star Chamber decree merely gave rise to secret presses and they provided the liveliest trade on the streets of London in the selling of occasional, and of course illegal, pamphlets. This had its most striking impact in the publication of the Martin Marprelate tracts which argued from a Puritan perspective for the introduction of an episcopal Church government. The printing press which the tracts were printed on was smuggled all around the country to avoid detection, indicating the limitations of a London-based system of licensing and the levels of support for Puritan opposition within the printing community. It stands as a prominent early example of belief preceding profit in the printing trade. The Martin Marprelate tracts combined satire with serious theological arguments and drew in a larger readership for these discussions, popularizing religious debate to an extent not seen before in England. They are significant in the history of journalism because of the radical breaching of the threshold of linguistic deference: 'By attacking the bishops in language hitherto used only for the personal, Martin Marprelate decoupled the decorum of language from the decorum of subject' (Levy, 1999: 33). It was often to be journalism's ability to use language in ways which innovated and destabilized convention which lent it much of its ability to retain a freshness and a connection to the patterns of private speech of its audience.

Political and Economic Imperatives

Another development facilitated by printing and driven by the appetite for news and opinion in printed form was the practice of news writers disseminating their reports on Parliament, thus destabilizing the privileges of parliamentary confidentiality. Siebert records that in 1589 the Speaker of the House of Commons warned members that: 'Speeches used in this House by the Members of the same be not any of them made or used as Table-talk, or in any wise delivered in notes of writing to any person or persons whatsoever not being Members of this House' (1965: 103). Anxieties relating to the political and religious stability of the country sometimes took subtle forms and influenced the monarch's view of what should be authorized in print and what should not. From 1578, Watkyns and Roberts received a licence to print almanacs after Elizabeth's government became concerned about the destabilizing potential of prognostications of her imminent death.

Towards the end of the sixteenth century, England was becoming a more dynamic economic nation and more prominent on the world stage. Its acquisition of colonies and the rise of England as a maritime power after the victory over the Spanish in 1588 led to an increase in commodity wealth in England and the corresponding rise of a commercial class to rival the landed aristocracy. The implications of the trade in news in early capitalism were complex and began only slowly to make themselves apparent in first reinforcing and then breaking open social patterns of communication:

> On the one hand this capitalism stabilized the power structure of a society organized in estates, and on the other hand, it unleashed the very elements within which this power structure would one day dissolve. We are speaking of the elements of the new commercial relationships: the traffic in commodities and news created by early capitalist long distance trade. (Habermas, 1992: 15)

These merchants depended on the provision of regular and reliable information. News was increasingly being traded as a commodity in lubrication of other commodities. This prompted an increased demand for all sorts of news, but because of the restrictions imposed through the Stationers' Company, it was not yet able to be channelled through print media. The means of transmitting this information was in the handwritten newsletters of the day. The writers of these letters were not yet referred to as journalists and their wares were far from regular. They were called intelligencers and the most prominent were John Chamberlain, John Pory, William Locke, Rev Larkin and Rev Mead. Many had started providing information services for particular families who paid them well but the trade was so much in demand and so lucrative that they soon became fully professional, able to live off their intelligence distribution and employing scriveners to copy material for distribution to a widening clientele. In addition to their written output, these writers were also highly prized for the networks of contacts and sources which they developed in pursuit of their information. What had begun as a family correspondence service for the wealthy had become professional newsletter writing. Newsletters contained among other things: 'corantos, proclamations, copies of letters, bills of mortality, verses, banned books, pamphlets, books of masques, and foreign newspapers' (Atherton, 1999: 52–3).

The increase of news became most noticeable at times of war or national crisis. The struggles with Spain first stimulated English interest in printed news in the 1580s and 1590s and the most famous intelligence gatherer of this era, John Chamberlain, began his work in 1588. From 1585 when the war with Spain broke out into open hostilities, the Stationers' Company was forced to take a much more assertive role in recording all printed matter produced and insisted upon pre-publication licensing. John Wolfe, a printer and publisher, was recruited by Lord Burghley, the principal Minister of the Queen, to distribute translations of Protestant propaganda to Catholic countries such as France and Italy. He also developed the first corantos translated into English, for example, *Credible Reportes from France, and Flanders. In the moneth of May. 1590* and experimented with the compilation of news pamphlets in a series, but one which lacked regularity. They were above all profitable ventures and provided recipients with 'an increasingly detailed insight into current affairs, much of it provided by semi-professional journalists with a reputation for accurate reporting' (Cust, 1986: 69).

John Pory, a writer of manuscript newsletters, aware of the potential of coupling printing with this demand for regular news, attempted unsuccessfully through the Court to be granted a monopoly on the distribution of printed news: 'to establish a speedy and reddy way whereby to disperse into the veynes of the whole body of a state such matter as may best temper it, & be most agreeable to the disposition of the head & the principale members' (Levy, 1999: 28).

From 1589, there was civil war in France which brought English involvement in the war with Philip II. Dozens of news quartos were printed in Elizabethan London, prompted by public interest in the religious strife and political instability in France which reflected real concerns about the danger of similar upheavals in England, underlining the appeal of foreign news as a barometer of domestic anxieties. In Elizabeth's Protestant land, much coverage emphasized the cruelty of Catholic forces. These quartos were essential in preparing an extended understanding of a community imagining itself as a national community, unified in the face of dangers from across the Channel, and the medium of print enabled that understanding to resonate across wider sections of the population than ever before. Voss points out that the 'news revolution', often described as taking place in England after 1622, actually occurred on a smaller scale, and for a finite period of time, nearly 30 years prior to the English corantos and periodical publications, since a quarter of all publications in England from 1591–1594 were concerned with the carnage and starvation of the war and that in one year alone, 1590, there were 38 newsbooks about events in France (2001: 15). There is much evidence in these quartos of the claims of this news to justify its veracity and reliability not just as a discourse, but as a commercial rationale with titles stressing 'newes', 'true', 'credible', and 'report'. They were the first rehearsals of 'journalistic truth as a commodity to be packaged and sold' (ibid.: 54).

The increased flow of information outside traditional elites accelerated the break-up of older patterns and hierarchies of deference and led to still wider dissemination of information, and the new technology of print meant that this information could flow quicker and more regularly than before. This created parallel constituencies of power outside traditional elite groups. By the early seventeenth century, a wealthy English merchant class was evolving and it needed a reliable flow of information upon which to base its commercial decisions. Not surprisingly, given the ambivalence of the authoritarian Tudor monarchs to the printing of news, the first regular news in England consisted of foreign imports such as *Mercurius Gallobelgicus*, which was printed at half-yearly intervals at best, in Latin out of Cologne from 1594 to 1635 and was the first periodical to use the Mercury title. Other translations followed from the Low Countries where political control was not as absolute as that in England and therefore less able to stem the flow of news. Domestic news which commented on affairs of state was absolutely forbidden at this time, although there was a regular supply of it in manuscript newsletters at considerable cost to recipients. This meant that news at home in printed form tended to be limited to the sensational, which was what Nathaniel Butter was attempting to capitalize upon with a single edition in 1605 concerning a couple of murders in Yorkshire, *Two most unnaturall and bloodie Murthers*.

The narrow dissemination of officially sanctioned information was at odds with the wider reality of the age which was that printed information was becoming widespread and increasingly difficult to police. Often prohibition and restriction were little more than belated attempts to prevent what was already happening. Despite attempts to stifle it, printed news was commonly in circulation by the middle of the sixteenth century. Where often medieval markets had provided the literal commodification of information and travelling hawkers and peddlers had long trod the routes which were to become more formalized paths of news dissemination, chapmen and mercury women facilitated the spread of print culture and news as part of it. Often the sellers of mercuries or pamphlets were the wives or widows of printers. It is not just the proliferation of printed news but also the variety of forms which news was taking which were remarkable. As well as pamphlets and newsletters, there were proclamations and ballads which dealt with plots, rumours, rebellions, battles and executions. Ballads were often, in effect, informal news-sheets although they had more heroic and hyperbolic features compared to more official and licensed sources. The Spanish Armada of 1588, for instance, provided countless opportunities of the patriotic type of heroic naval coverage in this form. Other informal material which was widely distributed had a sensational attraction to it, such as *News from Antwerp* (1580), which added an aura of adventurousness to its content by claiming that the letters it consisted of had been intercepted and that they proved the impossibility of negotiating a lasting peace with Spain. This willingness, even necessity, to experiment with various forms and combinations was forever to characterize successful journalism. It has been identified by

McLuhan (1995: 215) as a 'mosaic' mode of interpreting the world which illustrates something of the complexity and open-endedness of our experience. The late sixteenth century also saw an increase in the London trade in news pamphlets dealing in sensationalist news of murders, witchcraft and strange apparitions which were a favourite for printers and readers and less contentious than many other stories in that they avoided political and religious sectarianism, as in this report from Germany from 1601:

> First they were all sixe brought before the towne house of Manchen where the woman (being plaest between her two Sonnes) had both her Brestes cut off: and with the which Brestes the Executioner stroke her three times about the face; and in like manner her two Sonnes, who satt on either side of her were likewise beaten about the face with their Mothers Brests three times apiece. This being done in the presence of many people, the woman had six stripes given her with a Whip of twisted Wier: and after, had both her arms broken with a Wheel, and then set in a settle made of purpose: her body was immediately burnt. After this the other five witches had also six stripes apiece, and both thie arms broken with a Wheele, and foure of them tyde unto a stake in the same place, and burnt: But *Paule Gamherle*, the father and maister Witch of them all, was spitted alive, and so roasted to death. (Cranfield, 1978: 3)

Perhaps the most important benefit to print culture in the proliferation of formats was that it was becoming established as part of a more widespread literacy by the seventeenth century. Print reinforced and accelerated previous methods of communicating information about contemporary economic, political and military events. News became part of broadly defined social status – you were what you knew. At Court, in the Inns of Law and around the lanes of St Paul's, the vibrant culture of news and gossip exchange became more concrete than ever in written and then printed form as newsletters. Certain manuscript newsletters were simply translations of foreign events and others were reports of strange and sensational happenings, monstrous children, terrible earthquakes. These could be bundled or bound with other matter such as broadside ballads about events or famous political figures, but they all lacked a key ingredient of what was to become established as a central feature of the rhythm of news – periodicity. They were also more expensive and therefore more restricted in distribution than the printed newsbooks which followed, but they offered the exclusivity of a more intimate medium and were less likely to be read aloud to groups or to be sold on second-hand at a reduced price as the newsbooks.

The commodification of news in printed form meant that it was even more profitable if it could extend its reach from a private exchange between individuals to a more public availability based on an ability to pay. The intensity of political and military events on the European mainland combined with less effective regimes of censorship and licensing there meant that printed news in England of the early seventeenth century was by definition news from abroad. Periodical newsbooks and news-sheets started to spread across the cities of Europe: Strasbourg and Augsburg in 1609, Basel in 1610, Frankfurt and Vienna in 1615, Hamburg in 1616, Amsterdam in 1618 and Antwerp in 1620. The first to appear in England which survives is from 24 September 1621. This print revolution was accompanied by a 'news revolution' which also contributed from the seventeenth century onwards to the dispersal of older understandings of what constituted knowledge. Sommerville comments on this process that: 'a serial and factual news began as a luxury commodity, literally more than its weight in gold. It was an information system based on scarcity, helping elites to maintain themselves by monopolizing political and commercial intelligence. Eventually, this system would be challenged by one of abundance' (1996: 19).

Perceptions of Time – the Corantos

Sommerville emphasizes the radical role which 'periodicity' plays in the formation of the practice of journalism. This writing of news about the contemporary world, at regular intervals, which was defined by market demand for that information caused a reconfiguration of human understanding of the world which still has implications today. The periodical newspaper was the single most important element in the creation of modern cultural conceptions of information in time. It required a particular form of writing which was to distinguish itself from other related literary forms, one which was centred on the transitory and the contemporary and foregrounded the political and public aspects of writing like no other. Yet if journalism can be defined as such a form of public philosophy based in the contemporary, then it has always been a philosophy conducted with one eye on the balance sheet:

> Periodicity is about economics. There can be news without it being daily, but if it were not daily, a news *industry* could never develop. The industry's capital assets would lie idle waiting for news of significance to print. Periodicity is a marketing strategy, a way of holding property in information. (ibid.: 4)

Anderson adds to the debate on the emergence of printed newspapers in the seventeenth century an understanding of the structural changes in attitudes towards time which needed to be accepted culturally if the practice of journalism were to develop into a meaningful political and economic form:

> What had come to take the place of the medieval [i.e. 'Messianic' typological] conception of simultaneity-along-time is to borrow again from Benjamin, an idea of 'homogenous, empty time,' in which simultaneity is, as it were, transverse, cross-time, marked not by prefiguring and fulfillment, but by temporal coincidence, and measured by clock and calendar. (Anderson, 1986: 30)

There were certainly elements of that messianic perception of time in Burton's 1628 description of early news:

> I hear new news every day, and those ordinary rumours of war, plagues, fires, innundations, thefts, murders, massacres, meteors, comets, spectrums, prodigies, apparitions, of towns taken, cities besieged in France, Germany, Turkey, Persia, Poland, etc., daily musters and preparations, and such-like, which these tempestuous times afford, battles fought, so many men slain, monomachies, shipwrecks, piracies, and sea-fights, peace, leagues, stratagems, and fresh alarums ... New books every day, pamphlets, currantoes ... . (Burton, 1972: 18)

The increased prominence of news generated a critical resistance. Much of this criticism of news in its earliest printed form was related to its diminished status as knowledge as it became less associated with privilege and more with profit motives and a more general audience. There was also a common perception among critics that news was untrustworthy, prone to exaggeration and dependent on vulgar novelty for its profits, thus providing a recipe for deliberate invention and deceit. Atherton quotes one jest from 1626 about the unreliability of the news of the day: 'Currantes many tymes publish currant lies' (1999: 47). There was also a rather resentful snobbery in criticisms of printed news from elite circles. For them, this new commodified form of knowledge compromised their own privileged status. Previously the intelligence of diplomatic staff, for instance in metropolitan centres, had been digested into weekly reports for circulation among other professionals on the circuit and access to that knowledge was an indicator of informal ranking in political circles for both courtiers and men of more commercial bent. As news came to be more widely circulated, it threatened that privileged economy of communication.

Official attitudes in England towards printing and news dissemination were extremely cautious in the midst of the religious instability which had become endemic in Europe by the sixteenth century. Authority developed in England, as we have seen, with the collusion of the vested commercial and political interests of the printers. As England entered the seventeenth century, it was religion once again which shattered the uneasy and provisional settlement provided by the Tudors. It was the Thirty Years War which provided the spark which was to further stimulate the newly formed passion for printed news. The war broke out under the apprehensive gaze of most of Europe's major players. Its prelude had been typical of the troubled political manoeuvring of the era. In 1613 James's daughter, Princess Elizabeth, married Frederick, the Elector of the Palatinate. He had subsequently accepted the crown of Bohemia against the wishes of the Holy Roman Emperor. The question which everyone wanted an answer to was, how would James react on behalf of Protestant England? Many wanted an intervention on behalf of the Protestant forces. It is because of the increase of interest in speculation and news of these events and therefore in profitability for printers that newsbooks known as 'corantos' became established in England from 1620 on the outbreak of this war. Readers in England interpreted the events on the near Continent as a vicarious expression of the tensions and threats inherent in the religious divisions already well advanced in their home country. Religion kindled interest in foreign news and, as during every war since, news production fed a voracious increase in appetite. During this time of widespread military conflict across Europe, printed news had an essential role to play in forming commercial strategy. Interest in news was not only driven by idle curiosity. Often early newspapers would include lists of commodity prices and details of arrivals and cargoes in ports and other trading centres.

The corantos were digests of foreign news translated from foreign gazettes and corantos and from original letters, mainly concerning the religious wars which had broken out in mainland Europe, but they did not contain any domestic news partly because this was illegal and partly because they were printed abroad and then translated into English for purely commercial motives. They appeared approximately on a weekly basis if there was enough suitable material to reprint. From 1622 certain of the more successful corantos were numbered and Thomas Gainsford, on behalf of both Butter and Bourne as publishers, began to experiment with edited versions which attempted to provide a continuous narrative. Baron points out that these corantos were implicitly critical of James I's foreign policy by their very existence (2001: 44). Concern about the heated nature of political debate in England prompted James I to issue a proclamation on 24 December 1620 suppressing the spreading of news from abroad in the form of corantos. However, it was limited in its effect. Wars on the Continent and suspicions of the motives of Spain had brought to boiling point debates on the political situation in England and its likely outcome and the pamphlet was a widely disseminated way of engaging with that tumult: cheap, ephemeral and effective with a ready and profitable audience. After Gainsford's death in 1624, Butter continued his collaborative work with the newsletter writer John Pory.

Thomas Archer produced the first English coranto in 1621, a compilation of news out of the Low Countries translated from the Dutch and was promptly imprisoned for publishing without licence. More prudently, Butter and Bourne acquired a licence and began the authorized production of English newsbooks which soon, in their regular and numbered sequence, succeeded from the corantos of the early century. The newsbooks consisted of a quarto pamphlet of 8 to 24 pages, depending on supply. They kept this format until 1655. They were numbered from 1622 and had stable titles from 1624. There were usually between 400–500 copies of newsbooks in circulation. The first dated newsbook still in existence is from 23 May 1622, *Weekly Newes from Italy, Germanie, Hungaria, translated out of the Dutch copie*, published by Thomas Archer and Nicholas Bourne. The contents of the newsbooks and, before them, the corantos were distinguished from previous literary forms in that they claimed to be composed of facts. Ballads, poems and pamphlets were allowed great latitude which was a reflection of their more entertaining and provocative purpose. This new factual discourse was one rooted not in the eternal truths and symbols of religion but one rooted in the 'Absolute Present' (Bell, 1979: 48) of discrete, closed narratives, fixed in specific times and places and having a claim to authenticity and reliability such as in the following. 'For I translate onely the Newes verbatim out of the Tongues or Languages in which they are written, and having no skill in Prognostication, leave therefore the judgement to the Reader, & that especially when there are tidings which contradict one another' (*Mercurius Britannicus*, 28 June 1625).

Opinions of News Take Shape

Yet despite such claims, at this point, printers printed reports rather than composing them themselves and therefore they were often at the mercy of unreliable and contradictory evidence which did nothing for the reputation of the new medium. It seemed to traditionalists that they 'inverted all known truths and social decencies' (Raymond, 1996: 276). Conservative opinion was appalled at the idea that knowledge could be bought and sold in such a crude commercial transaction and was enflamed by the realization that news clearly destabilizes a certain hierarchical understanding of the status of knowledge among the learned classes in the Renaissance period. This shattering of the epistemology of knowledge was to provide an opportunity for innovation in the emergent discourse of journalism:

> News was a problematic form of knowledge in the seventeenth century, causing problems of writing and problems of audience, and raising conservative fears of 'licentious discourse' … The relationship between fact and fiction was a central literary problem of the seventeenth century, and the development of English newspapers has been placed in the context of the breaking down of the epistemological barrier between knowledge and opinion. (Atherton, 1999: 48)

Such anxieties were expressed in the work of playwright Ben Jonson. In 1620, the year in which English-language corantos first appeared in London, Jonson produced a play, *News from the New World*, which mocked the pretensions of the novelty of printed news. In 1626, he resumed his mockery in another play *The Staple of News* in which he pours scorn on a syndicate of newsmongers. Jonson is caustically dismissive about the dissemination of a certain sort of knowledge through printed news. He uses the term 'Staple' in the title of his play *The Staple of News* in a pointed way to indicate the fact that such information was very much akin to cheap food. In a withering section, he gives us the first sceptical variation on the theme that some gullible people would believe anything they read in the papers:

See divers men's opinions: unto some
The very printing of 'em makes them news;
That have not the heart to believe any thing
But what they see in print. (Jonson, 1816)

For Jonson, news is an effeminate form, born of the wasteful activity of 'tattling' and 'tattling is the forerunner of the "new" news, the fluid, costless, cottage version of the impulse and the industry that the Staple syndicate will seek to technologize, commercialize, and monopolize' (Sherman, 2001: 29).

Journalism has been formed by the convergence of many miscellaneous elements over several centuries and the variety of practices and the complexity of relationships between new writers and the publications they wrote for even at this early point were manifest in the range of different names by which they and their output was described: 'authors, curranters, mercurists, newsmen, newsmongers, diurnalists, gazeteers and (eventually) journalists' (Herd, 1952: 12) wrote Corantos, Relations, Newes, Posts, Gazettes, Proceedings, Accounts, Passages and Diurnals and the seventeenth century saw a great variety of descriptions for the phenomenon of news, occurrences, intelligences, advices, advertisements. Yet amidst all of the generic experimentation, the crucial component is that these regular printings of news and opinion on contemporary affairs were written for profit, in a regular cycle of periodicity. News was a commodity which was created according to the perceived demands of specific readers and survived or failed on the accuracy of its perception of an audience. This meant that a commercial dominant was always the driving force behind innovation and change in the production of news and it was this which attracted printers and publishers to invest in it in order to make a profit. The combination of profit, politics and curiosity in an easily reproducible printed form contributed to the creation of what Sommerville (1996) terms a culture of 'news consciousness' which was essential if the practices and discourse of journalism were to take hold in the public domain to the extent that they became a dominant form of cultural narration. Commodifying news to appeal to various markets in the form of readerships was an early and successful part of this process of discourse formation.

By the early 1630s, the Thirty Years War had reached a point of decisive interest with the victories of Gustavus Adolphus over the German forces, much to the delight of the printers and writers of the newsbooks who were supportive of the Protestant cause. However, such partisanship in the newsbooks of a country not formally involved in the combat displayed an insensitivity to foreign opinion and so displeased the Hapsburg ambassador in London that in 1632 the Privy Council decreed that the printing of foreign news was unlawful and all corantos were suppressed. This is another example within the zigzagging of the development of journalism mentioned earlier. The publishing of domestic corantos stopped and there was a return to the import of foreign versions already translated. It also heralded an increase in the flow of news in ballad form. Manuscripts, nevertheless, continued to be the more prestigious form of written news as late as the early eighteenth century as they were more plentiful than printed news, more accurate than ballad or broadsheet, less censored, and regarded as more authoritative (Atherton, 1999: 40).

The control of manuscripts was less severe than the blanket ban on the printing of domestic news in the 1620s and 1630s, but this was also monitored. The level of censorship does not explain by itself the lack of home news. In general terms, news from home was less interesting because it was more generally available through a range of social contacts and less of an attractive and exotic commodity. Foreign news tended, especially the religious sort from Europe, to be more sensational and gruesome with even more scope for embroidery. In apocalyptic terms there was more evidence in the reports from foreign wars that a great battle between the forces of good and evil was being enacted. Throughout the heyday of the newsbooks, the newsletters still continued to contain most of the controversial material, including reports from Parliament. Their writers had no licence to lose and were carefully shielded by their patrons. The content of the newsletters was also more provocative in that it dwelt on controversy and dispute in a way which the less opiniated newsbooks were unable to do. Many of the newsletter reports constructed the events as confrontational, prioritizing conflict and argument. This led, according to Cust, to 'a process of political polarization in the early seventeenth century' (1986: 87).

Some books and pamphlets which were out of print or prohibited found themselves copied by hand and circulated as 'separates' within the newsbooks. The trade was so lucrative that publishers could employ whole teams of scriveners to copy out versions and in the early century they kept pace with printed copies in price and circulation. Another significant feature of the early development of journalism was the way in which it was exclusively a metropolitan product. It was centred on and directed through the capital and Cust points out the role of London as articulating the nation through its news output: 'The news from London was, however, not simply London news. Rather the city tended to serve as a melting-pot for information from all parts of the country' (ibid.: 70).

Government control of the press has often been seen as the only significant form of control but often it was restricted, and remains so, by the cultural expectations of the society in which it exists. Journalism is as much defined by its resolution of the balance between information and entertainment as it is by its relationship to politics and commodification. This much is true even at this early stage. Journalism has always negotiated a complex and pragmatic relationship with varying forms of government control from autocratic to *laissez-faire*. Siebert puts a good deal of emphasis on the informational/normative-functional political model of journalism, but ignores the other complexities of its role in entertainment and profit-generation. Raymond is keen to stress the pleasurable aspects of news consumption: 'News was supposed to be consumed not only because it enabled social exchange, or facilitated rational behaviour, but as an end in itself' (1996: 2).

All narratives of journalism are historically and geographically specific. The characteristics of a particular English journalism are essential to understand its pattern of discursive formation and explain the stability of the genre over time. This is why this history of the emergence of journalism will focus on particular moments to establish what conflicts and continuities have locked into the struggle to define and develop the practice.

2

Journalism as Miscellany

Newsbooks and Mercuries

Domestic Policies in the Newsbooks

The next significant stage in the formation of journalism was a very clear-cut period between 1640 and 1660. It came as a consequence of the social and political upheavals of the period which saw the fall of the government, the execution of the king, the creation of a secular Parliament and a civil war between supporters of the Parliament and the Royalists. Although printed news concerning domestic politics up to this point was prohibited, manuscript letters had for some time been circulating intelligence on all major political issues including debates in Parliament. They were restricted by price and by social contact to an elite who could afford subscriptions, paid in advance, but they served to establish a broader market for this form of news: 'The manuscript newsletters thus laid the groundwork for the tide of printed domestic news that flowed out of the presses of London after 1641 – and they had done so well before the appearance of "Diurnall Occurrences"' (Baron, 2001: 54).

The distribution networks which were built upon by the corantos and newsletters meant that there was a ready market and a rudimentary supply infrastructure for the innovation of the printed newsbook. Furthermore, it was the newsletters, hand-written and irregular, unlike their more sober printed rivals the corantos, which had been quick to provide opinion and even propaganda which in generic terms were the precursor to the newsbook. The newsbooks of the 1640s formalized the spread of the reports from Parliament which had hitherto simply leaked from politicians via scriveners to the newsletters. In terms of journalism, they did something of probably even greater consequence. They selected a target reader, and addressed this reader, assuming that he shared an ideological community with the writers.

The corantos had been almost exclusively concerned with foreign news. They had also striven to distinguish themselves against accusations that they were inferior to the manuscript newsletters in their accuracy by attempting to provide neutral accounts of happenings overseas without entering into opinion or controversy as the newsletters did. This had meant that with the exception of the brief career of the proto-editorial writer Gainsford with the *Mercurius Britannicus*, they were very dull. They were also conducted entirely for profit whereas the first newsbooks of the 1640s, although financially rewarding for the printers, were also by definition on the side of Parliament and therefore explicitly political.

In the wake of the political crisis which saw the summoning of the Long Parliament on 3 November 1640, members of Parliament from all factions insisted on having their speeches printed and distributed and their criticisms of the speeches of others. This was politics in the raw, more topical and contested than anything which had been experienced before in print and it was available at short notice and for a fraction of the cost of the newsletters. Mendle states that:

> This was obviously a bonanza for the printers ... In spring 1642, the publication of the declarations and messages exchanged between the two houses and the king (the 'war of words') created yet another round of 'separates', as a half-sheet broadside or several sheets in quarto. Meanwhile, events outside the houses required treatment: first, events in Scotland and Ireland, then news of the armed confrontations of the king's partisans and parliamentary commanders at Hull, finally war news itself. (2001: 60)

This period had a highly significant influence on the way in which news-gathering and the spread of opinion and propaganda in printed form developed. For instance, from the early 1640s there was a radical reorientation of interest in and production of domestic news because of the tense and volatile political situation. In fact, during the English Civil War the practice of translating news from abroad into English, familiar to a generation, was reversed and *Le Mercure Anglois* was printed in London and sent to France from 1644 to 1648. In addition, the quantity of domestic news in circulation was increasing because of the weakening control of the king. In 1641 King Charles I lost control of his Parliament and the subsequent political turmoil in the land was the catalyst which enabled print to become a medium of genuinely public debate and information. Not only did the demise of Charles' authority mean that home news could be covered for the first time without risk of persecution, the volatility of the times also determined that there was much to be written about, not least the proceedings of Parliament itself. Printed accounts of the debates in Parliament were able to claim aspects of the authority that the king had lost and involved their readers in political debate and the formation of opinion on the state of the country as never before possible under an absolute monarchy. Newsbooks were creating a public channel for the regular circulation of domestic political information and debate where none had previously existed. Zagorin has emphasized the role of regular domestic newsbooks and their early forms of journalism as essential to understanding the new relationships forming across political life in England:

> The appearance of the newspaper in 1641 was an indication of how far
> political life had broken through its former limits. Opposition to the regime had
> engendered a broad public which wished both to participate and be informed.
> To mobilize popular support and stiffen conviction, the press was indispens-
> able. The systematized provision of news, the presence of the journalist and
> publicist, were the necessary adjuncts of an energized politics. (1969: 206)

The newsbooks, particularly in their partisanship, were to become the most
influential political material of the mid-seventeenth century, beyond the
combined influence of books, pamphlets, ballads and other means of communication. Their effectiveness was fuelled by the turmoil of the age which
the newsbooks ensured spilled over into the daily experience of their readers.
It is significant that Charles I was not inclined to use the newsbooks or
printed pamphlets to argue his own position. Prior to the collapse of his
authority, Charles did not employ the newsbooks as a form of propaganda
because he could simply not countenance that he should engage in a dialogue with his subjects. He would certainly have agreed with William
Cavendish who in the early 1650s expressed the view that: 'The pen is a
virgin, the printing press a whore' (Baron, 2001: 41). He was and remained
an absolute monarch. Consequently the newsbooks increasingly allowed the
parliamentary opposition to gain the upper hand as the Royalists left the
field of the propaganda war open to their highly articulate enemies. The fall
of the Star Chamber on 5 July 1641 ushered in a period of intense activity in
the creation of a politics in public form which was to remain one of the defining features of journalism. Once the Star Chamber had relinquished its
power, the Stationers' Company would never again hold the same monopoly position and the fact of news and discussion in print had been established. This print culture was advantaged by its blend of financial
motivation and political commitment. Many printers were Puritan or
Presbyterian by sympathy but there were also profits to be made from popular street literature and resentment at the monopoly of a few wealthy printers, illustrating Frank's point that: 'In the seventeenth century, as in the
twentieth, profits were usually more important than principle, though it was
pleasant when the two went hand in hand' (1961: 269).

The first newsbooks encouraged what has been described as a 'symbolic
leap in attitudes towards the polity' (Raymond, 1996: 122). They contributed
to the formation of a public discourse which demanded explanations for
political decisions, one of the core activities of journalism and a paradigm
shift towards the beginning of the modern era. The development of journalism as printed public reporting and debate was the logical consequence of
the critical impulses of the Renaissance which have been described as aim-
ing: 'to subject the power of rhetoric and the rhetoric of power to critical
scrutiny ... to draw authority itself from shadows of divine mystery into the
full glare of utilitarian rationalism' (Sharpe, 2000: 325–6).

The 1640s witnessed a rapid growth in the range and above all quality
of political debate through the distribution of printed matter and even more

importantly its discussion. The Civil War years were to have a pivotal influence on the development of periodical literature and journalism in England. Much of this is preserved by the collecting zeal of George Thomason with over 25,000 items, including 7,216 newsbooks, in the British Library. The period 1640–60 became an extended experiment in the politics of the press under conditions ranging from an almost absolute freedom to almost absolute control. Coming as it did at such an early stage in the development of 'news consciousness', these years gave a great experimental vitality to what shape and tone the news could take. The years of the English Civil War were the laboratory for the permutations of early journalism. They saw the birth of many modern techniques of modern political journalism: the planted item, the inadequately denied rumour, the inside story (Frank, 1961: 54) plus, in a world of suspected parliamentary and monarchical corruption, another staple of journalist-manufactured news, the exposé (Mendle, 2001: 58). Herd has observed how home news, especially parliamentary intelligence, became the main content but was complemented by editorial comment, articles on questions of the day, and special correspondence, which all became accepted features within the newsbooks (1952: 23). As early as 3 January 1643 in the *Kingdomes Weekly Intelligencer* there were short phrases indicating the content of reports printed below. This forerunner of the headline was soon a widely copied innovation. From 1643, it was the *Mercurius Civicus: London's Intelligencer*, particularly targeted at a metropolitan readership, which produced the first illustrations as woodcuts from its first appearance. Following this, the newsbooks were often interspersed with woodcuts using technology previously employed in popular broadsheets. They also began to use advertising to fill empty space and publicize other products from their printer.

Mendle points out how the application of ancient symbologies in 'brachygraphy' developed into a rudimentary version of shorthand which was used by reporters of trials and executions to boost the authenticity of transcribed speeches and the description of the settings of trials and executions (2001: 63) which could be noted in shorthand and then contrasted with other versions to produce a comprehensive synthesis. In the 1650s, a version developed by John Farthing was very influential. A good example even by modern standards of the abilities of writers at this time to capture the moment though these techniques, even when in the midst of momentous events, was the sober, factual report of Charles' execution from *A Perfect Diurnall* (29 January to 5 February 1649) which still has the power of great journalism to stir the emotions:

> Tuesday, January 30. This day the King was beheaded, over against the Banquetting house by Whitehall. The manner of Execution, and what passed before his death take thus. He was brought from Saint *James* about ten in the morning, walking on foot through the Park with a Regiment of Foot for his guard with Colours flying, Drums beating, his private Guard of Partizans, with some of his Gentlemen before, and some behind

bareheaded … after which the king stooping down laid his neck upon the blocke, and after a little pause stretching forth his hands, the Executioner at one blow severed his head from his Body. Then his Body was put in a coffin covered with black Velvet and removed to his lodging in Whitehall.

The rhetoric of the newsbooks was drawn from a variety of experimentation as the writers were in the main not classically educated, yet they quickly established the use of a language designed to incorporate a sense of wider community among their readers – direct, vivid, often colloquial – to draw on oral traditions of political argumentation. As they became more opiniated, they became more individuated. They canvassed and addressed readers in a confident voice with growing consistency of opinion. The newsbooks from the 1640s claimed exact dates for their news and contained domestic news and unchanging titles which gave them a greater sense of continuity and a distinct advantage over other printed matter: 'Where pamphlets, prints, ballads and verses were occasional, the newspaper offered the possibility of continuous communication and commentary on political events' (Harris, 1996: 4).

The Heads of Severall Proceedings in this Present Parliament from the 22 to the 29 November 1641, published by John Thomas, with its news of the proceedings of both Houses became the first recorded English newsbook with domestic news. It was written by Samuel Pecke who, as an illustration of the continuity between news formats, had until this point been a scrivener, writing accounts for distribution to wealthy clients in newsletters. This new venture consisted of eight pages of domestic news and was predominantly a retelling of events and discussions in Parliament. It was ordered under chronological headings and was the composite work of writers, editor and publisher. Each of these parties would expect a profit from the venture and competition between publications became fierce. The numbers of newsbooks increased, as the number of writers with an opinion to voice grew in number. The newsbook was to become a lucrative and specifically political and periodical form within a much wider proliferation of print culture which included books, pamphlets, chapbooks, ballad broadsheets, broadsides, almanacs and religious tracts. Poor printers, who, as we have seen, had long been excluded by the combination of royal privileges and the restrictions of the Stationers' Company, leapt into the carnival of experimentation, propaganda and disrespect for political opponents. Plagiarism increased as well as all attempted to provide the latest and most complete news for the readers.

The newsbooks were defined by being relatively inexpensive, weekly, and containing reports of parliamentary proceedings and debate. At the start they eschewed both the vicious prose of the pamphlet and the satirical approach of the ballad. They attempted to fashion a genre which depended on an authenticity in their style to capture the spoken nature of debate in its full flavour in order to distinguish their content as news, an ambition reflected in many of their titles. Despite these early good intentions their detractors still considered them to be intrinsically 'false and scandalous'.

At any one point in 1642 there were up to 20 of these publications and after the brief anarchy of the collapse of Charles' rule and the fall of the Star Chamber, Parliament itself in April 1642 decided to step in and limit the number of newsbooks by licensing some and prohibiting others. Pecke continued to produce the most widely respected and accurate account, *A Perfect Diurnall of the Passages in Parliament*, but this did not stop factions within the Parliament and other news writers from entering the fray. Some of them wished to publish their versions of events regularly, while others were content with an occasional contribution in the form of a political or religious pamphlet. Increasingly in the 1640s as the constitutional crisis grew, pamphlets were being produced and sold to the public on the streets by journeymen printers prepared to risk the wrath of the printing elite because the potential to make money or their commitment to a cause was so great. To temper claims for the undoubted revolution in terms of political debate and the increasing experimentation with content, Sommerville, more sceptically, comments of this frenzy of publication and the variety that it engendered: 'We cannot afford to forget that journalism is a business rather than a profession. The search for profits made news publishers ingenious' (1996: 36).

In 1642 from 10–17 June we see the appearance of the printer Humphrey Blunden's *A True Diurnall of the Last Weeks Passages in Parliament* which was the first newsbook with consecutive numbered pages. There appeared more and more Diurnall Occurrences as the conflict spread around the country and newsbooks became more dependent on correspondence from the provinces and therefore more dynamic than the court and Parliament-based reporting of their predecessors. The profusion of newsbooks meant that individual titles were in fierce competition for the patronage of their readers and stressed the topicality and reliability of their news. Other newsbooks tried for more pragmatic reasons of security to establish a reputation for factual and balanced reporting in an embryonic version of journalistic objectivity:

> A reputation for truthfulness and a concern to avoid antagonizing those in power continued to be the route to success among all editors and publishers who did not conspicuously ally themselves with a partisan group; and Pecke [*A Perfect Diurnall*], having sampled jail, never again fell off the political tightrope. (Frank, 1961: 43)

Printed news and opinion on contemporary domestic affairs became part of the spread of a written vernacular culture and part of this culture was an appreciation of the political perspectives which journalism could bring. Embedded in the discourse of the newsbooks, no matter how scrupulously they stuck to their sources and no matter how reliable those sources were, the issues of the prioritizing of sources, preferential readings and selectivity which contribute to the power of news as a social and political construction were already in evidence. In the newsbooks, as they developed during this period of political partisanship, there was an experimentation with form and genre in which news and opinion could scarcely ever be strictly separated.

The very publication of events from Parliament constituted one of those partial claims and it was this which detonated the Royalist response. Opposition to the single authority of the monarch was to a great degree constructed textually through the newsbooks and through their ability to tap into a public curiosity about political and religious affairs. Sharpe argues that the Civil War was every bit a war of words as a war of weapons (2000: 31–2). A war for the right to claim absolute authority for the word of the monarch against the diversity of opinion was lost by absolute authority. Yet the loss of absolute authority is reformulated in how various writers construct their authority *vis-à-vis* the reader. Authority is regained and reshaped through these early experiments in the formation of journalism.

By 1643 the authority of the Stationers' Company was in crisis when Parliament tried to re-establish it through the Ordinance for the Regulating of Printing on 14 June. It was a vain attempt to rein back in the feverish printing activity of the time. The Ordinance was an attempt by Parliament to support the Stationers in re-establishing control over this seemingly free flow of information and political opinion. The demand for printed material was at this point driving the market, however, and no amount of central control could stop the proliferation of presses and the production of material. It was in opposition to attempts at licensing certain sorts of printed material that Milton wrote his famous *Areopagitica*, itself published as an unlicensed pamphlet, and although he was not in favour of suspending censorship, he did not agree that the Stationers were best equipped for the job. This is widely seen as the first statement of the liberal view that in a free market of ideas, the good will supplant the bad and that all intelligent people need is access to the fullest expression of ideas for they themselves to distinguish the former from the latter. Yet Milton shared much with writers such as Jonson in his contempt for the new practice of printed news. His pamphlet, though often cited as the seminal argument for a free press, is so unconcerned with journalism that from 1651 he was able to take on the role of licenser of newsbooks. Siebert has commented on the content of the *Areopagitica*: 'Milton wanted freedom of discussion for serious-minded men who held honest, although differing opinion. He was not willing to extend this freedom to men of lesser standing with less serious purposes. To him, both Roman Catholic literature and ephemeral journalism were beyond the pale' (1965: 196). Censorship and control were so ineffective that Milton mocked them in his *Areopagitica*, mentioning how they were unable even to prevent the publication of *Mercurius Aulicus*: 'Do we not see, not once or oftner, but weekly that continu'd Court-libell against the Parlament and City, Printed, as the wet sheets can witnes, and disperst among us for all that licencing can doe?' (1979: 221). As Wheale points out: 'the publishing market outgrew the legislation which remained in all essentials the antique Tudor mechanism for the regulation of printing' (1999: 68). This had been sufficient when printing was a novelty and printed matter a relatively scarce commodity, but politics and economics had determined that this was no longer the case and journalism was entering the everyday life of a much wider section of the population.

The alternating successes of the Civil War meant that in the early stages of this proliferation of printed news and opinion, no party could establish a control which might restrict it.

From Reporting to Political Polemic

Following the initial success of the newsbooks of the early 1640s, the next movement in this exhilarating chronicle was much more radical in the weight that it gave to polemic and partisan political writing. It indicates that journalism, even in its earliest stages, was never narrowly focused on the simple reporting of the world but has always contained the potential to express opinion and have a proactive effect on the world it reports. The mercuries provided early and compelling evidence of this. The newsbooks moved rapidly from the sober reporting of 1641 to the battles of the mercuries from 1643, as the readers were exposed to attempts at opinion formation through satire, scurrilous innuendo about public figures and overt political propaganda. It is at this point that we witness the first attempt in periodical news format to create a public forum through a consistently partisan idiom. The Civil War mercuries may have sold approximately 1,000 copies a week, indicating the narrow field of reception within the population but their influence went far beyond this. The Mercury of so many titles was the messenger of the Gods and characterized the hyperbole of much of their output. Ironically, the power and reach of these newsbooks grew as their reputation for fairness and probity declined. This indicated the breadth of the market even at this stage, which ranged from those who wanted sober, balanced accounts to those who wanted the polemical fare of the mercuries. One solution in the battle to understand competing accounts of events was suggested from the market perspective of Clement Barksdale in 1651:

> As the *Armies* did against each other fight;
> Even so doe our moderne *Historians* write:
> Each for his *side*. The *Stationer* says, *Buy both*:
> Compare them, and you may *pick* out the Truth.

> (Raymond, 1996: 263)

There is a rapid movement from attempts to provide literal account of parliamentary proceedings to more whimsical and figurative accounts, as in this extract from the *Diurnall out of the North* from 1642:

> As the King was Bowling, there was scatter'd a paper with Verses, very scandalous against Mr. PYM, and shewed the King, who having read them, tore them in pieces, and with a sad looke said, *such libellous Rascals hath broke the peace of the Kingdom, and if Iustice did but lay hold of them, peoples minds would be quickly calm'd*, he that showed them very likely looked for better thankes. The Lords here sit at close, as the Houses of

Parliament doe at *London*, let every good heart pray their consultations
may meet in the Glory of God and this Kingdome. (Raymond, 1996: 133)

In fact, it was the measured and fastidious attempts by the official newsbooks at the start of this period to give impartial and accurate accounts as far
as they could that provoked opposition to them in the form of the first opiniated mercuries. Despite attempts at accurate reporting of the proceedings of
Parliament, King Charles and his court, having decamped to Oxford, felt
that in itself such reporting amounted to a provocative rationalization of the
Parliamentary cause and sought to counter it by launching *Mercurius
Aulicus*. In doing so, Charles was not only conceding that he needed to communicate to a wider public which he had been unable and unwilling to do
in the run-up to the constitutional crisis of 1641, but was also triggering the
first sustained inclusion of overt and partisan opinion into what had hitherto
claimed to be a purely factual discourse. This meshing of opinion and fact
was one of the most revolutionary leaps in journalism which the proliferation of mercuries was to bring.

Mercurius Aulicus (Oxford) was started on 8 January 1643 to counter
what they perceived to be the parliamentary propaganda of the London
Newsbooks. It was produced first by Heylin and then more emphatically by
Sir John Berkenhead with much editorial commentary and counter-accusations
of inaccuracies in reporting. Berkenhead pioneered the systematic smearing
of opponents, contradictions of other printed accounts and routinely
accused opposing newsbooks of lying, calling one of his rival publications a
'weekly cheat' (*Mercurius Aulicus*, 8 January 1643).

Whereas Pecke, for example, fastidiously checked his sources,
Berkenhead stressed splits in the Parliamentary faction in partisan fashion and
would include anything of benefit to the Royalist cause. *Mercurius Aulicus* was
full of scandal, insult and stories which dwelt on the life of the Royal Family.
It ran a section drawn from its parliamentary rival *Mercurius Britanicus* entitled 'London Lyes'. More salaciously, its tone can be gauged by the story it ran
on 23 December 1643 that a prisoner of the Royalists had been found bugger-
ing a mare and stressed that it was the worse for it happening on a Sunday!

Sunday Decemb. 17
You may remember this day three weekes, how the Rebels railed on us for
telling the world what they doe on Sundays. Their reason is (for some allow
Them to be reasonable creatures) this day revealed by an expresse from
Shrewsbury; wherein it was certified among other particulars, that on Sunday
last Decemb. 9. while His majesties Forces were at Church, one of their
Prisoners was missed by his Keeper, who searching for him, and looking
through a cranny into the Stable, he saw a ladder erected and the holy Rebell
(busie at a Conventicle) committing Buggery on the Keepers owne Mare.

Mercurius Aulicus was the first 'official' Royalist newsbook published in
England. It was immediately countered by the Parliament-sponsored

Mercurius Britanicus: Communicating the Affaires of Great Britaine: for the Better Information of the People by Thomas Audley and Marchamont Nedham which attempted to return the vicious rhetorical onslaught started by Berkenhead. The subtitle indicated the importance placed by the mercuries on calls to a people involved in politics. Its style, particularly that of Nedham, contributed much to the development of an opiniated journalism of political engagement. Yet it was not only Nedham's style which signalled a formative moment in the discourse of journalism during these years. It was also the fact that as a writer whose undoubted talents could be a big advantage for whoever paid him, he switched sides in the Civil War not once but twice, indicating that as a professional writer, not a professional zealot, he was willing to shift pragmatically depending on the circumstances and who was paying his wages.

The sly and sarcastic abilities of Nedham were soon in evidence, as in this brief extract:

> Where is King *Charles*? What's become of him? The strange variety of opinions leaves nothing certain: for some say, that he saw the Storm comming after him as far as *Bridgewater*, he ran away to his *dearly beloved* in *Ireland*; yes, they say he *ran away* out of his own *Kingdome* very *Majestically*. (*Mercurius Britanicus*, 28 July to 4 August, 1645)

In 1645 news production peaked with the production of 722 newspapers of various forms (Siebert, 1965: 209). The importance of this went beyond the quantity of material being produced. It was the interaction of this quantity with the opinion and discussion which it generated which created such an intellectual turmoil. The circulation of opinion on such a regular and widespread basis generated an extremely productive and provocative cycle of publicity: 'As news publications incorporated a greater number of people into the arena of political debate this debate was increasingly polarized. The production of news … generated conflicting opinions and permitted those divergent opinions already existing to become public' (Raymond, 1996: 115).

In the 1640s editors and printers intervened less and less in the ferociously partisan wars of the mercuries but still many of the freedoms demanded by this writing remained implicit. For the first explicit, philosophically principled demands for the freedom of news and opinion production as part of a truly radical perspective, we must turn to the Levellers and their petition to Parliament, backed by 40,000 signatures, of 11 September 1648. In this, which Mabbott printed in the *Moderate*, they demanded the establishment of a republic, declared themselves against the king and for the army as long as it supported the will of the people. It was most importantly written in language which was accessible to its target audience whether literate or listening to the petition read out loud: 'In actively preaching democracy Mabbott was smart enough to realize that his message had to be simple' (Frank, 1961: 156). Bearing in mind that estimates put the number of literate population in London at 70–80 per cent and nationwide at 30 per cent in the

1640s, this was testimony to both good journalism and good politics. The following extract captures a flavour of its polemical commitment to the freedom of political expression in the press as a fundamental and universal political right:

> As for any prejudice to Government thereby, if Government be just in its Constitution, and equal in its distributions, it will be good, if not absolutely necessary for them, to hear all voices and judgements, which they can never do, but by giving freedom to the Press, and in case any abuse their authority by scandalous pamphlets, they will never want Advocates to vindicate their innocency. And therefore all things being duly weighed, to refer all Books and Pamphlets to the judgement, discretion, or affection of Licensers, or to put the least restraint upon the Press, seems altogether inconsistent with the good of the Commonwealth, and expressly opposite and dangerous to the liberties of the people, and to be carefully avoided, as any other exorbitancy or prejudice in Government. (Siebert, 1965: 201)

No other writer of this period is a better indicator of the potential variety and pragmatism within early journalism than Marchamont Nedham. Nedham was imprisoned in 1645 for accusing the king of 'a guilty Conscience, bloody hands, a Heart full of broken Vowes and protestations' and in addition mocking his speech defect (Raymond, 1996: 43). After this brief period of imprisonment for his 'seditious libel', he was recruited to start the appropriately named Royalist *Mercurius Pragmaticus* from 14 September 1647. By the mid-decade the mercuries had established the pattern of their coverage and had shifted in their hostilities from King vs Parliament to Parliament vs Army. In 1647 Parliament decided to act against unlicensed printing and on 30 September issued an ordinance which prohibited anyone from printing any news-sheets without the approval of the licenser under pain of fine, confiscation of equipment, imprisonment or whipping. It is not clear that this had very much effect as one of its chief targets, Nedham, escaped punishment. *Mercurius Pragmaticus* was a potent mix of scurrilous invective as a clandestine publication, and Nedham's contributions have been described by Frank as constituting 'an anti-Puritan Cassandra' (1961: 140). It was produced and distributed while Nedham was constantly on the run from the Parliamentary authorities and the army. His importance to journalism in its early form is summed up:

> Nedham gave his readers a good many peeks at the machinations of a successful political faction ... If one looks at the London scene of 1647–48 through the lens of *Pragmaticus*, he sees a grimy landscape flecked with graft, violence, and cruel ambition. It is a distorted view, but it was well drawn and included objects and shadings that no other journal could manage. (ibid.: 141)

He contributed to the success of this publication until after the execution of his patron the King when, on 13 June 1649, he changed sides once again and began work on the Parliamentarian *Mercurius Politicus* which claimed in its sub-title to be, 'in defence of the Commonwealth and for information of the People'. In his opening preface, he asked in self-deprecation, 'Why should not the Commonwealth have a fool as well as the king had?' and proceeded to blend his own brand of earthy humour, appetite for gossip and trenchant wit with more thoughtful meditations on government and republican politics. From 1650 it was the dominant news organ in England. It contained foreign and domestic news and often including stirring republican polemic from Nedham. Fox-Bourne hypothesizes that at some point during the employment of Milton as censor of the press early in the 1650s, he may well have influenced if not even written for Nedham (1998: 21–2). In August 1655 Cromwell put into effect a series of laws against the press. There was little competition to official publications, given the scrupulous supervision by Cromwell's Secretary of State, John Thurloe, but Nedham's freewheeling days were over. From 1655–59 *Mercurius Politicus* enjoyed government sponsorship and he continued its impressive demonstration of the miscellany and vitality of early journalism, as well as confirming the commercial attractiveness of the newsbook format until it was finally closed down in 1660 as the Restoration with its more conservative and less polemical newsbooks took over under Muddiman and then Lestrange. Nedham was an important contributor to the development of journalism in his pioneering of editorial opinion and his facility for publicizing republican ideas in a language and rhetoric which combined political sophistication with an ear for a vernacular appeal to a relatively broad readership. As well as being an extremely effective writer, Nedham was astute enough financially to see the potential of the advertisements which had started to feature in most of the successful newsbooks of the period, as he became associated with the first advertising-only publication from 1657, the *Publick Adviser*. The inclusion of advertisements had started as a strategy by printers to use up empty space in their publications by placing announcements in their newsbooks for other publications of theirs, from books to pamphlets, but the practice soon became lucrative enough for the publishers to be canvassing outside their own business for advertising in order to boost their income. It would not be long until the interdependence of advertising and news became a characteristic combination of journalism, with all the benefits and compromises this brings. This period also saw the inclusion in the newsbooks on a regular basis of the movement and cargo of ships into London.

Throughout this period, the Royalist faction continued to retain a loyal community in their own mercuries even after the execution of the King, such as the polemically sub-titled:

> *Mercurius Militarius or Times only Truth Teller*
> Faithfully Undeceiving, The Expectations of the Vulgar, (who are daily abused by a Crew of brainlesse and brazen-faced News-scriblers whether Royall, Martiall, or Parliamentall) who have sold themselves for a penny to doe wickedly, relating the most perfect translations, both forraigne and domestick, collected with much labour from divers particulars, and here

presented in one bundle to the Reader. (From Tuesday May the 22 to Tuesday May 29 1649)

Some proclaimed their opinions through verse, indicating the generic variation in approaches to political reporting at the time and the intertextuality of print culture as it drew on a wide range of forms including ballad, poetry and, as we will see later, drama:

> *Mercurius Elenctius (For King Charles II)*
> From Munday April 30 to Munday May 7 1649
> Communicating Intelligence from all Parts, touching all Affaires, Designes, Humours and Conditions throughout the Kingdome. Especially from Westminster, and the Head-Quarters
>
> Tremble ye Tyrants, now the heavens appeare
> Serene, and radiant Phebus from his phere,
> … Breakes your black night of horror, with his rayes,
> And breathes us life, in hope of halcyon dayes.
> … And from the Ashes of our Martyr'd King,
> Charls our true Phenix on his Throne shall spring.
>
> 4 March 1650 *Royal Diurnal*
> Blush, shameless England, weep, drown'd in thy vile staine,
> Of Blood with Teares: shall damn'd Rebellion reigne,
> Whilst CHARLs his sacred Blood doth cry
> Aloud for Vengeance on the Blood-guilty?

This loyalty to the king's cause would remain an essential structuring dynamic within the press, through the Restoration, Glorious Revolution and through the eighteenth-century series of Jacobite rebellions. It is such binarism which from this point onwards through its expression in print becomes the focus for the adversarial politics which would generate the Whig/Tory duopoly characteristic of the British political system into the twentieth century and confirms the role of newspaper journalism in its development. The press was also the location for other manifestations of the effects of the social anarchy of the Civil War on the population. Friedman (1993) claims that the proliferation of news of strange occurrences indicated that in the wake of the execution of Charles, the world had been turned upside down. Almanacs were also given a great boost at this time of great uncertainty about the future and the genuine feeling among many was that they were living though an era of heightened cosmic importance as the king whom many believed to be a divine representative on earth had been removed by force from his throne and executed (Capp, 1979). Almanacs foresaw many equally disturbing events to come as God rebuked the population. For all their desire to be involved in political and religious controversy, there was no lack in the mercuries of what would become a staple of a certain sort of sensational journalism, the strange and inexplicable occurrence under a title which clearly indicates claims to veracity despite its content:

A perfect Mermaid was, by the last great winde, driven ashore nere Greenwich, with her combe in one hande and her lookinge-glasse in the other. She seemed to be of the countenance of a most faire and beautiful woman, with her armes crossed, weeping out many pearly drops of salt tears; and afterwards, she, gently turning herself upon her back againe, swamme away without being seen any more. (*Mercurius Democritus; or, a True and Perfect Nocturnal*, 2 November 1653)

There was a nearly insatiable demand for domestic news at this time of public political debate. In deference to the growing awareness of a more public scrutiny, parliamentary debates appealed more explicitly to the people of the country and the newsbooks and mercuries eagerly amplified this trend. Both sides in the run-up to the outbreak of hostilities in the Civil War made arguments to the people in print and called on their support with reasoned argument, invective and counter-argument. The sub-title of the *Scottish Dove* of 1643 is of interest in the way that it locates its purpose in opposing Royalist propaganda and in so doing lays claim to its own discourse of reliability. Such claims were commonplace, despite the widespread use of invective as each of the mercuries sought to establish itself as the most reliable for its particular readership: 'The *Scottish Dove*, sent out and returning; bringing intelligence from the Armies, and makes some Relations of other observable Passages of both Kingdoms, for Information and Instruction. As an Antidote against the Poisonous Insinuations of *Mercurius Aulicus* and the errours of other Intelligencers.'

Generic Experimentation within Early Journalism

This period also witnessed the development of a more scatalogical form of periodical publication descended from oral traditions of gossip and ribaldry which has maintained a continuous presence within the traditions of journalism ever since. Fervent Royalist, John Crouch, provided smut and scandal but with the political edge that they were often at the expense of Puritan personalities. He was prolific at the height of the Commonwealth's attempts to impose a severe public morality and yet for all the profanity of his and many other similar publications, the Puritan government seemed happy to tolerate them as long as they did not commit the more serious crime of political sedition. He produced the worst offender in terms of content with the 1654 *Mercurius Fumigosus, or The Smoking Nocturnal*. It combined news of a sort with dirty jokes and ditties. It was very popular and very much imitated by rivals eager to exploit a profitable market at the entertainment end of the spectrum of printed periodical material. Its sub-title indicated the 'world-upside-down' nature of its endeavour with the frisson of its promise to reveal what was hidden even by the depths of night:

> *Mercurius Fumigosus or The Smoking Nocturnal*
> Communicating Dark and hidden Newes Out of all Obscure Places in the
> *Antipodes*, whether in Fire, Aire, Earth or Water For the right understand-
> ing of all the Mad Merry *People* in the Land of *Darkness*.

It starts with a reasonably straightforward version of contemporary events
as if to better contrast its later subversion of the serious newsbook style with
a section called, 'The Diurnal News' before moving swiftly through, 'News
out of Bedlam' and the main attraction, 'Now for our Nocturnal Newes'.
Archly, Crouch, confident of his reader's tastes, recommends to them:

> Of Country Newes I now must Prate,
> and something rare and new,
> I meddle not with Church nor State,
> but News more pleasing you.

> (13 June–20 June 1655)

This section consists of a veritable carnival of lewd miscellany including
Letters, Jokes and Ballads which include such characters and topics as
Cuckolds, Codpieces, Lifted Skirts, A Dog's Execution, A Public Rat Burning,
Bawdy Bakers, City Dames, Tankard Women, Merry Maides, and Py
Women. The content of the Nocturnal News can often seem alien to our con-
temporary tastes but a flavour is captured in the short extract below:

> A merry Maggot-monger not long since coming home late from the Sack-
> shop with a rattle at his tayle ... to save Coals, he down with his breeches,
> and dropped so much *yellow Frankincense* thereon, that raised such a
> smother, that the Smoak choaked Six hundred and fifty Ratts ... and fifty
> Mice. (19 September to 3 October 1655)

In an earlier venture from 1649 by Crouch, there is a premonition of a certain
kind of investigative muckraking in the *Man in the Moon*'s promise to expose
'knavery' among politicians and then, as now, a market ready to buy it. The
carnival inversion of his nocturnal perambulations is captured in the
announcement:

> Make room there for the *Man in the Moon*, that his Nocturnall walkes, hath
> discovered more *knavery* than ever (before these prodigious times) was
> acted by my People under the *Sun*; I visit the *House of Commons* every day,
> the *Counsell of State*, the *Counsell of Warre*, nay the Common Counsell can-
> not keep me out; I see all their deep Conspiracies, heare their closest
> Debates, understand their slyest *Plotts*, can Paraphrase upone them.

> (16 April 1649)

One fascinating addition to the variety of generic devices for commenting on
public events in these years was the printed pamphlet play. The generic variety
of many of the newsbooks allowed satirical content to be foregrounded.
Poetry, and even more so play pamphlets, where sexual innuendo could be

indulged in, undermined any fledgling claims to objective reporting. News in the almanacs had already become history by the time of its consumption and space left over was often left for readers' comments and observations. Pamphlet plays, however, presented themselves to their readers as both news and a sort of entertainment that could be repeated much like the ballad form. They were often bound together with newsbooks to further emphasize the mingling of printed genres. They, like more formal news categories, addressed their readers as participants in a vibrant dialogue of political formation as citizens which characterized this period of print culture's emergence. They had an additional effect in promoting discussion of printed material because of their controversial and provocative illustration of many of the debates of the day. One of the best-known writers of these pamphlet plays was Richard Overton. A characteristic example of his work *Articles of Treason* is cited by Wiseman:

> a dialogue between Master Papist 'a profest Catholike' and Master Newes 'A Temporiser'. Wiseman has pointed out the connotations of news as a 'temporiser', acting as a mediator between news and public and turning the times to its own economic advantage, both as political opinion and as commodity. This ambivalence is at the core of the way playlets popularized political debate and were also categorized as news in the 1640s. (1999: 68)

By the emergence of *Mercurius Politicus*, the newsbook had become a truly multi-generic text. Often satirical treatment of the issues and personalities of the day pushed the events themselves out of the spotlight. The Civil War mercuries provided an exuberant inversion of the hierarchies of the early seventeenth century during two decades of irreverent experimentation and snubbing of authority. The contribution of individual authors to the generic dynamism of the journalism of this formative era demonstrates the perceptiveness of Fox-Bourne's comment that 'journalism has progressed as a phase of authorship, no less than as a powerful engine for the political advancement of the community' (1998: vi).

Women's Contribution to Early Journalism

Much of the narrative of early journalism is dominated by male writers and this reflects the gender divisions of the age. Nevitt has commented that the discourses of the time towards women in print media were informed by highly gendered and misogynistic language (1999: 84). These divisions were evident in the production and consumption of news. There were certainly women readers and in the lower classes women mercury sellers, but there is no evidence that there were women writers of newsbooks. As might be expected, one exception to this pattern comes from the Levellers with their radical philosophies of equality, and we know of the reputation of Katherine Chidley as a pamphleteer in her own right. Yet there were significant numbers of women printers – 300 between 1580 and 1720, the majority after 1640 according to Wheale (1999), but none claimed the title of Masters or even Mistresses of the trade. The complex and co-operative process of publication which blurred the boundaries of author, printer, publisher, editor, or book-shop owner in journalism's early history becomes shattered by narratives which foreground one significant person, usually a man, and occlude the contributors further down the social scale and especially women. Thus Sheppard, Nedham, Pecke, Crouch, Border and Walker are remembered as individual names over the collective exclusion of the numbers of anony-mous women and the other co-operators of the Civil War, Grub Street and beyond.

One woman who has escaped the eroding tendencies of patriarchal histories is Elizabeth Alkin, who played her part as an intelligencer for the Commonwealth and circulated information on Royalist sympathizers. Because of her intimate knowledge of the book trade she was able to track down the producers and distributors of unsympathetic publications. Between 21 June and 30 September 1651, according to Nevitt (1999: 94), she was involved in the production of no less than ten newsbooks, including one in which she is referred to by name, *The Impartial Scout*, which specialized in naval and military news. Between September 1650 and September 1651 Alkin was also involved in the production of single issues of *The Moderne Intelligencer*, *Mercurius Anglicus*, and *The Modern Intelligencer* (ibid.: 98).

As an outspoken anti-Royalist, Alkin became known as Parliament Joan for her part in supporting the parliamentary side. Between May and June 1650 she sold counterfeit Royalist newsbooks to identify who peddled the authentic ones and was so successful that both she and the soldiers returned from Cromwell's suppression of the Irish rebellion cleared the streets of London of these publications.

The Establishment of a News Culture

Siebert has concluded that by the time of the Commonwealth, 1649–51, 'Journalism, controlled or uncontrolled, had become a permanent social and political phenomenon' (1965: 220). This book would agree that many identi-fiable features of journalism could be seen at this time. Readers were being targeted as participants in politics but also as consumers who could deliver profits to the printers and publishers. This meant that the new medium was not solely political but identifiably part of the generic hybrid between pub-lic information source, communal identity and profit which constitutes jour-nalism. Political opinion in this era of the mid-seventeenth century was formed from a wide range of sources including gossip, rumour, broadside, ballad, pamphlet, book, and news-sheet, thus forming a complex and multi-ple textual community of political debate at an everyday level. The fact that, increasingly, printers and booksellers sought out this readership as profitable indicates something of its scale and the newsbooks were central in providing a forum in which the readership could become familiar with the blending of this miscellany of print culture: 'Newspapers (and earlier newsbooks) played an important part in constructing readers' sense of neighbourly and national identity by spanning linguistic constituencies and geographical entities ... the newspaper constructed the basis of a series of interlocking and overlapping spheres of political debate and action in different communities of readers' (Raymond, 1999b: 130).

The increasing use of the terms 'Spy' and 'Scout' in the titles of newsbooks indicated a shift in the ways in which news gathering was being perceived by some practitioners; rather than reporting the world, they were intruding upon aspects of it which were not by rights theirs to access. For the first time, in the process of its own creation, the public discourse of journalism, the 'first draft of history' becomes as much as part of that history as a simple commentary on events. The newsbooks did this by 'furnishing a language with which to describe history ("diurnal occurrences", and "exact journal", a "perfect diurnal") and establishing the content of that history' (Raymond, 1996: 312).

By 1655 the temporary suspension of decorum and deference was almost at an end. In this year Cromwell saw to the enforcement of the Ordinances on Printing and effected them in ways which were as stringent as controls of the press had been in Elizabethan times. The more contentious content of certain newsbooks did not disappear but was suppressed into other printed forms including the newsletter. The increase in weekly postal services to three by 1655 meant that even with the increasing control of official publications under Cromwell's Commonwealth, the thirst for news could be satisfied by an increased and more regular flow of newsletters. The public dissemination of political information which the newsbooks had pioneered retained some of its vitality through newsletters which continued news circulation to a wider post-revolutionary social audience. Throughout this period there were concerted attempts to force errant printers and writers to restrain the vitriol of their attacks on religion, politics and personalities. Fines, imprisonment, whippings were to be meted out to those who broke the often hastily changed statutes on licensing and libels. The sellers, writers and distributors could all be held responsible in the increasingly effective attempts to control content and distribution of controversial material. By the Restoration the return to a situation of central control over journalism may have become established practice once again, but the news culture in which journalism would continue to extend its influence had become a much more widely accepted constituent of social life. Even under repressive conditions, the logic of this embryonic culture of communication was to find ways of re-negotiating its public presence.

3

Periodicals and the Formation of the Bourgeois Public Sphere

The Consolidation of Journalism

The news culture of the Civil War period had provoked a pullulating range of experiments in the forms and styles of journalism. The years which followed the Restoration provided a time of quieter consolidation for both printers and writers and also for politicians adapting to the implications of a wider reach of information flow. Harris and Lee (1978: 44) point out that there was no political or commercial drive to produce journalism for a wider audience at this stage, although there was clearly a readership for it. The scale of this readership was demonstrated by the wide circulation of broadsides, chapbooks and ballads as the mainstream political press was forced by legislation to concentrate on the respectable commercial classes as its constituency. The readership of newspapers may have addressed the 'nation' or the 'people', but in effect it was restricted to a predominantly metropolitan stratum, a narrow elite in contact with the actual business of government and conduct of the economy. Much of what had constituted the formative diversity of journalism during the Civil War and much of what was later to re-emerge as an essential part of journalism's vitality were hawked to the lower classes for profit and entertainment, as a journalism which concentrated on a restricted range of information was targeted towards the upper middle classes by booksellers anxious to maintain their profits and their good standing with government. Ultimately, such a division was always going to be too restrictive for the commercially orientated and generically varied practice of journalism. Just as the evolution of journalism is no smooth and continuous transition from ignorance to public enlightenment, neither is it a series of simple pendular swings of progression and regression. Macdowell sees the post-Restoration years as a time of coalescence in which 'The printed news and public debate of the new Journals, Medlesy, Mer'cries was inseparable from an older oral culture in which news and opinions were still spread primarily by conversation and gossip in the marketplace, coffee-house, and street' (1998: 124–5).

Some commentators consider the time from the Restoration to the lapsing of the Licensing Act in 1695 to have been a 'bleak period for English journalism' (Smith, 1979: 41) and yet in many less spectacular ways it constitutes an equally important formative stage for journalism. It may have seen the return of many regressive features such as the loss of parliamentary reporting for over one hundred years, the return of direct censorship and control by an autocratic monarch, but Sutherland (1986) stresses the steady, if unspectacular, contribution of the period, especially when its suppressed potential bursts into view between 1679 and 1682. The barrenness of this period for journalism has been overstated. First, the return of a more rigorous censorship of the press on the Restoration of the monarchy is something of a red herring, considering how after 1655 Cromwell had already recognized the dangers to authority of unrestricted periodical publishing and had Nedham running the *Mercurius Politicus* and the *Publick Intelligencer* as uncontentious publications, disseminating foreign news and Parliament-approved material. Second, many commentators, including most prominently Habermas, have identified the period following the Restoration as being characterized by the initial grouping of what he termed the 'bourgeois public sphere', the historical crystallization of the bourgeois class and its expression in print (Habermas, 1992). Charles II realized the dangers as well as the political advantages of bringing a larger section of society into the flow of public communication. This larger section was the rising bourgeoisie and the story of journalism over the next two centuries was to be an account of the ways in which this class negotiated its central role in society through print culture and the impact that this had on the formation and discourse of journalism.

Journalism in these years began to move from a 'stratum of literary output' (Harris, 1978: 82) to a form of mediated political information, and the increased regularity of this flow meant that it began to take on the altogether different energy which came from the expectation of increasing numbers within society of an involvement in news on an everyday basis. In the seventeenth century, it was difficult to be exact about what constituted a 'newspaper' given the many varied formats and styles in print, but the term 'newspaper' is first recorded in 1670 and the newspaper as a specific form of journalism emerged, sober and prudent under the renewed gaze of monarch and licenser, after the Civil War, as the content and structure of the newspaper press began to take on a more regular pattern. However, the regular discussion of news was just as important for the formation of a public as the increasingly regular supply of news. Habermas sees this 'public sphere' as an arena between the individual and the state where a compromise between the conflicting interests of the aristocratic and bourgeois classes was negotiated and won in the face of authoritarian state traditions by 'the critical judgement of a public making use of its reason' (1992: 24). Journalism was the catalyst for the creation of this public sphere and was structurally linked through the period of the Restoration to the creation of what Habermas has called, 'the thoroughly bourgeois idea of the freely self-actualizing personality' (ibid.: 13). These bourgeois individuals were bringing themselves into history by the exercise of their critical judgement on the information supplied through various forms of early journalism. Therefore the link between this public sphere and journalism is strongly reinforced. Journalism became defined as inclusive of the debate and opinion of its readers as part of its own process of 'self-actualization'. It is important to stress that this was a process, not an event. The consequences of the turbulence of the Civil War had left a state whose claims to absolute authority continued to be eroded despite the Restoration, because a bourgeoisie whose confidence in its own place in the social and political fabric was growing despite restrictive measures like press control which were intended to impede it. The period from 1660 saw a narrow section of the bourgeois public struggling for a stake in political authority and print is the terrain upon which this struggle becomes most evident in contesting the absolute authority of the monarchy and its political allies. This would continue, according to Habermas, until 'the public … held together through the medium of the press and its professional criticism' (ibid.: 51).

The public sphere also enabled a dominant liberal version of journalism to establish its main political claim which asserts itself as attempting to align with, yet retain a distance from, political power. This balancing act between the press's relationship with political power and its unwritten pact with the structural contingencies of the economic – the need to make a profit – is essential to journalism's commercial legitimation. The fact that it claims to conduct this business on behalf of the public is its political legitimation. Unlike Jürgen Habermas whose public sphere tends to be a concrete space of exchange, often linked with the coffee house, Levy, drawing on the work of Halasz (1997), interestingly for our purposes, puts the public sphere entirely within the realm of discourse:

> Such discourse is an abstract entity, a limitless source on which capital draws in order to produce textual property, a property then commodified by being put into as wide a circulation as possible to maximize profits. Such circulation is not free of constraints: the state, the church, the market, even an intimate private sphere, all try and control the flow of textual property for their own ends. Instead of lying in an intermediary position between the sphere of the state and the private sphere, this 'public sphere' is (not only) inseparable from state, market and 'intimate sphere,' it is the medium of their interweaving. (Levy, 1999: 33)

This perspective endorses the view of this study that journalism, woven within this public sphere, emerges as a range of claims on power and authority and is not wrested from authority but becomes part of those complexes of power. Since the growing economic power was that of the bourgeoisie, journalism's claims to represent that public cannot be disassociated from its own claims to authority. We must now consider how journalism attempted to align itself favourably within the newly emerging bourgeois model of authority.

Let us return to the claim that the era from 1660 constituted an important period of consolidation for journalism and its dominant clientele, the bourgeoisie. Renewed restrictions on press freedom masked the growth of opposition which would culminate in a renegotiated place for journalism in public life. We need, therefore, to consider briefly developments in journalism from the time of the Restoration to the Stamp Act of 1712. In 1660, General Monck invited Henry Muddiman, a Royalist supporter, to issue an information sheet called *Mercurius Publicus*. Its purpose, indicative of the function that the incoming regime planned for the press, was to prepare a loyal England for the return of its monarch. On the Restoration, 31 May 1660, Berkenhead who had proved his loyalty and his credentials as a news writer and editor on *Mercurius Aulicus* became Charles II's first supervisor of the press. Control over the number and content of licensed publications was increased. One consequence of this was a reciprocal increase in the circulation of handwritten and printed newsletters and the return to the import of news from the Low Countries. With the genie out of the bottle, the thirst for a wide range of alternative news sources could not be simply corked up and the news culture sought other provisional discursive channels.

Printing was to continue to be limited to the 20 master printers of the Stationers' Company of London and the universities, but this limitation was to be better policed. One thing was certain; the new regime certainly had an appreciation of the subversive potential of the press and a sustained range of policies designed to improve the central management of news. They were quick to pass an 'Act for preventing the frequent Abuses in printing seditious, treasonable, and unlicensed Books and Pamphlets, and for regulating of Printing and printing Presses' on 10 June 1662 and this remained the basis of control until 1694. A resolution was passed on 25 June 1660 to restrict what had become the prerogative of the English over the previous decade and a half until Cromwell's crackdown on newsbooks in 1655, access to printed accounts of Parliament: 'that no person whatsoever do presume at his peril to print any votes of proceedings of this House without the special leave and order of this House' (Herd, 1952: 27).

The *Mercurius Publicus* was soon supplemented by a second official newsbook, *The Kingdom's Intelligencer* and these provided a limited range of news, including sympathetic accounts of the king and his family until they were suppressed, most probably because they were not being conducted with the rigour expected. In order to remedy this, Berkenhead was replaced by Lestrange as Surveyor of the Press from 24 February 1662. Lestrange was well positioned to act as Surveyor because he had experience of printing and writing during the Protectorate, which meant that he knew where to look for illicit publications and presses and understood the printers' motivations in breaking regulations. He founded two new newsbooks whose didactic subtitles reveal much about what the king and his Surveyor of the Press expected the function of the press to be. These were '*The Intelligencer, published for the Satisfaction and Information of the People, with Privilege*' which appeared from August 1663 on Mondays and '*The News, published for the*

Satisfaction and Information of the People' which was to appear from 3 September 1663 on Thursdays. The appeal to the people was an indication that at least rhetorically Charles II's press recognized that it had to engage with a broader constituency. There was no doubt in the minds of some influential policy-makers in the aftermath of the Restoration that the widespread dissemination of opinion and propaganda among the population had been a direct contribution to the demise of Charles I. Chief among these was Sir Roger Lestrange who took a homeopathic view that the cure for the evils of unrestrained printing was in dispensing small doses of the poison to effect a cure: 'Tis the *Press* that has made 'um *Mad*, and the *Press* must set 'um *Right* again. The Distemper is *Epidemical*; and there's no way in the world, but by *Printing*, to convey the *Remedy* to the *Disease'* (Raymond, 1999b: 109).

Lestrange was supported by the full weight of judicial authority. This was notoriously demonstrated by the arrest and brutal execution of Twynn, a printer of unlicensed and seditious material. In endorsing the work of Lestrange and its bloody consequences, Lord Chief Justice Hyde stressed the need for examples in Twynn and others in 1663: 'The Press is grown so common, and Men take the Boldness to print whatever is brought to them, let it concern whom it will; it is high time Examples be made' (Sutherland, 1986: 2).

In the years 1662–79, Lestrange as the Surveyor of the Press became a significant power in the land and worked a complex combination of licences, seizures, sureties, punishments and limitations on apprenticeships. Siebert describes some of the complexity of his motivations:

> Lestrange typified the seventeenth-century official attitude toward printed news. He decried the public demand for more information concerning affairs of state but condoned the publication of such news provided no untoward reactions were precipitated. As both publisher and censor, responsible to the crown through the secretaries of state, he held his monopolistic privileges only on condition that he exercised discretion. His income, on the other hand, depended largely on the popularity of his wares. On more than one occasion he was forced to expand his services to satisfy public demand. (Siebert, 1965: 293)

Siebert gives an example of how in 1665 Lestrange doubled the size of the *News* when war with Holland broke out. This provides us with a fair indication of how even a restricted form of journalism continued to display the self-interest of the publisher and his desire to make money out of what the readers were willing to buy. Despite his economic motivations, he remained wary of the democratic implications of a widening of the base for political information. This was evident when he set out his views on the independent newsbook, the rival journalism medium, which he disapproved of as expressed in the first edition of his *Intelligencer* of 31 August 1663: 'it makes the multitude too familiar with the actions and counsels of their superiors, too pragmatical and censorious, and gives them not only an itch, but a kind of colourable right and licence, to be meddling with the government'.

Clearly this was something unacceptable to both monopoly newswriter and autocratic government.

However, even within such attempts at constraint, the demand for more independent sources of information provided a lucrative market for alternatives. Muddiman may have been deposed as the official newspaper publisher but retained the privilege of free postage. In order to make the most of this commercial opportunity, he developed a renewed system of newsletters and the subsequent success of his service demonstrated that there was a market which wanted a broader range of news than a monopoly could provide. Lestrange's venture was profitable chiefly because of his power to close down formal avenues of news circulation, but the fact that he needed to keep to the restrictions placed on him by the government determined the nature of alternative news provision. The reliability of Muddiman's newsletters and their political content meant that Lestrange's publications were forced into including at least some reporting of the Acts passed by Parliament, if not the details of the debates, and to conform to some notion of reliability and veracity beyond the authority of the government. Muddiman's reputation as a journalist was rewarded when, despite having lost the lucrative role as licenser for the government news publications, he was given the task of founding the official government paper, the *Oxford Gazette*, which was published in Oxford until it moved back to a plague-free London and became the *London Gazette*. From 1665 the *Oxford Gazette* was published twice weekly by Muddiman who was the principal influence behind its style and structure and who ran it during its first formative year. It was produced in an entirely different format from the earlier newsbooks. It was a half-sheet with two columns on each side, meaning a more economical use of paper. Herd comments on its importance: 'In the history of journalism its significance lies in the fact that its single leaf form (technically a half sheet in folio), with its pages divided into two columns, broke away from the news-pamphlet form to a style that is a recognizable link with the newspaper as we know it today' (1952: 33).

Despite the official ban on newspapers other than the official *Gazette* from 1666 to 1679, the effect of the proliferation of public news in print form during the Civil War years meant that the government at least felt obliged to supply an official outlet for news, something which had not been provided under any preceding regime.

The *Gazette* returned to London as the *London Gazette* in 1666 after which time it was no longer edited or written by Muddiman but by a collection of government writers, and from then until 1679 it was the only official newspaper providing government announcements and, in addition, a combination of court and foreign news. It had a good reputation especially for its foreign service principally because of its privileged access to diplomatic sources. It was, however, handicapped because of its lack of most domestic political news although it did contain regular briefings on the activities of the Royal family. From 1671, indicating an increase in commercial opportunities, it began to carry advertisements. It expressed its official nature through a cool and considered mode of presentation. As a self-conscious newspaper of record, its anonymous authorship and professional style could not have been more different to the personalized polemic of the mercuries of a few years before. Yet any truly interesting domestic news continued to circulate chiefly by means of the manuscript newsletter and that is why readers would pay a premium for it. In similar ways to the preceding generation of newsletter writers, Henry Muddiman continued to exploit his wide range of contacts to maintain the range and credibility of his output. His newsletters contained among other things, foreign newspapers, correspondence from sources close to the government, extracts from parliamentary discussions, copies of private letters and pamphlets. Journalism was informed as much by style of writing and contents, as by the networks of communication to which the newswriters had access. In demonstrating his ability to build these networks and exploit them through the efficient editorial sifting of material and his astute targeting of his work to a specific readership willing to pay regularly for it, Muddiman is perhaps the first modern journalist.

Despite the efforts of official printed publications such as the *London Gazette* to maintain a bond between the word of authority and the truth, print culture itself had already loosened that relationship. In part, this had been precipitated by the dissemination of a wide range of interpretations of contemporary events in the Civil War, but it was also part of longer trajectories of change throughout the Early Modern era. It was this break in the perceived unity between language and truth which enabled the flourishing of opinion and constituted an important cultural shift which enabled a legitimation of many of the practices which would lead to the fuller development of journalism. One explanation for this is provided by Sharpe, writing of the late Renaissance period: 'the revival of the classics and the teaching of classical oratory reinforced the close association between rhetoric and power, but simultaneously exposed the possibility of a gap between language and truth, the capacity of words (and their authors) to mis-represent as well as represent' (2000: 30). Journalism was, from the start, inextricably involved not only with the circulation of reliable information about the world, but also with selectivity concerning which information to include and a range of opinion about the merits of such information.

The Crucible of the Coffee House

From the late 1650s a new phenomenon began to establish itself in the pattern of English urban culture which was to have a remarkable effect on the dissemination of information among the bourgeoisie (Pincus, 1995). The coffee house is seen quite literally as the space of exchange which corresponds to Habermas' public sphere and it is here that we must look for one of the fundamental factors in the enhancement of news consciousness and the creation of a discourse of public opinion which would shape how journalism emerged. The functions of the coffee shop illustrate how a continuation of a news culture through other means became possible and how this era of close scrutiny and control of the press was not as arid a period for journalism as might have been imagined. Largely because of the coffee shop, journalism was not synonymous with the official newspapers and it was through the period of 1680 to 1730 that the coffee house was to have its most marked effect. At a time when the newspapers had returned to a dull routine and were heavily controlled by government, the coffee houses provided a location for a social exchange of information in a comfortable and non-domestic environment. In the years of the early Restoration, they flourished in the lanes and streets around the Royal Exchange in London, once again the hive of news and gossip activity and by the mid-1670s coffee houses had established themselves in all the major urban centres of England. Just as they drew customers eager to discuss politics, they also attracted newswriters eager to be involved in further refining gossip and disseminating the latest information, alert to the possibility of gathering fresh intelligence or opinion on matters of the moment. These places were considered to be dens of argument and dissent and were recognized as incontrovertibly Whig and oppositional. They reinforced the assumption made by critics of the news culture that it necessarily provoked adversarial views of politics. The stimulant nature of coffee led to furious disputations on live political issues communicated by word of mouth, but such discussion was also very often provoked by the unauthorized newsletters, advertising sheets and lists of published and banned books which were regularly delivered to the coffee houses. This textual miscellany further increased the appeal of the location to the clients. The emphasis in discussions moved quickly from information to opinion and, as Park has indicated, this is the real communicative imperative at the core of news as social exchange:

> Once discussion has started, the event under discussion soon ceases to be news, and, as interpretations of an event differ, discussions turn from the news to the issues it raises. The clashes of opinions and sentiments which discussion invariably invokes usually terminate in some sort of consensus or collective opinion – what we call public opinion. It is upon the interpretation of present events, i.e. news, that public opinion rests. (1940: 677)

This proactivity from readers and listeners in the development of the culture of journalism has been also identified by Raymond: 'Readers were always capable of using texts for their own ends, of improvising arguments on the basis of printed texts. It was perhaps by encouraging this that the newspaper made the strongest contribution to the informed and reasoned debate in seventeenth century Britain' (1999b: 132).

As with news in general earlier in the century, there was grave concern from some quarters about the kind of knowledge being fostered in such discussions and in such an environment characterized in terms of: 'Tobacco,

Lyes, and Lac'd Coffee' (Sommerville, 1996: 78). Coffee houses had become such dens of gossip and illicit trading in news that the king decided on dramatic action. Disapproval reached its peak in 1675 when Charles II proposed to close them down. This was discreetly announced in the *London Gazette* of 27 December 1675 but by January the proposal had been withdrawn owing to fears of a backlash from the patrons and owners of what had become such a popular and lucrative cultural activity. As a compromise, he decided to ask the owners to report anyone using their premises for the distribution of incendiary material in print or oral form. This marked a refinement of attitude from prohibition to monitoring.

The coffee house, this arena of the free exchange of information, provides an essential background to understanding developments in the production and consumption of news among the bourgeoisie in the late seventeenth century. Political opinion in this era was formed from a wide range of sources including gossip, rumour, broadside, ballad, pamphlet, book and news-sheet, all forming a complex and multiple textual community of political debate on an everyday basis. The fact that increasingly printers and booksellers sought out this readership as profitable indicates something of its scale and the fact that the coffee houses could act as such popular arenas for the exchange of information and opinion further underlines the strength and vitality of this culture. Such was the proliferation of ephemeral and unlicensed material that the authorities were forced to step up their policing of it. On 2 May 1674 *A Proclamation to Restrain the Spreading of False News* was published. From the printers' perspective, the appearance from 4 November 1675 of *The City Mercury: or Advertisements concerning Trade* indicated that there was profit to be made not just in the circulation of news but also in terms of the advertising revenue attracted by it. However uncomfortable for the ruling classes, the economic interests of the bourgeoisie as articulated in the practice of journalism were proving too powerful to be simply suppressed. A solution was needed which would allow journalism to develop its full bourgeois potential without endangering the security of the state.

The Popish Plot: the Materialization of Dissent

From the late 1670s, rumours of the king's alleged Catholic allegiances began to gather a certain amount of credible momentum, especially in the coffee houses as they became established at hotbeds of Whig dissent. This culminated in the propaganda war of the 'Paquets' starting with the *Weekly Paquet from Rome*, issued on 3 December 1678. These were short, political pamphlets centring on allegations about the king's religious preferences or refutations of these claims. They were naturally unlicensed and although limited in circulation they indicated the extreme levels of anxiety about the relationship between politics and religion in England at this time. In 1679, to avoid the passage of the anti-Catholic Exclusion Bill, Charles II prorogued Parliament and the propaganda war reached new heights as the Licensing Act was in effect suspended. There was a marked increase in the production of newspapers with 17 titles coming out up to 1682 (Atherton, 1999: 55). The Popish Plot caused unlicensed material to flood out to meet the unprecedented demand for information and, just as importantly, rumour and an equally unprecedented demand for interpretations of the facts of the matter. The entrepreneurial nature of a capitalist press in a period of divided opinion was such that it ensured that the instabilities of the monarchy's position were profited from and experiments in format blossomed. The Popish Plot demonstrated the suppressed popular demand for news in this period and the willingness of publishers to meet that demand which erupted each time formal restraint was removed. The boom in alternative newspapers to the official *Gazette* brought with it the first clear articulation of the division along political lines in the country between the Tories loyal to Charles and the opposition Whigs. Both sides produced polemical propaganda which engaged interested readers in the full details of opinion and debate. Some argue that these unlicensed papers acted as a safety valve which prevented the sense of political dislocation from degenerating into civil strife as it had done 40 years before and Atherton points out that the papers were: 'a response to political division, not its midwife' (1999: 59).

Whereas Charles II had sought to suppress Whig opposition and its representation in the press by the creation of a privileged official newspaper monopoly and the vigorous pursuit of his opponents and rivals through prosecution for seditious libel, from 1685, James II responded by having the Printing Act revived, relying more upon legal constraint than overt censorship at a time when the introduction of the penny post in 1680 had made it easier to distribute printed matter than ever before. Nevertheless, the imposition of centralized control could not prevent the dissemination of a wide range of views and reports, given the amount of interest in politics and the number of printers willing to take risks for profit or conviction. Although the Crown re-established formal control over printed news, the challenges thrown up by the freer expression of the range of conflicting political opinion had fatally damaged the autocratic ambitions of Charles II and James II was not able to revive them. It was this period of newspaper experimentation which, according to some historians, was to ensure that the 1688 revolution was such a peaceful transition which comprised 'essentially a series of defections from the Crown in each of which an assessment of popular opinion, and a calculation of other persons' moves, were deciding factors. Without the extraordinary development of unlicensed newsmongering that preceded it, the Revolution could hardly have taken such a smooth course' (Fraser, 1956: 132). This was quite an achievement for the press during a period when it was subjected to a great deal of state intervention and it indicates the importance of the impact of the culture of news dissemination in the coffee house culture which preceded the short flourishing of oppositional newspapers between 1678 and the reimposition of licensing in 1685.

Bi-partisan Politics and
the Shaping of Journalism

After the Revolution of 1688, one institution which began to establish regular political exchange through the press was William III's mixed Tory/Whig ministries. In such a heterogeneous political environment, rhetoric was employed by conflicting parties to establish arguments to present to the government. The press encouraged this and continued to play an important role in establishing politics as essentially a process of debate and disagreement rather than consensus. Journalism was to become an attractive arena for politically ambitious writers to establish their rhetorical credentials on behalf of the party of their preference. One consequence of these debates with regard to the press was the lapsing of the Licensing Act between 1694 and 1695. It happened not because of a political will to establish a free press but more because of the inefficiencies of the Stationers' Company in controlling the press and the difficulty in establishing what constituted 'offensive' material in legal terms. There were also difficulties in assessing the appropriateness of punishments for printers and writers which would not outrage the public. The divided Houses of Parliament could not decide on these issues and the Act was simply allowed to lapse. This happened not because the elite political and social classes felt any great regard towards the activities of a press free from their control, but more because it could no longer be administered efficiently. The 1695 lapse of the Printing Act did not usher in any explicit rights for the printers and writers of pamphlets and news-sheets but simply marked an end to formal restrictions on the process of printing itself. Nevertheless, there remained many highly effective means of control on the outcomes of printing which the authorities were quick to impose and consolidate if they felt that their authority was being undermined. The law retained ample leeway for legal action against publications deemed seditious or blasphemous. There were, in addition, other less formal ways in which the wronged could claim redress and printers made to suffer for impertinence, as writers and publishers were frequently beaten or had their property attacked by the aggrieved subjects of reports. In general, however, legal prosecutions throughout the century were difficult and unpopular and the publicity often had the effect of raising interest and sales in the publication being prosecuted. Most importantly for journalism, from 1695 and the final lapse of the Licensing Act, there is a vigorous resumption of experimentation with political news and opinion in print.

The Lapse of Direct Control

After the era of direct licensing up until its lapse in 1695, we move to a period dominated by official and unofficial subsidies and bribes from politicians to newspapers, when the content of the press was determined less by threats of imprisonment or censorship but more by the promise of preferential financial conditions. At this point, newspapers often lacked the financial stability for long-term success without the support of financially powerful politicians. The most effective of these early controllers was Harley, who ran a range of spies and correspondents on most of the London papers in the reign of Queen Anne (1702–14). The government could offer privileged access to information, financial reward for direct political support or for the suppression of stories and also advertising and therefore was an invaluable sponsor for newspapers who wanted to be involved in the mainstream of political information and survive economically. From 1695, journalism begins to consolidate its position as an official constituent of political opinion-making outside the narrow circle of policy-makers of the previous era. Political opinion and, through the work of more culturally orientated publications, social expectations were to become much more dependent on the circulation of periodically produced printed matter whether in the form of news-sheets, newspapers, essay sheets, pamphlets or any of the other genres which flourished after 1695. Although there is uncertainty about the actual effect of the press on the opinions of the people at any one moment, there is nevertheless a generalized sense that newspapers dependent on capturing the feelings of their readers needed to be able to match their assumptions against actual sales if they were to be able to retain credibility and their market. This has led observers such as Hannah Barker to remark on the 'complex interplay between press and popular politics' (2000: 1). Amid discussions of parliamentary coverage in the press, newspapers increasingly found ways to join and even lead the debate, particularly because people wanted to read political news and not just of the official sort in the government-approved *Gazette* exemplified below:

Westminster, October 20
The Parliament met this day, and the King being come to the House of Peers and Seated on the Throne in his Royal Robes with the usual Solemnity, the Commons were sent for up by Black Rod … His Majesty made a most gracious Speech to both Houses of Parliament which follows:

My Lords and Gentlemen,
I have call'd you together as soon as was possible, and I think it a great Happiness that this year has pass'd without any Disadvantage Abroad or Disorder at Home, considering Our great Disappointment in the Fonds given at your last Meeting, and the Difficulties which have arisen upon the Recoining of the Money … But I am sure, We shall all agree in Opinion, that the only way of Treating with France is with Our Swords in Our Hands, and that we can have no reason to expect a Safe and Honourable Peace, but by shewing Our Selves prepared to make a Vigorous and Effectual War.
(*The London Gazette*, Monday 19 October to Thursday 22 October 1696)

This sort of deferential, formal reporting served a function but a limited one, as a broader public needed a more varied diet to its journalism. In the last decade of the seventeenth century, scriveners and clerks around Westminster wrote up news and gossip from messengers, clerks and parliamentary ancillaries such as doormen. John Dyer, the Tory newsletter writer, was very prominent in this development. These scriveners attached themselves to one party or another, sometimes out of allegiance but more often than not out of the convenience of narrowing down the quality of their sources. Coffee houses were their networks of distribution and gossip. After 1695 there was a great range of experimentation in form and style. It was, to a large extent, the interaction of this variety with a reading public expecting to select and interact with textual constructions of the contemporary world which inexorably led to the consolidation of the public sphere.

A wide variety of essay papers appeared alongside the first experiments in more popular formats such as question and answer correspondence and the popularizing periodicals which were to develop into the early magazines. In addition to variety, regularity became a key factor of journalism once again and proved its worth in establishing an important aspect of its institutionalization and therefore commercial viability: 'the regularity with which newspapers appeared guaranteed a continuity of information and therefore of debate ... This is more likely to develop patterns of remembering and active involvement' (Raymond, 1999b: 132). The attractions of regularity meant a move to more frequent and reliable patterns of news publication from the thrice-weeklies based on the three posts a week to the first daily, the *Daily Courant*, from 30 April 1702 written by and distributed by government employees but with a definite Whig agenda. This defined its role in the following terms in its first issue:

> the proper and only Business of a News-Writer; first, by giving the freshest Advices from all Quarters, which he will certainly be able to do (let the Post arrive when it will) by coming out Daily: and next, delivering Facts as they come related, and without inclining either to one side or the other: and this too he will be found to do, by representing the same Actions, according to the different Accounts which both Sides give of them ... And thus having fairly related, What is done, When, Where, by which Side reported, and by what Ends transmitted hither, he thinks himself obliged not to launch out of his province, to amuse People with any Comments or Reflections of his own; but leave every Reader to make such Remarks for himself as he is capable of.

The *Daily Courant* was started by Samuel Buckley with an eye on the public appetite for news of war which had been amply illustrated in previous years. This time it was the War of the Spanish Succession in Europe against France. It drew on the needs of the government for their policies and involvement in the war to be understood more widely among an increasingly interested and involved society. It was not the form that was impressive but the regularity of its appearance which distinguished it in the history of the development of journalism. It was a half sheet on one side of paper, with two columns all made up of foreign, second-hand news. It developed over the first months of its production into four to six pages and came to include advertising and shipping news. In many ways it was a continuation of the tradition of the coranto in its claims to deal impartially in fact and its concentration on digests of foreign news without overt commentary. After the excesses of the Civil War years and the venom of the pamphlets and periodicals during the period of the Popish Plot, there was a return to a convention of reporting as factually as possible in the regular press as newspapers attempted to and to a large extent succeeded in clawing back some reputation for their factual credibility. This meant that there was a general lack of editorial comment in the early eighteenth century. It was nevertheless commercially orientated and aspired to independence from direct government control, both features which enhanced their viability. This made it easier for them to raise money through advertising, although they remained dependent financially on government sponsorship and privileges. These moves within newspapers left the field, for the development of opinion so necessary in this new social formation, open to the pamphleteers and journal writers and this is something that the politicians were not slow to capitalize on, as they demonstrated by hiring many of the best writers of the early century to ply their trade in opinion broking. Pamphlets, broadsheets and ballads could still be employed for more scurrilous one-off assaults at potentially high profit, good effect and little risk.

Despite the success of the *Daily Courant*, it was the thrice-weeklies which set the dominant pattern in an era of slow transport and limited print technology. The first significant thrice-weekly paper of the 1690s was the *Flying Post* begun on 11 May 1695. It was certainly one of the first profitable benefactors of the lapsing of the Licensing Act and managed a good combination of reliable information and lively style:

Hague, March 11.
The Heer Brand van Cleverskerke, our Ambassador in England, did in a Letter of the 6th Instant, N.S, give the States General an Account of the Discovery of the Assassination, etc, designed upon His majesty, to the effect following, viz ... wicked and unmanly Design ... Godless Miscreants who had agreed to attack the King, on Sunday 25th of February last, N.S. either as a Hunting at Richmond, or in his Passage ... If this horrid Treason had succeeded, a signal was to have been given by fire from Dover Cliffs, that the late King James, and others, might have immediately Embarked for England with the French Troops; and they were to have been received at Dover, or Rye, by some Squadrons and Battalions of Jacobites and Papists. (*The Flying Post*, Saturday 7 March to Tuesday 10 March, 1696)

It was soon followed by the *Post Boy*, and the *Post-Man*. Postscripts written in the margins for late news became common in the competitive environment for news after 1695. Advertisements prominently included thefts and losses with rewards for return of goods and were often framed as a sort of crime news with a vicarious thrill about much of it. The *Post Boy* started the practice of leaving a blank page for readers to become correspondents in filling in their news for circulation to contacts around the country by post.

It could provide a good deal of colourful detail in its foreign reports:

> Constantinople, January 20th.
> The Bassa of Babylon has notified to the Sultan by an Express that the revolted Arabians have not only possessed themselves of the Kingdom of Basora but also of the Fortresses and Castles about Basora and Babylon ... they entered Ispaham in triumph with Drums beating, Colours flying, and Trumpets sounding etc, after the Turkish manner. (*The Post Boy*, Saturday 21 March to Tuesday 24 March, 1696)

During Queen Anne's reign, adversarial politics engendered a partisan and often acrimonious press not seen since the heyday of the wars of the mercuries. Propaganda and counter-propaganda flew in both directions. Writers of great reputation and skill were employed by both sides to fight the war of words over the location of the press on the nation's political landscape. At this time, journalism continued to draw the hegemonic balance away from aristocratic dominance to a settlement with the vested interests of the new commercial entrepreneurs which included the printers and publishers as central participants in the bourgeois public sphere. Its success prompted warning voices which expressed concern about the dangers of this proliferation of printed news and opinion: 'In 1703 the Tory writer Charles Davenant warned that "the liberty of the press will be the ruin of the nation and I must confess anything that doth but look like an appeal to the collective body of the people is of very dangerous consequence to the constitution" ' (Black, 1991: 10).

Any definitions of news formats at this point in history are complicated by the diversity of practices engendered by the newly emancipated press. There was much cross-pollination in generic terms as news output experimented with patterns most likely to appeal to readers and transmit their authors' and owners' views most effectively. Raymond cites this very diversity as one of the most important factors in the development of critical debate: 'Precisely because they juxtaposed unrelated items, newspapers offered a textual space which required the reader to make sense of, to recognize and synthesize diversity' (Raymond, 1999b: 132). He lists some of the cornucopia of their content:

> War stories, parliamentary proceedings, travel accounts, political editorials, book adverts, lost property, bills of mortality, cargoes of ships, biographies, bibliographies, Hebrew anagrams, lottery numbers, assize reports, literary criticism, and social comment all stood side by side, and in doing so invited rather than compelled the reader to construe a view of the world from the page before them. (ibid.)

Such a gamut deflected attention from great inconsistency in the coverage of news which was irregular and still suffered from unreliabilty. This applied particularly to the dailies post-1702 which often had difficulty filling their pages on a regular basis.

This diversification within print culture was not only confined to the practices of journalism. The novel could only have emerged within a culture atuned to periodical news. Sommerville comments on this generic transfer:

> The pace of the novel was the pace of news, which had come to seem the pace of life itself. The ordinary lives of novelistic characters were anchored in a social and physical world that had been made literary by periodical publications. And novels often returned the compliment, by masquerading as journalism. Daniel Defoe is the most notable example of a newsman who could step over into fiction – or novelistic fact. (1996: 114)

As this diversity of practice emerged at the cusp of the seventeenth and eighteenth centuries, there was no automatic coupling of news or of journalists and printers with forces which supported social change. Despite the fact that news and print were having a radical effect on the restructuring of society and the renegotiation of relationships between political authority and a wider bourgeois public, there was nothing about the production of the news that was politically radical beyond the support for one political faction or the other. Journalism, although varied, remained primarily profit-driven. The freedom of journalism was a freedom shaped, even in its early emancipation, by the influence of advertising which dictated that the content and tone of newspapers in particular should be reasonably in tune with the emerging bourgeois culture. As early as 1705 Daniel Defoe would write: 'the principal support of all the public papers now on foot depends on advertisements' (Downie, 1979: 11–12). There were writers and printers who, despite supporting conservative social and political positions, believed in the efficacy of print in distributing knowledge, opinion and information about the events in the contemporary world from their own perspective. For their part, the elite classes were also ambivalent about the role and potential of these news organs. They could, in theory, control newspapers and they were able to demonstrate this at times over the next one hundred and fifty years but they were also keen to be associated with the rhetoric of freedom which the news organs claimed as their own. They were confident that they could manipulate sections of this new press to present their own views in a persuasive manner and thereby garner popular support while being able to take action against seditious influences when they saw fit. A glance at the titles of newspapers and journals of this time is enough to indicate the ways in which they saw their own role in society. For instance, John Dunton's *Pegasus* from 1697 was so called to show it could 'keep Pace' with rival publications. The press was able to begin to develop a dual function which both represented the people and their interests as well as keeping them informed about matters in their interest (as construed by the publishers and validated by the circulation), but the first attraction of its journalism was topicality. Although there was of course an element of opinion exercised in selecting and editing news, the specific opinion-forming function of the newspaper was to develop later after being first developed through the medium of the journal or essay paper.

In the early eighteenth century, newspaper readership was metropolitan and low. This soon picked up as the variety and consequent competition intensified. Public reading became commonplace. Taverns, coffee houses and barber's shops, which spread throughout the land at the same pace as the newspaper and news-sheet, were all part of a complex network of outlets for newspapers and informal discussion groups which gathered to read and to exchange opinion on their reading matter. Papers encouraged reading and this virtuous cycle provided an exponential market for all forms of printed matter as literacy grew to match the curiosity of ever-widening sections of the population for the latest that the printed form could supply.

Periodicals and Social Communication
- -

The most important indicator of the growing maturity of the public sphere came not with the early newspapers, however, but with the development of the literary and political periodicals of the reign of Queen Anne (1702–14). The two party politics of the Whigs and the Tories which emerged coincided with the high point of press autonomy after the lapse of the Printing Act and the rivalry of journals over issues such as foreign policy and the relationship between Church and State. Defoe's *Review* was the first influential journal of political comment and its main rivals were Swift's Tory *Examiner* and Mainwaring's Whig *Medley*. Politically this period witnesses England's annexation of Scotland in 1707 and the acquisition of a large amount of over-seas colonial territory which began to raise important questions of national identity and colonial trade. In the peace which followed the defeat and decline of the major European power, France, the emphasis shifted to the rivalries between political parties at home and the need for the increasingly powerful bourgeoisie to be involved in debate not only about politics but also what was in good taste in terms of literature, fashion and manners. As trade flourished and the self-confidence of the metropolitan nation grew, its com-mercial classes were increasingly seeking out voices which could represent their views and aspirations as they entered into this unchartered territory. It was a century of 'increased social intercourse' (Siebert, 1965: 305) and into the fractured set of older social hierarchies stepped writers able to articulate the political volatility and social ambition of the era. This cultural moment was the culmination of the set of activities which have become known as the public sphere but certainly the preceding 40 years had played an essential part in enabling them to crystallize in this form. The era saw the increasing involve-ment of particular writers such as Defoe, Swift, Steele and Addison who were to define the contours of the role of political journalist and social commenta-tor for the first generation of full-time journalists in the 1740s.

It was Daniel Defoe who first displayed the political acumen and versatility of the modern political journalist in his *Review* which ran from 1704 to 1713. He had started it in inauspicious circumstances in Newgate Prison where he was serving a sentence for a satirical pamphlet *The Shortest Way with Dissenters*. He described the birth of his periodical as having taken place 'In tenebris' and some have thought that this was a reference to his recruitment to work through the *Review* as spy, informer and propagandist for the Home Secretary, Harley. The title of his journal *A Weekly Review of the Affairs of FRANCE: Purg'd from the Errors and Partiality of News-Writers and Petty-Statesmen, of all Sides* indicates three important claims of journalism at this time. The first is that it is informed about the important foreign issues which were driving the foreign policy of an increasingly world power; second, its claim to superiority over other newspapers, and, third, the implication that its author had 'purged' all his reports of error and bias. It is perhaps this final editorial claim, along with the articulation of political positions in its pages, that distinguished the *Review* as a milestone in political journalism. Its circulation probably never exceeded 425–50 copies but these were very influential at the time. It was a hybrid production consisting of a serious essay on the contemporary affairs of France and then 'Advice from the Scandalous Club', with much satire and exposure of inaccuracies of other reports. Later it became a twice-weekly paper. Defoe revived the tradition of political persuasion in his tightly and accessibly argued pieces but in a way shorn of the excesses of the political pundits of the Civil War. His first aim seemed to be the articulation of rational political positions and in this way he contributed powerfully to the development of a sort of persuasive and principled journalism. Fox-Bourne claims: 'It was a better sort of journalism that Defoe undertook to introduce, a journalism that would be critical and instructive, exposing follies and falsehoods, enforcing truths, and elucidating principles' (1998, Vol. 1: 63).

His eulogy to the merchant was characteristic of his contribution to the formation of a rational public sphere which privileged the bourgeois perspective as well as his championing of plain speech:

> I wonder sometimes at the ignorance of those people and nations whose gentry pretend to despise families raised by trade … If we respect trade, as it is understood by merchandising, it is certainly the most noble, most instructive, and improving of any way of life … A true-bred merchant is a universal scholar … his foreign exchanges, protests, and procurations speak all tongues … the merchant makes a wet bog become a populous state; enriches beggars, ennobles mechanics, raises not families only, but towns, cities, provinces, and kingdoms. (Defoe, *The Review*, Vol. iii, No. 2)

Defoe was an arch-pragmatist, either a moderate Whig or a moderate Tory, so had no difficulty in playing both sides against the middle or in shifting his allegiances occasionally. His own explanation is a lucid rationalization of a very modern political journalism:

> It occur'd to me immediately, as a principle for my conduct, that it was not
> material to me what Ministers Her Majesty was pleas'd to employ, my duty
> was to go along with every ministry, so far as they did not break in upon
> my constitution, and the laws and liberties of my country: my part being
> only that of a subject, (viz.) to submit to all lawful commands, and to enter
> into no service which was not justifiable by the laws. (*An Appeal to Honour
> and Justice*, 1715)

Defoe was not immune from the dangers run by journalists even in the era
following 1695. Despite his earlier experience of Newgate Prison, he was
arrested again in 1713 and imprisoned because of comments in the *Review*
and warned about future conduct on account of his three pamphlets on the
Succession Question. Later in his career, his thirst for journalistic adventure
not sated, he contributed to the notoriously Jacobite *Mist's Weekly Journal*.
Throughout his career as a journalist, Defoe defined his approach to language as central to his ambition of making political information as accessible as possible. In this he is a true communicative democrat whose lineage
extends back to Mabbott and forwards to Paine, Cobbett, Dickens, Stead,
Orwell and Pilger. In his demotic style, he could be writing of the appeal of
many forms of popular journalism today: 'If any man was to ask me what I
would suppose to be a perfect style or language, I would answer, that in
which a man speaking to five hundred people, of all common and various
capacities, idiots or lunatics excepted, should be understood by them all'
(Herd, 1952: 51).

   Another famous literary figure who played an important part in these
developments in journalism was Jonathan Swift who was also employed by
Harley to contribute to the *Examiner* (1710–13) as a Tory rival to the success
of Whig-leaning publications. Swift was a true Tory and more consistent
than most. He wrote over 30 essays for it, and helped in its editing and management. It gave rise to the Whig *Examiner* of Addison from 14 September to
12 October 1710, and the *Medley* of Arthur Maynwaring and John Oldmixon
from 5 October 1710 to 6 August 1711 (Graham, 1926: 78). The polemic conviction of his journalism is laid out in the opening issue of 3 August 1710:

> I meet with a great Variety of Papers, neither so Correct, so Moral, nor so
> Loyal as they ought to be: I see the Town every Day impos'd upon by false
> Wit, false learning, false Politics, and false Divinity: These sort of Writings,
> thou' they are in contempt among the Few that judge well, yet have their
> Influence upon the Generality of Readers; and many of them are adapted
> by the Cunning Men who contrive them, to the capacities of the Weak, who
> are to be misled by them. Some of these Papers I intend to Examine, and
> set people right in their Opinions.

The most important moment in the consolidation of public debate came in
another series of journals, the *Tatler* and the *Spectator*. The *Tatler* first
appeared on 12 April 1709 and was written at first by Richard Steele and
later with significant contributions from Addison. Steele had previously

enjoyed a successful career as a dramatist and included a good range of literary and dramatic criticism which was enlived by his acquaintance with many of the leading writers of the day. He also put his writing skills to use in broader ways which were to inflect the conversational tone of much of his work: 'From his comedy-writing, Steele brought to his essays a good ear for living speech and a witty way of setting it down' (Ross, 1982: 31). Steele was the official government writer of the *Gazeteer* which appeared twice weekly and this allowed Steele to be as informed as anybody about the state of the news but it was to be the essays in this new venture, published three times weekly, which were to be the decisive component for contemporaries and posterity. Steele made it clear that his journal would not strain to produce news if there was nothing of interest: 'we shall not, upon a dearth of news, present you with musty foreign edicts, or dull proclamations' (*Tatler*, 12 April 1709).

Milic points out (1977: 37) that news had been a masculine preserve, concerned predominantly with power, war, trade, material and men, but Steele found a new way of presenting it which widened its appeal and later when news was dropped altogether from the eighty-third edition onwards, he discovered other ways of contributing to the politicization of English life without direct reference to politics. The *Tatler*, planned from the start as 'a coffee-house and tavern oracle' (Graham, 1926: 62) compartmentalized its contents to reflect the coffee house culture which it drew on and informed. 'Accounts of gallantry, pleasure and entertainment', were reported from 'White's Chocolate House, poetry from Will's Coffee House; learned debate from the Grecian, foreign and domestic news from St James', and any miscellany not suitable for the other sections were included in a section 'From my own Apartment'. Strong editorial direction embodied in the figure of Isaac Bickerstaff as the *porte parole* in the *Tatler* helped in making it consistent and successful.

There may well have been another more pragmatic reason why news was dropped:

> the increase in advertising, and the difficulty in keeping news fresh and timely, in the face of much competition from the newspapers, were reasons enough for eliminating this department. Add to these the fact that the single essay type had become a favourite form with writers and readers. Richard Steele was enough of a journalist to give the public what it wanted. (Graham, 1926: 68)

As with many journalistic innovations, novelty lay less in the original features of the *Tatler* which had been seen before but in the overall tone and direction of the journal. It had an overtly didactic mission to educate the tastes of its readers and, from the seventh isssue, Steele began soliciting letters to the editor as an important way of establishing the community of taste and opinion he sought. Winton considers that journalism was an ideal vehicle for Steele in that it was a provisional medium which allowed for topics to be changed, extended, contracted and repeated (1977: 25–6) and this process of experimentation and discovery was extended when with his fellow contributor Addison he started the *Spectator* on 1 March 1711. It was produced every weekday until 6 December 1712. As the *Tatler* had its Bickerstaffe, the *Spectator* was shaped around the silent and retiring 'author', Mr Spectator, and was addressed to the reflective hours of the civil servants and merchants represented in its subscription list (Ross, 1982: 37). It was in no modern sense of the word a newspaper, but has had a defining effect on what we understand as journalism in its broadly educational and cultural impact, particularly in its acute observations of its social milieu. This observation even extended to ironic commentary on the fascination for news itself:

> There is no Humour in my Countrymen, which I am more enclined to won-
> der at, than their general Thirst after News. There are about half a dozen
> ingenious men who live very plentifully upon this Curiosity of their Fellow-
> Subjects. They all of them receive the same Advices from Abroad, and very
> often in the same Words; but their Way of cooking it is so very different,
> that there is no Citizen who had an Eye to the public Good that can leave
> the Coffee-House with Peace of Mind before he has given every one of
> them a Reading. (*Spectator*, 8 August 1712)

Both the *Tatler* and the *Spectator* established a discreet and authoritative tone with their readership. They sought to educate the bourgeoisie in the ways of a polite society far removed from the excesses and authoritarian nature of the aristocracy but they did this in ways which obscured the central charac-teristic of the new social hegemony of the bourgeoisie and its historic com-promise with the older ruling classes. Eagleton has observed that these journals, as central institutions of the public sphere, provided 'a consensus around newly emergent bourgeois norms of taste and value and specifically one in which the very defining feature of this new class, property, was occluded, a public sphere based on a radical dissociation of politics and knowledge' (1991: 16–17).

Sommerville also cautions against a triumphant view of the journals of the public sphere at this point:

> they reduced the effort needed to participate in public opinion, by mar-
> keting news and discussion as a product. No longer did readers need to
> search out a wider world when they could find it on their own doorstep ...
> Readers could begin to live in a more subjective world, encouraged by a
> news industry whose expertise was in the knowledge of its customers
> rather than some outer reality. (1996: 146)

Journalism had enabled a new form of social communication to become established in English urban life. It was one which blended political with wider cultural information across a range of publications and representa-tional styles. It culminated in increasing demands on the political institu-tions of the country but on terms defined from the perspective of the bourgeoisie. The history of journalism was to become from this point onwards the pragmatic negotiation by the bourgeoisie for a dominant role in the commodified information flow of this public sphere. In this process, journalism, in all its miscellaneous potential, becomes the site where politics, profit and the public converge.

4

Profit, Politics and the Public

The Position of the Press in 1712

The seventeenth century and early eighteenth century had already, during periods of political upheaval and uncertainty, defined the potential range of journalism. The eighteenth century was to determine how that potential would crystallize in practice under very specific economic and political constraints. From the imposition of the Stamp Duties from 1712, journalism was to evolve in ways which continued to address contemporary cultural and political concerns and which extended the experimentation with style and content. It is best to divide this evolution into three overlapping phases: (1) coming to terms with the implications of the Stamp Act and the imposition of advertising duty; (2) the revision of the discourse of political journalism; and (3) the formalization of journalism as a political economy. The newspapers and journals which were most prominent in these processes across the century did not enjoy the unfettered latitude of the period between 1640 and 1660. They had to constrain their writing to more closely defined political and cultural norms and needed to be aware of the increasing importance of their position within a market economy of print. Journalism develops as a pragmatic negotiation between the demands of three interest groups: (1) readers who increasingly perceived themselves as both private individuals and as part of a wider public; (2) advertisers who were also keen to profit from the wider circulation of newspapers; and (3) politicians who had an ambivalent attitude to exposure in the news, fearful of criticism yet craving the popular acclaim and legitimation which only the newspapers could provide.

The governing class could, in theory, control newspapers and they were able to demonstrate this at times over the next one hundred and fifty years. Black (2001) stresses that attempts to supervise the press were responses to the very real fear of violent insurrection provoked by first the Jacobite, and later the Jacobin rebellions, and the fear of what panic a notoriously inaccurate and sensational press might spread across the land. There were also benefits for the press in steering a moderate course, as politicians were more inclined to restraint in their dealings with it if they could enjoy the publicity of a commercial press in the hands of an enlightened bourgeoisie. Politicians became increasingly confident that they could manipulate sections of this new press to present their own perspectives and thereby garner popular support while being able to take action against seditious influences when they saw fit. Michael Harris has concluded that in its broad reach by the time of Walpole as Prime Minister: 'the London press had long been accepted as an important and legitimate component of the political system' (1987: 113).

Over the eighteenth century journalism developed a much more consistent response to the political and economic pressures of the age and the ensuing shape of the practice became by the end of the century not only the dominant paradigm for the journalism of the modern era, but the institutional presence against which alternative views and practices would be tested when calling the political or cultural norms of journalism into question. Some newspapers were written in an overtly rhetorical style so as to enhance the effect of reading aloud to groups and began to rival other fora for the public dissemination of ideas, that is, the pulpit and the public meeting. The newspapers were to begin to play a role in the education of a population into citizenship with all of the implications and demands of this status. This chapter will explore these developments through a selection of prominent moments and contributors which began to articulate a place for the people, through journalism, at the heart of the political process:

> Newspapers were thus vital not only in putting the 'people' into English politics, but in politicising and uniting sections within the increasingly powerful body of 'the public'. By so doing, the newspaper press not only altered the manner in which politics was conducted at the centre, but also in the way in which it operated at every level of English life. (Barker, 2000: 5)

The Implications of Stamp and Advertising Taxes

It must not be forgotten that the Licensing Act had merely lapsed. The government had not ushered in positive legislation freeing the press. It was not immediately confident that developments in journalism were in its own best interests, although Black argues that over time the political impact of the press, or at least ministerial concern about it, was reduced as politicians became more accustomed to newspapers (1991: 141). Such was the state of public interest in affairs of state in the reign of Queen Anne that there was a flood of separate political pamphlets. There was at this time an air of alarm about the growing audacity of the press and what the government could do about it. Despite the fact that it was the pamphlets, with their largely uncontrolled and disruptive effects on public opinion, which were the chief target of the legislation which was introduced in 1712, the timing of the legislation indicates that it was finally, in April 1712, Samuel Buckley's critical comments in his *Daily Courant* on the conduct of the war with the Dutch which forced Parliament into action. There was also a strong economic motivation for legislation. In addition to concerns over the influence of erroneous or seditious material, at the start of the eighteenth century, there was a pressing need for government to raise funds via commodity taxation, and newspapers by this time very conveniently fell into this category as commodities. The legislation was the Stamp Act of that same year, introduced by Lord Bolingbroke. It applied taxation to cover size and advertising content of both newspapers and pamphlets. It represented a pragmatic combination of control and fiscal opportunism rather than a simple attempt to introduce another explicitly censorious measure and newspapers adapted and evolved within these new frameworks, frameworks which made them more responsible, respectable and ultimately more lucrative propositions to publishers. However, libel laws, government prohibition on reporting Parliament or disseminating seditious material were also still available to authority. When serious opposition emerged in the eighteenth century, particularly with regard to the Jacobite invasions in 1713, 1719 and 1745, and the serious Jacobite conspiracy of 1723, the government had to resort to cruder methods of control and punishment to ensure effective policing and deterrent. John Matthews, for instance, a 19-year-old journeyman printer, was hanged for treason for his role in the production of the Jacobite pamphlet *Ex Ore Tuo Te Judico: Vox Populi, Vox Dei* of 1719.

According to the Stamp Act, pamphlets were taxed at two shillings per sheet per edition, had to be registered at the Stamp Office and include the printer's name and address. Because of their content, which was often political or religious and therefore controversial in nature, pamphlets were unlikely to carry advertisements but newspapers had to pay a penny per full sheet and a tax of one shilling on every advertisement they carried. It made the publisher ultimately responsible for the content, even if the author remained unknown. This was particularly expedient in terms of pamphlet publication where most controversial material appeared, leaving Cranfield to observe: 'If the author of a pamphlet could rarely be identified, at least the printer could be suitably dealt with' (1978: 39).

If, as Harris has suggested, the Act was designed as a policing measure and was expected 'to shatter the newspaper press' (1978: 60), owners demonstrated resilience and raised their retail price from 1d. to 1½d. and increased their charges for advertisements. They judged astutely that the appetite for news was now well enough established to tolerate a little inflation. There was plenty to keep its popularity on the rise as topical events and personalities, controversies surrounding Walpole's ministry and the continued growth of bi-partisan party politics drew readerships and made news a commodity which increasing numbers were willing to pay for. The restrictive effects of the Stamp Act mainly impacted upon daily newspapers which could not guarantee enough copy to fill the pages economically enough to survive nor generate enough advertising revenue to offset the cost of the increased taxation. The weekly papers and the thrice-weekly papers intended for country-wide distribution remained successful but by and large the stamps delivered a death blow to the ambitions of the daily paper in the early century. Swift noted ironically the passing of much of what had made the press so vibrant in the years between 1695 and 1714 when he wrote that there would be: 'No more ghosts or murders now for love nor money' (Herd, 1952: 44).

The pamphlet form, however, continued to flourish. In fact, it was the unofficial and therefore illegal, irregular and incendiary, hawked material which most benefited from this creation of the category of officially stamped newspapers. It could undercut officially sanctioned news-sheets and boasted the attraction of a greater freedom of expression. Journalism could not have emerged as it did through the middle years of the century if the mainstream press had not felt obliged to enter into competition with this style of unofficial publication in its claims to represent the interests of the public and to provide them with fresh and provocative intelligence. Thus journalism was shaped both inside the mainstream and as a competitive response to forces outside of that mainstream.

Newspaper readership and ownership remained within the control of the propertied classes. Despite a clear demand for political news among the lower classes, this was not addressed directly by the owners or writers of the newspapers and these classes continued to buy the more transitory ephemera of the age such as almanacs, ballads and pamphlets. The political education of the lower classes was feared by people of property and restricting the poor to a diet of ephemeral entertainment ensured they were kept at a distance from anything likely to contribute to their dissatisfaction or political education. This meant that there was no attempt by the regular newspapers to break into a wider market. They kept their diet restricted to political and economic news and let the burgeoning unofficial and ephemeral media aimed at lower sections of the population deal with other aspects of print culture such as songs, poems, witty anecdotes, gossip, crime and humour. This segmentation of the market brought a divided public into existence, differentiated between bourgeois and popular, reinforcing Sommerville's observation that: 'If a "public" is defined as a group that shares a common source of news, then these journals were creating the possibilities for new social divisions' (1996: 151).

The development of journalism in this century is sometimes seen as intimately bound up with the emergence of a politically independent newspaper but it was an independence very much brokered in the interests of a commercial elite. Easy narratives about progress within journalism tend to underestimate the cyclical and miscellaneous nature of much of its content and practice. Independence of the press generated the same need for financial stability that any other serious economic undertaking required. This led journalism to become an increasingly respectable institution, owned and directed by men of wealth and often social ambition. Black aligns himself with E.P. Thompson's distinction between polite and popular culture with regard to the press, seeing it definitely as 'a facet of the former' (1991: 297). The consequences of this emergent political economy of journalism was that, although newspapers had the potential to foster radical political debate, their ownership and intended market made them inherently conservative in their world-views.

Yet the Stamp Act was not able to curtail all of the perceived scurrilous excess of the press. There was, for instance, reprinted in 1722 in the *St James's Journal*, a sermon read before the Commons by a Whig cleric demanding action against the excesses of the press: 'Among the many ways taken to poison the minds of the people, and to alienate their affections, the most dangerous and diffusive, has been the insufferable licence, which has been of late so scandalously taken of spreading seditious papers and libels thro' the Kingdom' (ibid.: 123).

For all the criticisms of its distribution of information to classes unable to deal maturely with such knowledge, a criticism which echoed Lestrange's in a more authoritarian age some 50 years before, from 1725 most papers were respectable, four pages long, adequately provided with news and dependent upon advertising revenue, as well as the beneficial subscriptions of coffee house owners, all of which allowed them a modicum of medium-term financial security. However, this list of virtuous practice fails to include the most important single constituent in their financial stability: the good will of government subsidy and intelligence.

Subsidy and Privilege: the New Controls

After 1712, with the legitimate press a contributor to the exchequer as well as to public debate, the consideration of politicians focused increasingly on the most effective ways of harnessing it within the communication system. It received significant support from political sponsors which ranged from direct bribes and other financial assistance to the preferential distribution of political information. Regarding the regular taxed newspapers, Siebert has commented: 'By making it difficult to operate newspapers at a profit, the government forced the publishers to accept subsidies and political bribes' (1965: 322).

Regular income and reliance on government funds, information sources and party success might have provided short-term security but in the longer term it was increasingly the pursuit of profit through the good opinion of the readers, who needed to believe in the distinction between the official information of the government and a more impartial news, which drove the newspapers away from this direct patronage. Political sponsorship also extended to the activity of the journalist within the evolving two party system, riven by factional disputes within and between the parties, which was very closely allied to the fortunes of the party his paper supported:

The preoccupation of the journalist lay quite outside the accurate reporting of facts; there were no facts more important, nor more urgent, than the fate of factions; it was these that provided the revenue, the market and the intellectual compulsion behind the product. The journalist, as a soi-disant professional processor of information, did not yet exist. (Smith, 1978: 157–8)

The official *London Gazette* which boasted that it was 'Published by Authority' had a wide range of official news, proclamations and news of financial transactions and was understandably well supplied with information from abroad, given its privileged access as an official newspaper, but it was dull and obsequious regarding internal politics as the following extracts illustrate:

Most Gracious Sovereign
We your Majesty's most loyal faithful and affectionate Subjects the Deputy-Lieutenants of your Majesty's Tower-Hamlets, cannot but look back with the utmost Pleasure and Gratitude on the Ease and security we have enjoyed under your Majesty's most mild just and prudent Reign; and at the same time be surprized and fired with Indignation that any neighbouring Powers should vainly imagine that Britons thus made happy by your Majesty, should tamely suffer an abjured bigotted Popish Pretender and Imposter to invade them, or that we should submit our Consciences to a barbarous Spanish Inquisition, exchange our Liberty for their Slavery, or yield up our Property to be the Plunder of our Enemies ... we beg Leave to assure your Majesty, that we shall think no taxes too heavy which shall be found necessary to promote your Majesty's Happiness and the Welfare of your Subjects.

Madrid Feb 17 N.S. Count Conigseck is still indisposed of the Gout, so that he has not been able to go to the Pardo to have his usual Audiences of their Catholic Majesties; nor is his Courier so long expected from Vienna arrived yet ... Letters from the camp before Gibraltar of the 9th Instant relate, that the bad Weather and continual Rains had made it impossible to bring up the Battering Pieces of Brass Cannon which lay upon the Road from Cadiz, and had so occasioned dangerous Sicknesses among the Troops. (Tuesday, 21 February to Saturday, 25 February 1726)

The *Daily Journal* had a similar range of material, together with prominent letters and deductions drawn from the arrival and departure of warships in foreign ports. Miscellany had been a feature of the late seventeenth-century newspapers and continued to be so into the eighteenth century even in the formal official publications. Advertisements indicative of the local market of the time featured clockmakers, private schooling, the arrival of fish, theatre, opera and gentlemen's outfitters. News was divided into sections with subheadings such as Home News, Port News, London News and occasionally News from Ireland. It was better provided for in terms of crime news, which because of its apolitical nature was reported in a lively enough manner:

Last Weeke one Mrs Welsh, near the Seven Dials, attempted to hange herself; but was cut down by the Man that keeps the Crown Alehouse, before she was quite dead ... The same Day an Hostler at the Nag's-Head Yard in Orange-Street, fetching a Pail of Water from the Pump, fell down, by which Accident he bit his Tongue, so that a great Part of it hung only by a bit of Skin; It was immediately sew'd together by a Surgeon; yet notwithstanding he is so very ill, that his Life is thought in great danger. (Wednesday, 1 January 1729)

As with the *London Gazette*, there was also news of the marriages and social lives of the gentry and royal news: 'Last night his Royal Highness Prince Frederick, was at the Theatre Royal in Lincoln's Inn Fields, to see the Beggar's Opera acted by Lilliputians, where there was a very numerous Audience' (*The Daily Journal*, Thursday, 2 January 1729).

The economic ambitions of the owners, combined with their conservative assumptions, meant that the daily press which had survived the introduction of the Stamp Duties were efficient but monologic: 'There was little suggestion of anything to be discussed. Most pieces displayed a certainty that reflected an attitude that the reader would share the suppositions and intentions of the author' (Black, The English Press 1621–1861: 246).

Oppositional Journalism Reconfigured

The political sponsorship of newspapers was streamlined by Horace Walpole. Between 1715 and 1742 Walpole developed a network of direct and indirect controls over a vast range of the press. He provided free post and subsidies for government papers as well as pensions and sinecures for his loyal writers and editors. Under Walpole, 'author by profession', became a term which categorized the favours, perks or pensions which the professional journalist could expect to receive after a career in what amounted to political service. Walpole preferred professional journalists and publishers in general rather than more partisan literary figures or zealots such as Defoe, Swift or Crackenthorpe who had been cultivated to varying degrees by Harley a decade before. There was considerable opposition to Walpole's tactics. The *London Journal* with 'Cato's Letters' and *Mist's Weekly Journal* were the first to fully explore the potential of regular political essays in a newspaper as a response to Walpole's interference. These were followed by the *Craftsman* with considerable contributions from Bolingbroke and Pulteney.

In an early example of the call of a newspaper for accountability from senior politicians, the *London Journal*, edited by two dissatisfied Whigs, Trenchard and Gordon, called for an investigation of the South Sea Bubble investment disaster and 'public justice' for the managers of the scheme. Its most venomous pieces were signed CATO. By 12 August 1721, it was selling

10,000 copies. In the case of the *London Journal* the pragmatic stand-off between politicians and commercial journalism had clearly been shattered. Consequently, in 1722 Walpole exercised a more direct option, bought the paper, dismissed the editors and changed the line of the paper to something more acceptable to the government including the pro-government Hoadly's essays signed, 'Britannicus'.

Ministerial papers sought to destroy the reputation of opposition papers by making guarantees to its idealized reader that:

> [they] may depend upon having, in the course of these papers, an impartial, unbiased way of writing, neither courting friends nor making enemies; the placing things in false lights shall be avoided, which seems to have been the greater art, and only merit, of *some writers*, with whom (whether they speak of private persons or of public) the character of no man is safe; but scandal and calumny are dealt about like dirt, without regard to things or persons, either sacred or civil. (*Honest True Briton*, 21 February 1724)

Notable opposition newspapers in the first half of the eighteenth century which were not willing to bow to political pressure or accept government sponsorship were *Mist's*, *Fog's* and the *Craftsman*. They were all economically attractive because of the independence of their stance and the lively style of their political contributions. These were the exceptions within a predominantly compliant press. They had owners who adopted critical, political stances and thereby gained a credibility and a vitality not always in evidence in their more sedate contemporaries. Mist was the leading Tory newspaper figure of the period. His paper was enormously influenced by classical learning, most visibly in the signatures on the many letters and other correspondence which were selected on the basis of classical credentials: 'The following is a Thought upon the Inconstancy of Man, and as it seems to be writ after the Manner of Seneca, we conceive, that it is sufficient to recommend it' (*Mist's Weekly Journal*, Saturday, 4 March 1727). It featured a wide range of letters and topical political contributions often signed anonymously by the likes of 'Briton' or 'Englishman', and penned in Will's Coffee House or some other well-known gathering place. It saw its mission broadly, 'to instruct as well as entertain your Readers' (Saturday, 15 July 1727). In miscellaneous fashion, home affairs included crime news and deaths, highwaymen, shipping news, and deportations. There was a regular section on foreign affairs, and its popularity made it an attractive location for the advertisers of tinctures, ointments, treatments for gout, sales of property, letting of houses and other printed publications. Advertisements for items such as pet birds and blinds for windows reflect the increasing leisure and affluence of its readers and indicate one of the ways in which the newspaper and advertising formed part of a virtuous economic circle for the bourgeoisie. A strong supporter of free trade, Mist was adamant that taxes should not be levied to fight a war he disapproved of and that these taxes were hindering the trade of the nation which he saw as its strongest asset:

> The Accounts we receive from Abroad so often differ, that of late we have seen one Foreign Gazette speak of nothing but War, while the next, perhaps, gives us strong Assurances of a Peace ... Thus I believe it is pretty plain, that Manufacturers are frequently gain'd and lost by Wars; for which Reason England, whose Support is her Trade, should follow the Lacedemonian Policy, never to make War long upon one Enemy; for as they did it, lest their Enemies should learn their Art of War, our Policy should be, lest they should acquire our Arts of Peace.
>
> I knoe that some sanguine People who fight all Battles by their own Firesides, will condemn such pitiful Advice, and tell us, that let what Nation soever set up Manufactures, we must beat them out of them; but besides to such I must answer, that such a Cause of war being altogether unjust, I should be sorry to see the Prosperity of our Trade depend upon the Event of a Battle. (Saturday, 11 February 1727)

It was in its audacious pieces on public figures where it best displayed the prescient popular appeal of critical writing on contemporary issues. 'There is nothing that concerns the attention of a private man as much, as the actions of persons in the administration of public affairs' (*Mist's Weekly Journal*, 17 January 1728). The most notorious example of this was when *Mist's Weekly Journal* printed a vicious libel on George II, as a Persian Letter on 24 August 1728. Mist was constantly in trouble on account of the audacity of his journalism, until in January 1728 he fled to France to avoid further conflict with the authorities. The paper nevertheless continued until his death in 1737. *Fog's Weekly Journal* was founded as an immediate successor to *Mist's* in February 1728 after Mist had fled to France. It continued Mist's project as an anti-Whig paper, opposed to Dissenters. The arrest of printers, booksellers, searches of the post, even the imprisonment and later self-imposed exile of Mist, all had relatively limited effects on the sales and subversive reputation of both publications. Their pages display the positive commercial advantages of a certain style of notoriety and there was no shortage of advertisements, for example, for lawyers, gloves, ink powder and lamps, frequently with woodcuts to highlight the advertisement and make it stand out. It comments confidently on the power of the people informed by the good intelligence its engaged journalism purports to provide:

> It was the saying of a very wise man, that the Speculation of Political Affairs, is a much honester Task, than the Practice of them. This, we presume, is a Truth, in which Men of all Parties will agree, and therefore we hope it will serve as a standing Justification, for Us and Others, who may now and then enter into Controversies of such a Nature ...
>
> And it happens in Politics as in other games, where the Lookers on frequently see more than those that Play the cards – The people can easily see when their Prince is abus'd by selfish Counsellors; and the Reason is plain, for 'tis they who must feel the Effect of such a Conduct: A Knave in Power may find Means of obscuring Things (at least for some Time), from an indulgent Master; but the Multitude is an Argus with a Thousand Eyes,

and some of those Eyes are endued with a most penetrating Sight. (*Fog's Weekly Journal*, Saturday, 2 November 1728)

Another example of the trend for strongly worded oppositional journalism came on 7 December 1726 in the form of the *Craftsman*. It was launched as an essay paper written under the pseudonym of Caleb D'Anvers. This was Nicholas Amhurst, a former Whig now employed by William Pulteney, an opposition Whig, to write in opposition to Walpole and particularly his control of the press. Sommerville has commented on the impact of this publication on political journalism: 'This much-admired paper created the expectation of an absolutely relentless journalistic opposition to overbearing authority' (1996: 133). It was an oppositional paper but certainly not Jacobite in its sympathies, unlike *Mist's*. Ironically, the most significant contributor was the very instigator of the Stamp and Advertising Duties which had made the press so dependent on political subsidy, the rebel Tory, Lord Bolingbroke. Most notably he contributed the 'Oldcastle Letters' – 'Remarks on the History of England', an anti-Whig version of English history which Fox-Bourne has described as: 'until the time of Junius, the most brilliant and memorable specimens of this sort of journalistic work produced in England in the eighteenth century' (1998: 117).

The *Craftsman* was motivated by ruling class fears of the political dominance of Walpole's party and set out to mobilize elements of public opinion which had remained outside the reach of ministerial control. As well as a satirical approach to politics, it addressed the full range of contemporary political debates, as did the other essay journals of the time, such as taxes, foreign policy, trade and political scandal. Its pinnacle of notoriety and provocation came in the form of a letter, reputedly translated from Persian, which was a common device in the eighteenth century for addressing domestic issues while avoiding the official wrath of politicians which would have befallen a more literal approach. On this occasion the savagery of the satire was enough to cause outrage even in this disguised form, as it clearly attacked Walpole and impugned his ambition and financial probity:

In the midst of these execrations enter'd a Man, dress'd in a plain habit, with a purse of gold in his hand. He threw himself forward into the room, in a bluff, ruffianly manner. A Smile, or rather a Snear, sat on his Countenance. His face was bronz'd over with a glare of Confidence. An arch malignity leer'd in his eye. Nothing was so extraordinary as the effect of this person's appearance. They no sooner saw him, but they all turn'd their Faces from the Canopy, and fell prostrate before him. He trod over their backs without any Ceremony, and march'd directly up to the Throne. He opened his Purse of Gold, which he took out in Handfulls, and scatter'd amongst the Assembly. While the greater Part were engaged in scrambling for these Pieces, he seiz'd, to my inexpressible Surprize, without the least Fear, upon the sacred Parchment itself. He rumpled it rudely up, and crammed it into his Pocket. Some of the people began to murmur. He threw more Gold, and they were pacified. No sooner was the parchment taken away, but in an instant I saw that august Assembly in Chains; nothing was heard through the whole Divan, but the Noise of Fetters and Clank of Irons. (*The Craftsman*, 27 January 1727)

Reporting Parliament: Privilege Regained

The next significant shift in the discourse of journalism was the renewal of attempts to report Parliament, which had been outlawed since the Restoration. Unlike political commentary and criticism which, within the limits of libel and sedition, were developing in the essay papers, parliamentary reporting flouted the law, no matter what its content. This emerged not in the essay paper or the newspaper but in another and newer genre, the miscellaneous magazine. Parliamentary reporting was a very popular feature so it was in the interests of the press to find ways around official prohibition. Abel Boyer published *The Political State of Great Britain* between 1703 and 1729 as a monthly, always being careful to postpone the details of parliamentary debates until after the session they had taken place in had concluded. The coverage was also wisely tinged towards approval of the government so that it could act as a *post facto* rationalization of the power politics of the day. The information which informed it was smuggled out of Parliament via clerks and ancillaries.

A more robust challenge came from the *Gentleman's Magazine* which was founded in January 1731 by Edward Cave. It was a digest of news, literary and political comment and presented itself as a response to the feeling that the world was becoming too rapid in its pace and too crammed full of novelties for an individual to be able to follow them in detail. Its most innovative feature, however, was the reporting of Parliament through the remarkable memory of their political reporter Guthrie who would attend sessions and then return to the offices of the magazine to write up his account. Doormen were bribed to allow access to him and other reporters. It was the first periodical to report live parliamentary proceedings since the Civil War. This reporting started in issue 5, May 1731, and Cave made it the main selling point despite the other attractions of his miscellany. By June 1738, it had been forced to drop the explicit coverage of Parliament but reported its debates as the Parliament of Lilliput which included transcriptions of speeches penned by no less a personage than Samuel Johnson. In addition to its claims to fictional status, it employed techniques such as blanking out letters of names so that it could not be considered a verbatim report of actual Parliament with real politicians. An example of the allusive style of its parliamentary reporting is captured in this extract which deals with news of the ban itself:

> The Publick several Years ago received a great deal of Entertainment and Instruction from Capt. Gulliver's elaborate and curious Account of the newly discovered Empire of Lilliput; a Relation which (however rejected at

its first Appearance, by some as incredible, and criticis'd by others, as partial or ostentatious) has, with the Success almost always attendant on Probity and Truth, triumphed over all Opposition, gain'd Belief from the most obstinate Incredulity, and established a Reputation in the World, which can fear no Diminution, nor admit of any Increase...

But as the Hope conceived by the Publick of feeling this immense Undertaking successfully compleated, has been frustrated by Indolence, Business, or perhaps by the unexpected Stroke of sudden death; we doubt not but our Readers will be much pleased with an Appendix to Capt. Gulliver's Account, which we received last Month, and which the late Resolution of the House of Commons, whereby we are forbidden to insert any Account of the Proceedings of the British Parliament, gives us an Opportunity of communicating in their Room (June 1738).

In July 1738 it wrily observed that: 'Mr Gulliver, [was] astonished at the wonderful conformity between the Constitution of England and Lilliput'. This was popular stuff indeed, made the more pleasurable for the fact that it was toying with the boundaries of legality and official approval as well as providing a service which was much sought after by those who wanted to be kept abreast of these parliamentary affairs. By 1739 it had a circulation of 30,000 for its mixture of letters, essays from weekly papers, foreign news, poetry and parliamentary proceedings from Lilliput. The location of this parliamentary reporting within the magazine format and the parodic lengths to which it went illustrate the generic flexibility of journalism once more as it emerges as a highly pluralistic set of practices. The proceedings of the Parliament of Lilliput ran until 1743.

The magazine also had a rival from May 1738 as the *London Magazine* ran accounts of Parliament this time as a Roman Assembly. It reported Parliament as an imaginary political club with politicians sporting classical names such as Tullius Cicero and M. Cato. An index was appended for those readers unable to make connections between historical and contemporary characters. It was not until 1771 when Parliament opened its proceedings to the press, forced by the provocative publication of its dealings in the *Middlesex Journal*, that the right to report Parliament was tolerated for the first time outside the Civil War years and the next stage of the debate over journalism's relationship with democratic procedure began. It had been given much assistance by Cave's provocative toying with convention in his magazine some 30 years earlier.

The Middle Years of the Century

As regular newspapers and journals gained respectability, the less reputable press continued to draw the hostility of the political establishment. In 1743 an Act was passed against the selling of unauthorized printed matter. Hawkers were driven by law from the streets because of the success of unstamped news-sheets and pamphlets and other material lucrative to printers but not conducive to peace of mind among ministers. Although profitable for the printers, and certain of a sure and ready market, the most effective remedy was to hit the indigent street traders who sold the unlicensed material and to imprison them for three months.

At first, it had been the novelty of topical information which had provided the impetus for the development of newspapers and journalism. Steadily, the range of information in circulation was growing so that by the middle of the eighteenth century gossip, shipping news, court reports, social commentary, parliamentary debate and political opinions were all well developed in the newspaper. In addition to formal politics, poetry, parables and epigrams which alluded to political affairs made them more accessible to readers and linked them with more general entertainment values. As newspapers developed socially and culturally, it was this breadth of appeal which became as important as the extension of political debate to a larger public sphere. The inclusion of the miscellany of entertainment, consumerism particularly regarding fashionable tastes and advertising also endorsed a belief in the liberty and freedom of expression of English public life which was enhanced by the patriotic discourse of all the newspapers who were each vying for the ears of the people of England. A reciprocity between newspapers and readers was expressed particularly in the communal addresses of the newspaper to the people as belonging to a nation and the identification of the readers with this community through letters signed 'one of the people' or 'an Englishman' which were common, according to Barker (2000: 25).

Newspapers increasingly throughout the eighteenth century were responsible for the dissemination of ideas but also increased the feelings of involvement in political life among their readership, especially in letters published on matters of topical concern and in the general response of the papers to popular protest and dissent. There was no automatic coupling of news or of journalists and printers with forces which supported social change. The news was not naturally radical. The Jewish Naturalization Bill of 1753 was a good illustration of how the press, in particular, the *London Evening Post*, acting in tune with the public mood and sharing their prejudices, could also be involved in highly reactionary campaigns. It followed the outbreak of anti-Semitism and stoked that outbreak by its own coverage of the debates as well as in the language of its own opinion on the matter under discussion.

Even though the essay papers were those which were in retrospect the most dashing and perhaps the most important in the development of journalism, stylistically and as a political force, the thrice-weeklies and the advertisers were the organs which were economically prosperous in the longer term and did more to establish the institutional shape of journalism. By the middle years of the century, journalism was beginning to attract more consistent approval for its contribution to the political culture of the nation – one hundred and fifty years before Stead's 'Government by Journalism'. Targett reports an independent MP for Totnes, Joseph D'Anvers, commenting in 1738:

I believe the people of Great Britain are governed by a power that never was heard of as a supreme authority in any age or country before ... it is the government of the press. The stuff which our weekly newspapers are filled with, is received with greater reverence than acts of parliament: and the sentiments of one of these scribblers have more weight with the multitude than the opinions of the best politicians in the kingdom. (Barker, 2000: 24)

From a Victorian perspective this was also a highly significant phase of journalism's formation. Fox-Bourne sees the mid-eighteenth-century newspaper as a key to the development of a discourse of public opinion from 1760:

their modern history only dates from that reign [George III 1760–1820], and their recent progress has been in large measure due to the new contest, or the old contest under new conditions, forced upon them as champions of popular rights and exponents of public opinion in opposition to the efforts of the crown and its advisers to maintain an authority, and perpetuate institutions, that were becoming intolerable to the nation. (1998: 149)

In the 1750s John Gurney provided a newly systematised shorthand which was to reinforce technical claims to veracity on the part of the journalist as witness of what was said to herald the separation of the correspondent from the reporter (Smith, 1978: 162).

A renewed burst of influential literary magazines including the *Rambler* and the *Idler* took off from the 1750s. Samuel Johnson has already been mentioned as a key contributor to the political journalism of the *Gentleman's Magazine*. His other major contribution to the development of journalism was in his writing for literary periodicals which he helped become an influential medium from the 1750s and which became a further indicator of the growing maturity of journalism as it straddled politics and culture. Among other topics, he wrote perceptively about the trials and challenges of writing for a living as a periodical journalist who:

condemns himself ... to compose on a stated day, will often bring to his task an attention dissipated, a memory embarrassed, an imagination overwhelmed, a mind distracted with anxieties, a body languishing with disease: He will labour on a barren topick, till it is too late to change it; or ... diffuse his thoughts into wild exhuberance, which the pressing hour of publication cannot suffer judgement to examine or reduce ... No man but a blockhead ever wrote, except for money. (*The Rambler*, 1750–52, No. 208)

The *Idler* from 1758–60 also provided Johnson with an outlet for social and cultural commentary including more sceptical comments on contemporary journalism:

The compilation of newspapers is often committed to narrow and mercenary minds, not qualified for the task of delighting or instructing, who are content to fill their paper with whatever matter is at hand, without industry

> to gather or discernment to select ... The tale of the morning paper is told in the evening, and the narratives of the evening are brought out again in the morning. (*The Idler*, 27 May 1758)

Although they were priced beyond the pocket of many ordinary men and women, newspapers aimed in their style and miscellaneous content to provide a broad and generally accessible diet for their readers. Some newspapers reported eagerly on criminal cases, most often in moralistic tones in keeping with the way in which most newspapers and other periodicals presented themselves as opportunities to improve the mind as well as keep abreast of the latest information. From the 1760s, the importance of the letter, signed, as part of political comment becomes noticeable. In the second half of the eighteenth century there is an increasing emphasis on pastimes such as sport, with horse racing and cricket being among the first reported. For example, in the issue of *The London Evening Post* of Thursday 13 September to Saturday 15 September, there are various cricket reports including:

> On Monday last the great match at Cricket, so long depending between the gentlemen of Hambledon in Hants, called Squire Lamb's Club, and the gentlemen of Chertsey was play'd on Laleham Borough. Chertsey went in first, and got 48 notches, Hambledon got 76. Second innings, Chertsey heade 87, John Edmonds and Thomas Baldwin turned the game, by getting upwards of 40 notches: time expired, and they postponed it till the next morning, when Chertsey went in and got 12 notches; Hambledon went in, three out for four notches, the next five won the game. Chertsey had three men much hurt, and Hambledon had two, Mr Steward having his finger broken, and his knee sprained. On this match great sums of money were depending.
>
> During the Cricket match a gentleman of fortune at Weybridge was taken up by a warrant for a bastard child, which caused a great deal of diversion; the gentleman drew his sword on the occasion, and afterwards presented a pistol, and went off in triumph.

Advertisement growth was a significant feature of newspapers through the eighteenth century. Many early newspapers of the late seventeenth century had none at all. The word *Advertiser* became a common name for newspapers reflecting the increasing influence of advertisements on newspapers and their revenues. So important were advertisements and trade news that: 'in the 1660s London newspapers had been produced carrying no political news and simply containing advertisements and news of trade' (Black, 1991: 66). Advertising was part of a wider system of intelligence and opinion at whose centre was positioned the respectable, bourgeois newspaper as an intertextual, miscellaneous intermediary. The newspaper was increasingly providing what Bakhtin (1996) has called in a different context, a dialogic space.

  We can see the formation of the shape and structure of modern news in the papers of the mid-eighteenth century. It is laid out into regular grids with titled sections for LONDON, PORT NEWS, IRELAND, BANKRUPTS.

In terms of layout, large bold capitals were already used for initial letters of stories and reports. There are brief reports on the debates and motions of Parliament and local regional news, chiefly of a police kind. Letters from readers were already selected to emphasize an identifiable editorial identity. Other contributions from anecdotes to poems were included to reinforce points made by letter writers. Articles of intelligence and postscripts of other leading London papers are included in all titles as they plagiarize from each other. Prices, stocks, high water marks, theatre announcements and reviews are published regularly as well as the arrivals of ships. Distinctions sometimes made between the important political content and the trivial and sensational news included in papers have always missed the point that a judicious blend of these two was always the optimal requirement for a popular and successful paper, written for a broad and general readership not solely for scholars or politicians.

Politically, the newspapers were much less stable than the Whig/Tory duopoly might first indicate. This is because of the rivalries and splits within these political camps which gave rise to dispute and manoeuvring rather than propagandist authoritarian party lines. Politics was in flux although criticism until the French Revolution was only of politicians and of the political system which was perceived as open to reform. There was no call for reform or radical change to the social system or the franchise. The daily newspaper of the mid-century was maturing in its coverage of commercial and financial news while the weekly newspapers took a more general overview of the news and were better served by the political essay, often on the front page, in the tradition of the essay sheets. The quantity of information available often made continuity of news and the background to news stories difficult. However, in their coverage of foreign news, both were becoming better able to cover important events abroad such as the Lisbon earthquake in 1755 and the capture of Quebec from the French in 1759. News from abroad, especially in time of war, was an essential staple as an attractive ingredient which contributed to the vitality of any newspaper.

Despite the apparently more liberal tolerance of newspapers and journals by authority, other forms of resistance and control persisted. Threats to damage printers, whipping of hawkers, breaking of presses, duels between publishers and wronged victims of libel, actual bodily harm against printers and publishers occurred. This had an impact on the content of journalism and its style: 'The threat of persecution forced newspapers to adopt an allusive style and an allegorical approach, rich in innuendo and code words and letters' (Black, 1991: 165).

The mid-century also saw further restrictions on the press through increased taxation. The second Stamp Act of 1757 on the outbreak of war with France, which doubled the stamp duty on newspapers and was then increased up to a penny halfpenny in 1776, was principally a fiscal, tax-raising measure rather than an attempt to solely restrict the circulation of papers, but these increases nevertheless forced newspapers into more conservative relations with political supporters and advertisers in order to survive the increase in costs. Such increases restricted the potential readership still further.

Wilkes: Journalism as Political Opportunism

The career of John Wilkes and his rise to become a Member of Parliament, indicate the potential for building bridges between an individual's political motivations and the people and the way in which journalism was able to transmit those interests through direct, topical and powerful writing to a wide and regular readership. From 1762, in his essay paper the *North Briton*, Wilkes claimed to champion English liberty and the rights of the individual, particularly through a populist campaign of ridicule of George III's Scottish first minister, Lord Bute. He claimed that his paper had been brought out to counter the *Briton* being published under the royal coat of arms, and he wondered whether this was meant as an intimidation which indicated that its opinions had government or even royal approval like the *Gazette*. By issue number 2 he was already criticizing Bute, his place in Parliament and casting doubt on his financial ability to run the Exchequer. For Wilkes, drawing on populist anti-Scottish prejudices, the Scots are rebellious by nature and their chieftains are despots.

Issue 45 of 23 April 1763 caused the so-called 'Wilkes' Affair' to break into the public domain in sensational fashion. When Bute was subsequently removed from office, it was the first time that the press had played such a dynamic part in removing a politician from power and showed that it was possible for opinion to become the news. Wilkes accused Bute in the strongest possible terms:

> A despotic minister will always endeavour to dazzle his prince with high-flown ideas of the *prerogative* and *honour* of the *crown*, which the minister will make a parade of *firmly maintaining*. I wish as much as any man in the kingdom to see the *honour of the crown* maintained in a manner truly becoming *Royalty*. I lament to see it sunk even to prostitution.

In this issue he also makes a strong claim for his own interpretation of the freedom of the press:

> The liberty of the Press is the birthright of a BRITON, and is justly esteemed the firmest bulwark of the liberties of this country. It has been the terror of all bad ministers; for their dark and dangerous designs, or their weakness, inability, and duplicity, have thus been detected, and shown to the public generally in too strong colours for them long to bear up against the odium of mankind.

Wilkes based much of the popular success of his paper on his willingness to tap into Franco-Scottish Jacobite rumours and their perceived threat to the British state. Issue 45 was, in the arrest warrant of 26 April 1763, prosecuted because the authors, printers and publishers had produced 'a seditious and treasonable paper', and on 30 April when the execution of the arrest was ordered, it was alleged to be 'tending to inflame the minds and alienate the affections of the people from his majesty and to excite them to traiterous insurrections against the government'.

Popular unrest following the Wilkes' Affair finally caused General Warrants to be declared illegal in 1765. This indicated how popular support for Wilkes had made it untenable for the Courts to continue to pursue such prosecutions where they were unpopular and difficult to draw to a satisfactory conclusion. The deployment of the press by Wilkes as an advocate of his own position was a publicity stunt with which the legislature could not compete and was an indication of the extent to which journalism could claim to form part of a community with a broad readership representative of public opinion. There was an increasing resonance around the discourse of public opinion which the newspapers themselves fed into, often out of sheer self-interest in presenting themselves as first and foremost the champions of the public, their customers. Barker has observed of this period of journalism's development that it was clear that 'public opinion was increasingly associated with those who read newspapers and other forms of printed matter and that this was a trend encouraged by the newspapers themselves' (2000: 28). In fact along with the formation of political opinion, one of the prime functions and appeals of the newspaper became the way it created a community of readers in fact and in imagination (Anderson, 1986). This had an effect in the construction of both metropolitan and national identities and could be called upon for patriotic purposes, or in the case of Wilkes and others who followed him, for radical ends. Yet in other parts of the press, Wilkes was cautioned against excessive confidence in his anti-establishment games:

> To Mr Wilkes
> Be cautious, Wilkes, and bear with steady Head
> Those blooming Honours that around thee spread.
> Honours superior far to Stars and Strings,
> The Judges' s Ermine, or the State of King!
> Now let each proud, impetuous Thought subside,
> And glide with easy Sail along the swelling Tide;
> Nor trust too much to popular Applause,
> The breath may blast thee that supports thy Cause.
> Oft will the Multitude of this mad Town
> Set up an Idol just to throw it down. NEW INN

> (*Public Advertiser*, 6 January 1769)

This was published in the *Public Advertiser*, soon to become synonymous with the letters of 'Junius', the latest in a series of eloquent political critics and commentators who lent authority to the essay papers of the day, as they provided the impetus for the evolution of an engaged and critical form of political commentary as an essential contributor to journalism.

Junius's Letters

The relationship of the *Public Advertiser* to its significant number of readers, its advertising scope and its public service on behalf of the police in apprehending thieves were noted explicitly on the front page of its Friday, 6 January 1769 edition:

> From the Police
> The extensive sale of The PUBLIC ADVERTISER ... has always been the Means of detecting of many ROBBERIES, and of apprehending so many OFFENDERS, that it may be proper to give THIS PUBLIC NOTICE, That, for the Future, all Informations of this Kind, sent to BOW-STREET, will be constantly inserted in THIS PAPER: And if SUCH INFORMATIONS are properly attended to, by PAWNBROKERS, JEWELLERS, SILVERSMITHS, STABLE-KEEPERS, BUYERS OF SECOND HAND CLOATHES etc, few Robberies will escape Detection; especially if ALL PERSONS ROBBED make use of THIS PAPER to advertise their Losses in.
>
> J. FIELDING

Its front page was dominated by advertisements, as was becoming the fashion, as the advertisers accrued greater influence the more their financial input increased. The advertisements were in fact better laid out than the news. There were the results of prize draws, news from various government departments such as the Navy Office, the Stamp Office and Shipping news. There was news of polite society, criminal news from the courts and news from abroad, but it is most renowned for its exchanges of letters on the politics of the day. Rusticus, Cassius, Nestor Anglo-Saxon were all notable and regular anonymous correspondents. Beyond its appeal to advertisers, its prominent display of letters to the newspaper, a practice which was becoming commonplace by the mid-century, brought it great success. The anonymous 'Junius' made full use of this tradition. Junius's Letters, it is said, 'raised journalism to a far more important position than it had ever held before' (Fox-Bourne, 1998: 190). They began to appear, signed 'Junius', in the *Public Advertiser* from 21 January 1769 although Andrews claims a letter from 28 April 1767 signed Poplicola was in reality Junius's debut. These letters were vitriolically critical of the government and within the year they had doubled the sales of the newspaper:

> To Sir William Draper, 7 January 1769
> ...The Last and most important Question remains. When you receive your half-Pay, do you, or do you not, take a solemn Oath, or sign a Declaration upon Honour to the following Effect? That you do not actually hold any place of Profit, civil or military, under his majesty. The Charge, which this Question plainly conveys against you, is of so shocking a Complexion, that I sincerely wish you may be able to answer it well, not merely for the colour of your Reputation, but for your own inward Peace of Mind.
>
> Junius

On 19 December 1769 he wrote to the king via the pages of the *Advertiser*: 'Sire – it is the misfortune of your life ... that you should never have been acquainted with the language of truth, until you heard it in the complaints of your people. It is not, however, too late to correct the error'. Because of the letters, the *Public Advertiser* drew influential correspondents and became an important opinion maker, developing 'the superior eighteenth century manner' of political commentary and polemic (Herd, 1952: 103).

Newspapers at the End of the Century

At the end of the century there was a consolidation of the position of the daily newspaper as a rival to the essay paper in terms of its ability to intervene regularly and effectively in the realm of ideas, opinions and public affairs. The increased take-up of advertising in the later years of the century meant that new newspapers were better able to offset the expense of stamp duty, and the *Morning Chronicle* (1770), the *Morning Post* (1772), and the *Universal Daily Register* (*Times*) (1785) were launched. The *Morning Post*, under the Rev. Henry Bate, nick-named 'The Fighting Parson', developed the tradition of scandal journalism but with an even greater economic opportunism which provided a certain form of limited economic independence. As editor he perfected the system of 'puffs', 'correction fees' and 'suppression fees' whereby the subjects would pay for the publication or the suppression of stories depending on whether they were complimetary or not. From 1783 under a new editor, the Rev. William Jackson, known ominously as 'Doctor Viper', it added political subsidy to its coffers as well. At the cusp of the eighteenth and nineteenth centuries the influence of booksellers and printers begins to recede and editors and newspaper owners begin to appreciate the newspaper as a valuable product in its own right. In 1784 the mail coach was introduced by John Palmer and three years later in 1787 the Post Office created an office dedicated solely to the distribution of newspapers which added to the rising preference for daily papers and meant that by the end of the century the dailies had taken the lead in the market over the thrice-weeklies and weeklies. The *Morning Chronicle*, edited by James Perry, and the *Morning Post*, edited by Daniel Stuart begin to demonstrate what independent newspapers could begin to achieve although it was not until 1802 that the term 'editor' was used to describe the managerial control of a whole newspaper which Perry and Stuart had introduced. Soon credibility and respectability returned to the fore as equally important to financial success. The *Morning Chronicle* became 'the greatest paper in England' (Herd, 1952: 91) after Perry bought it in 1789 and it was the predominant Whig paper of the period, employing such luminary figures as Sheridan, Ricardo, Coleridge, Charles Lamb, Sir James Mackintosh, Thomas Moore and William Hazlitt. Nevertheless, such was its growing reputation that Perry had to compromise between finding room for Whig propaganda and fitting in the advertising which its increasing status was attracting (Smith, 1978: 165), eventually conceding that the miscellany or non-political features were the 'the soul of a newspaper' (Asquith, 1978: 107).

Rapidly, advertising was becoming a more reliable barometer of respectability than bribes or political subsidy. Daniel Stuart endorsed the overall effect of the advertisements on his *Morning Post*:

> I encouraged the small and miscellaneous advertisements in the front page, preferring them to any others, upon the rule that the more numerous the customers, the more permanent and independent the custom. Besides, numerous and various advertisements interest numerous and various readers, looking out for employment, servants, sales, and purchasers, etc. Advertisements act and react. They attract readers, promote circulation, and circulation attracts advertisements. (Cranfield, 1978: 84)

Such economic acumen heralded the arrival of the era of the independent commercial newspaper which was able to chart a course unimpeded by specific party pressures or political concerns. This was to see the rise of the centrality of advertising and the broadening of the ambition of the newspaper to cover more of a miscellany than simply commercial or financial news. The editorial or leading article was a device which enhanced this appearance of autonomy. The importance of the single owner and his relationship with a strong editor became another key component of the editorial character and consistency of these end-of-century newspapers.

Another commercially-minded proprietor, John Walter, launched his *Daily Universal Register* on 1 January 1785:

> the Register of the times, and faithful recorder of every species of intelligence; it ought not to be engrossed by any particular object; but, like a well covered table, it should contain something suited to every palate; observations on the dispositions of our own and foreign courts should be provided for the political reader; debates should be reported for the amusement and information of those who may be particularly fond of them; and a due attention should be paid to the interests of trade, which are so greatly promoted by advertisements.

In 1790 the *Times* could still complain that the ministerial *The True Briton* had better and quicker access to government news which was furnished by arrangement. It too was in receipt of bribes and sponsorship in its early years like every other successful paper of the era. The only way to compete was to rival government information networks, and to do this a newspaper needed to build a commercial base which would enable it to afford to rival government sources and to claim an independence from them which would further enhance its reputation. This is the process which began at the turn of the nineteenth century in the commercial press: the race for independence and commercial autonomy. Another crucial moment for the shape of journalism was the passing in 1792 of Fox's Libel Law which meant that henceforth it would be the jury, not a judge, who would decide whether something was libellous. This would enable newspapers to consolidate the relationship they had built up with the reading public, as champions of the freedom of expression against the control of the governing classes.

The Impact of the French Revolution

The economically successful daily press was initially sympathetic to some of the grievances which led to the French Revolution of 1789 but it was in no way deflected from its chief aim, which was to continue its productive relationship within the existing British political system. A ban on hiring newspapers from hawkers was imposed because of fears of revolutionary influences from France coming through such a cheap and unlicensed channel, not through the mainstream daily press. The essay papers and pamphlets were more influential than daily newspapers on the political implications of the French Revolution and later parliamentary reform and newspaper taxes. The daily newspapers continued to corroborate the conservative integration of journalism into the economy and polity: 'Sympathetic to popular distress but opposed to popular action, newspapers displayed little interest in any significant change in the hierarchical nature of society, whatever their views on changes in France might be' (Black, 1991: 272).

The French Revolution introduced 'democratic and demotic' newspapers to Britain (Barker, 2000: 176). The press and pamphlets played a significant part in creating a mass debate on social and political issues. In addition, newspapers provided an up-to-date account of the battles and main events of the Revolutionary Wars (though sometimes with inaccuracies) and were among the leading voices in campaigning for peace from 1807. News continued to arrive six or seven days after the event until the French Revolution gave impetus to the newspapers gathering their own information and rushing it back to London. The impetus thus shifted from Post Office official translations to the newspapers themselves. Journalism became an essential contributor to the formation of political opinion, not just a purveyor of news. In this respect, early nineteenth-century journalism was not so much displaying mere commercial progress, as reviving a radical tradition which had been eclipsed by economic and political pressures over the previous one hundred and fifty years, but it was only when this moved from the established press into the unstamped that it made its permanent mark on the discourse of political debate in English journalism.

5

Radical Journalism

Its Rise and Incorporation

Social and Political Conditions

The nineteenth century saw three trends within journalism become more divergent: (1) the publication of radical opinion; (2) the consolidation of the profitable and influential bourgeois press; and (3) the emergence of the Sunday and weekly popular newspapers as the staple fare of the lower classes. This chapter will examine the contribution of the radical press to the discourse of journalism as it attempts to reinscribe the interests of ordinary people in periodical form. As one set of developments were moving newspapers towards commercial respectability and therefore a particular sort of political independence, another, a long suppressed radical impulse, was about to gain renewed momentum. This found an outlet in a radical journalism which sought to contest the political status quo and foment revolutionary change. *Blackwood's Edinburgh Magazine* identified it in full awareness of its disruptive intent to the status quo: 'Radicalism is subversion, total excision and overthrow, the substitution, not of one order of polity for another, but an utter destruction of the present state of things' (*Blackwood's Magazine*, 8 1820: 329). The legacy of this radicalism expressed in unstamped journalism was the restructuring of the language of political analysis and a major contribution to the creation of a sense of working-class identity.

Previously it had been assumed that all newspaper readers were from a relatively homogeneous middle class, so newspaper owners and contributors had no interest in targeting the reading poor. Most newspapers and journals were tailored to this assumption. The lower classes were catered for through the more irregular publications such as ballads, chapbooks, broadsides and almanacs. Yet, under pressure from the impact of political and social events abroad, such as the American and French Revolutions, and at home, in the wake of the pressures of unemployment and urbanization in the early Industrial Revolution, readerships were being increasingly politicized along class lines. Newspapers began to address their readers in one of two ways: as a market for economic purposes, or as a social class for political purposes. Hannah More's Cheap Repository Tracts are indicative of concerns about the possible influence of radical public writing on the working classes. They were explicitly designed to drive seditious and immoral publications from the market, and, priced at a penny or a halfpenny, are estimated to have sold over two million copies between March 1795 and March 1796. They attempted a moral education to secure the loyalty of the lower classes to Christian virtues.

Smith has written of the limitations of the sort of journalism on offer in the late eighteenth century:

> The press could record public events and it could enliven debate among the politically involved. But as a means of social communication it was, in the eyes of many, a non-starter ... The social structures were too solid to admit of any new agency. Journalism was kept from communicating between classes, from spreading its truths in such a way as to allow the crowd to set up in judgement against the governing classes. Their curiosity was to be slaked, if at all, by the illegal unstamped newspapers, which began to circulate in greater profusion, the tighter the laws to tax and contain the ordinary press. (1978: 164–5)

At the start of the nineteenth century, journalism was renewing an acquaintance with political controversy unseen on such a scale since the English Civil War almost two hundred years earlier. Raymond Williams writes that what the nineteenth century brought was 'a new kind of campaigning political journalism' (1978: 47).

We may start by sketching a brief chronology of the political, social and economic conditions which led to the growth in radical ideas in the early nineteenth-century press in England and their contribution to the extension of the range of journalistic discourse into a mode of polemic not read since the time of the Levellers. The 1776 American Declaration of Independence was an obvious clarion call with its insistence on 'no taxation without representation' from the British. Building on the tradition developed by Wilkes with his political essay sheet *North Briton*, an important figure in the propaganda war which preceded the War of American Independence was the English émigré Thomas Paine who created a form of what Smith has called 'popular agitational journalism' (1979: 75). Shuttling because of political circumstances between Britain, America and France, he produced a wide range of polemical journalism, including his three main publications *Common Sense* (1776), *The Rights of Man* (1791) and *The Age of Reason* (1795). Jones captures the oppositional flavour of Paine when he writes: 'Print for him was essentially a publicly accessible and accountable medium of communication, not a tool under the monopolistic control of government, journalists or printers' (1996: 12). Such was the ambition which informed all of the chief contributors to the nineteenth-century radical press.

Opposing Radicalism

The 1789 French Revolution was in many ways more worrying for the British ruling classes, first, because of the proximity of France and, second, because its radical ideas chimed with issues which were urgently relevant to the politically and economically disenfranchised of Britain. The French Revolution demonstrated, as in the USA, the ability of print to generate mass action through its presentation of opinion on political matters and events, making abstraction concrete (Gough, 1988). To varying degrees, the *Morning Post* and the *Morning Chronicle* in England supported the ideas of the Revolution and only drew back once they perceived its violent excesses. To curb the spread of revolutionary ideas and enthusiasm through the press the government raised the stamp duty to 2d in 1789 and later in 1797 to $3\frac{1}{2}$d but still their influence persisted. Between 1793 and 1815 the newspapers played an increasingly strident role in opinion formation and in the polarization of popular political debate throughout the years of Revolutionary turmoil in France and the subsequent Napoleonic Wars. Press and pamphlets played a significant part in creating a mass debate.

Throughout the 1790s, anxiety about the spread of radicalism through the newspapers caused a limited return to the practice of subsidising newspapers, but even at this point the newspapers which were successful were more inclined to attempt to boost their reputation by demonstrating their independence from political sponsorship as an essential part of their public integrity. There were also attempts to present polemical alternatives as a means of fighting the power of political journalism with articulate refutations. Such was the influence of the combined attention of all varieties of journalism to events in France that Canning's *Anti-Jacobin; or, Weekly Examiner* was launched as a weekly six penny political journal which only produced 36 numbers (20 November 1797 to 9 July 1798) but had a huge impact in terms of influencing public opinion opposed to radical change. Its self-delegated task was to combat both radical and mainstream support in newspapers for revolutionary and republican ideas. It declared on its launch:

> Prospectus of *Anti-Jacobin or Weekly Examiner*
> Novelty indeed We have to announce. For what so new in the present state of the daily and weekly Press (We speak generally, though there are undoubtedly exceptions which we may have occasion to point out hereafter) as THE TRUTH? To this object alone it is that Our labours are dedicated. It is the constant violation, the disguise, the perversion of the Truth, whether in narrative or in argument, that will form the principal subject of our Weekly Examinations ...
>
> We vow ourselves to be partial to the Country in which we live ... We are prejudiced in favour of her Establishments, civil and religious: though without claiming for either that ideal perfection ...
>
> Of Jacobism ... We are the avowed, determined and irreconcilable enemies.

It based its appeal on a call to tradition and patriotism and, in addition to its eloquent conservative polemic, it provided appropriate poetry, anecdotes concerning recent events on the military and political fronts at home and abroad, and a listing of 'mistakes' and 'lies' from the daily press:

LIES OF THE WEEK
Last week Mr Smith, an eminent Watchmaker in Bunhill-Row, was deputed to wait on Mr Pitt, to misrepresent to him the danger of any further duty on Watches. He said a great number of journeymen would be entirely out of employ. – The Minister very coolly answered, there was employment enough for them in the Army and Navy. *Morning Post*, Nov 21.
(Monday, 27 November 1797)

MISTAKES
The *Morning Post* is out of its element. In falsehood, in calumny, in zeal for the pure faith of Jacobinism, it is not inferior to any of its Brethren; but it must yield to the *Morning Chronicle* in the work of Blasphemy.
(Monday, 19 February 1798)

In addition to the political and military challenges facing the British across the Channel, there was a set of more intractable and home-grown issues which threatened the stability of the political nation. The industrialization of the country had been gathering pace with an increase in the population of towns and cities. Older forms of life and economic production and the social relationships which accompanied them were breaking down as new forms of social and political awareness began to take their place. There was an increasing awareness of corruption within the political system and wide-spread scepticism towards a government unwilling to combat it. A new form of journalism developed, centred upon the editorial essay and concentrating not upon a relation of the events of the time but on building radical opinion on political issues. In its polemic, it sought to introduce politics to a reader-ship excluded from other formal channels of political expression.

Early Radical Journalism

Overt political campaigning (anti-corruption, anti-slavery, anti-Corn Law, pro-Reform) became one of the new, defining functions of journalism as it developed throughout the nineteenth century. The concerted attempt to shift policy by the support of popular causes through campaigns in the press becomes as much a marker of journalism as the much-heralded arrival of objectivity. The reasons why newspapers chose to support such campaigns lies in their special combination of commercial and populist motivations. The campaign was a key genre in the construction of a collective identity through popular and contemporary issues. This was a paradigm shift in the discourse of journalism which the radical press was to make for a while its own special area of expertise. In its earliest manifestation, radical journalism was identified by its strident campaigning on a wide range of issues concerned with what has been identified as the 'old corruption' (Hollis, 1970) but over time, and in dialogue with other social and political forces, it developed an increasing awareness of social class and, indeed, contributed much to the articulation of distinctly class interests (Thompson, 1979). The style of the early radical journalism was as broad as its range of targets. Carlile's republicanism, serious and principled, may have contained echoes of the Levellers while the satire of Wooler's *Black Dwarf* certainly had more correspondence with the ribaldry of certain of the English Civil War mercurists.

It was William Cobbett who first combined concerns over political corruption and favouritism with an awareness of the threat of new economic practices as they impacted upon the quality of ordinary people's lives. He drew these together in a journalism which was written in a declamatory style, suited to the eye or the ear, designed for the new proletarian public sphere which was growing around the country. Having started his writing career with the *Porcupine* in America as a provocative conservative, loyal to the British Crown, he returned to England and founded the *Weekly Political Register* in 1802 to escape from the persistent attention of the American authorities. His paper was originally conceived as a conservative organ with support from prominent Tory politicians. However, he quickly became alarmed at the deteriorating state of the country and sought to develop a critical position through his public writing. His politics may have changed but the provocative nature of his writing and its appeal to the common reader had not. His journalistic voice is a fiercely independent one and critical of the collusion between the state and the press demonstrated in his parable of the dog and the wolf where Cobbett clearly identifies himself with the wolf:

> 'What's your fancy,' says he, 'for making that mark around your neck?' 'Oh,' said the other, 'it is only the mark of my collar that my master ties me up with.' 'Ties you up?' exclaimed the wolf, stopping short at the same time; 'give me my ragged hair, my gaunt belly, and my freedom!' and so saying he trotted back to the wood. (Quoted in Herd, 1952: 105)

He often wrote explicitly on the failings of the press in England with regard to ordinary people:

> If ever there was in the world a thing completely perverted from its own design and tendency, it is the press of England: which instead of enlightening, does, as far as it has any power, keep the people in ignorance; which, instead of cherishing notions of liberty, tends to making the people slaves; and which instead of being their guardian, is the most efficient instrument in the hand of those who oppress them. (WPR, 11 April 1807)

Cobbett's critics have stressed both the personalized and the unsystematic nature of his writing: Charles Knight called him 'half knave and half enthusiast' (Jones, 1996: 106) and probably intended the allegation of enthusiasm to be as unflattering as the knavery. Hazlitt bemoaned his generalized attacks on the system and his overbearing oppositional nature: 'Wherever power is, there is he against it … His principle is repulsion, his nature contradiction: he is made up of mere antipathies' (Hazlitt, on the Character of Cobbett, 1822; Gilmartin,1996: 158). Yet what stands out in Cobbett in his contribution to the emergence of political journalism is his success in establishing in plain language a political rapport with a clearly identifiable audience – '*truth* in *clear language*' (Cobbett's Political Register 18, 1810). To this end he was explicitly didactic:

> I teach them how to know the cause of all the misery they see amongst the poor. I point out to them those who are the real cause of it, and, then I beat at their breasts till I force out loud indignation and bitter curses against the guilty party. (Cobbett's Political Register 21, 1812: 168)

Radical journalism, in the main, continued through this period unstamped and weekly, although David Lovell's *Statesman* (1806–24) was an exception as a stamped and daily paper. In most cases the organization of the radicals only permitted a weekly publication and, as they did not pay Stamp Duties, they were both profitable and within the reach of anyone who cared to read them.

John and Leigh Hunt

The *Examiner* was launched in 1808 by John and Leigh Hunt as a weekly paper. It constituted a radical and aggressive assault on the political status quo. In the opinion of Gilmartin, they 'joined other radical editors in a dangerous and disruptive form of guerilla journalism' (1996: 198). The paper was a strong and consistent supporter of extra-parliamentary direct action to achieve a more equitable social system. Both John and Leigh were prosecuted on several occasions for their publications, most notably in December 1812 when they were found guilty of libelling the Prince Regent. They were sentenced to two years in goal and ordered to pay a fine of £500 (Andrews, Vol. 2, 1998: 73). The Hunts' paper was also supportive of other key journalists and propagandists of the time, especially Richard Carlile. The Hunts bemoaned the economic priorities of the contemporary press and deemed them damaging to fully democratic debate: 'Our former periodical politicians, then, wrote to establish their own opinions and to acquire reputation; our present, simply to get money' (*Examiner*, 6 August 1809). To combat this they had proposed that they would do without the support of advertisers and in the Prospectus to the weekly *Examiner* it proclaimed this independence: 'No ADVERTISEMENTS WILL BE ADMITTED' (3 January 1808).

Gilmartin has commented perceptively that given the *Examiner*'s middle-class appeal, the Hunts were among the few radical editors for whom refusing advertisements was a realistic and economically viable strategy (1996: 205). This policy continued until 1820 when reeling under increased taxation and declining circulation, they too had to accept advertising.

With 1815 came victory at Waterloo and peace with France but also the return of soldiers to a country racked by economic depression and un-employment. Stamp duty was increased to 4d, further excluding the poor and the unemployed from reading about the political events which were deter-mining the material conditions of their everyday lives. The volatile atmos-phere was amplified between 1815 and 1819 by a whole range of radical and unstamped newspapers and journals which burst on the scene to exploit the demand for alternative and cheap forms of information and opinion. Cobbett's work was complemented by that of Wade, Wooler and Carlile, among many others. Such was Cobbett's influence that a publication, the *Anti-Cobbett*, or *Weekly Patriotic Register*, was issued to directly refute him in 1817. These radical journalists were engaged in a wide range of roles as writers, editors, printers, publishers, and booksellers, demonstrating the enormous vitality and commitment they brought to their ideological work.

The radical weeklies of the second decade of the nineteenth century appeared frequently enough to maintain coherence and loyalty with a rapidly evolving, politically concerned readership and they were able to do this without the costs associated with more frequent and more varied com-mercial publications. They also escaped the duties imposed on other news-papers as they did not contain news but only political comment and opinion on the news. Despite the fact that this had always been an essential part of journalism's range, it was not considered to be part of the narrow definition of a newspaper employed by the authorities at this time, much to the tempo-rary advantage of the radical and unstamped weeklies. The unstamped weekly became available to working-class readers for the first time with Cobbett's *Twopenny Trash* from November 1816. It was a cheaper weekly version of the stamped *Register*.

Despite enthusiastic support from readers and an ingenious system of distribution, the long-term success of radical alternatives was to be increas-ingly hampered by the clash between the commercial interests of advertis-ers and the narrow political agenda of the radical publicist/journalists. If the future of the newspaper depended on its ability to attract advertising, then the radical weekly would have none. As late as 1821, Cobbett finally accepted advertisements in the *Register*, but soon found himself confined to printing notices for other radical publications. While the government was increasingly dependent on laws and taxes against the press to restrict politi-cal and social change, the concept of a free press became linked by the radi-cal writers to a position of deeply held principle against the ruling class. It was in their political and discursive coherence as oppositional, not only to the government but increasingly to the entire British political infrastructure of the early nineteenth century, that they were to be distinguished from their more pragmatic journalistic relatives, the mainstream commercial newspapers. The early radical press was restricted to a very narrow range of political journalism which attempted to challenge the broader range of commercially successful journalism. It has been argued that commercial and conservative tendencies were actually embedded in the visual and structural syntax of bourgeois journalism: 'The newspaper is built by addition of discrete, theoretically disconnected elements which juxtapose themselves only in response to the abstract requirements of "layout" – thus of a disposition of space whose logic, ultimately, is commercial' (Terdiman, 1985: 120).

The whole structure and self-imposed limitation of the radical press were a political provocation. Yet in its concentration on one aspect of the increasingly miscellaneous range of the newspaper, the journalism of the radical press was in danger of becoming monotone in comparison with its more varied and marketable competitors. Political decisions, economic contingencies and the increasing expense of running periodical publications were all to define the ways in which radical journalism would become incorporated into a commercialized mainstream.

Discursive Experiments in Radical Journalism

As in many eras of journalism's history a glance at the titles of these radical papers (The *Cap of Liberty*, *The Destructive and Poor Man's Conservative*, *The Red Republican*, *The Working Man's Friend*) indicates the ways in which they saw their own role in society. Between 1815 and the 1830s, and to a lesser extent until the 1850s, there was a continuing process of political polarization in the country at large expressed in the unstamped. Economic hardship, social and cultural dislocation, all led to an identifiable clustering of class consciousness, the beginnings of organized labour, demands for reform, protests against newspaper taxes and against the Poor Law Amendment Act of 1834, the Corn Law and many other issues.

A significant contributor to this radical political journalism was Richard Carlile. He was very much heir to Paine's heritage in terms of his style, conviction and consistent republican political analysis. In 1819, he launched the *Republican* as an important essay-style paper in the wake of the Peterloo Massacre. Rejecting anonymity and setting himself on a collision course with the authorities through his version of the events of that day:

THE CRISIS No 1
The massacre of the unoffending inhabitants of Manchester, on the 16 August, by the Yeomanry Cavalry, and Police, at the instigation of the Magistrates, should be the daily theme of the press, until the MURDERERS are brought to justice by the Law Officers of the Crown, under the instruction

of the executive, or in default thereof, until the People have obtained their proper rank and station in the legislature, by an equal representation, and thereby the means of enforcing the execution of justice, which in all probability will now be withheld ...

Bloodhounds of Manchester ... The wholesale murderers say that before they began to use their sabres, a pistol was fired and a brick-bat thrown. This is false. Hundreds had felt the sabre before the slightest resistance was made.

Fellow Countrymen, rouse from this fatal apathy, and play the MAN – if you the creatures, be no longer the slaves of circumstances. (Friday, 27 August 1819)

His new venture was explicitly dedicated to the introduction of republican political structures and set out its programme in characteristically robust terms from its very title and motto:

The Republican
From the bottom of my soul I hate
Despotic kings, and ministers of state.

Swift

TO THE PUBLIC
... a continuation of that entitled *Sherwin's Weekly Political Register*, which has been invariably the bold advocate of the only rational system of Government, namely, the REPUBLICAN ...

no correspondence or essays be admitted into the pages of the *Republican*, unless accompanied with the real name and address of the author. Most periodical publications of the day, are filled with anonymous essays, correspondence and information on various subjects ...

Indeed it is apparent and evident, that the tree of liberty, which was planted, and which grew and bloomed in France, although its blossom was blasted, yet it has taken a root deep and wide, spreading over the Continent of Europe, a root that will baffle the despot, who attempts to eradicate it. (Friday, 27 August 1819)

To reinforce the continuities between the Painite tradition and the work of the *Republican*, Sherwin's edition of the *Life of Thomas Paine* and other radical tracts were advertised in the pages of the *Republican*. There were a variety of converging items included on a regular basis such as records of prosecutions of political allies, extracts from other papers when pertinent, copies of ministerial letters and dispatches, responses to correspondents. Money was sent in and accounts published of financial support from supporters for fines and production costs. Sympathetic letters were printed from named supporters such as the following:

To the Editor of the Republican
ON THE LIBERTY OF THE PRESS

Without the Liberty of the Press, the public authority can neither be enlightened, or responsible; and if this liberty has, like all human things, any inconveniences, it may be said that, like the lance of Achilles, it heals all the wounds it has caused.

   This liberty is even more necessary in Monarchies than in Republics, because there is always found round every throne, even those upon which the best kings are seated, a crowd of courtiers which prevents the voice of the upright from penetrating to the monarch ... John Sidney, Inner Temple. (From Letter to Editor: 10 December 1819)

Indicating the vigorous miscellany used in propagating his republican agenda and echoing the textual and stylistic variety of the Civil War mercuries, Carlile was quite willing to include a piece of polemic verse in his pages:

THE TRIUMPH OF REASON
With silent step bright Reason walks,
Diffusing light throughout the land;
And conscious Error fearful stalks
To claim Oppression's tyrant hand.
For Reason's beam has open'd wide
The den where Superstition dwelt,
Shorn the dark monster of its pride,
And Error Reason's pow'r has felt ...

GS (The *Republican*, 4 February 1820)

There were even international news items when they fitted with the precisely defined contours of the newspaper's political agenda:

MASSACRE AT CADIZ
A MASSACRE has occured at Cadiz in Spain, which equals in atrocity the late massacre at Manchester. The circumstances were not dissimilar ... It appears that about twice the number have been killed and mutilated at Cadiz, of those who were the dead or living victims at Manchester. (The *Republican*, Friday, 14 April 1820)

Carlile was never short of convictions, fines or other trouble with the authorities for the forthright publication of his radical opinions. He was convicted of blasphemous libel in 1819 for printing *The Age of Reason* and *The Principles of Nature*. He was fined £1,500 and sentenced to three years in prison which was extended to six when he could not pay the fines. This was draconian punishment indeed and a measure of the threat of this propagandist form of journalism to the establishment, as it sought 'to displace the distinction between whig and tory with a more ominous one between the people and corrupt government, and to make the press a forum for mobilizing this distinction on behalf of radical parliamentary reform' (Gilmartin, 1996: 1). He continued his publishing and printing from Dorchester Gaol. On 11 February his communication TO THE ADVOCATES OF PARLIAMENTARY REFORM is signed R. CARLILE *Dorchester Gaol, February 7th,* 1820. The *Republican* was suspended for a whole year in 1821 as many of his printers, hawkers, publishers and shop-assistants were arrested and some imprisoned.

A very different contribution to radical journalism came in Wooler's *Black Dwarf* from 29 January 1817. This was a rich combination of political engagement and satirical, textual experimentation in advancing both conventional and parodic arguments in favour of Reform and against the corruption of politicians. Its motto made this explicit:

> Satire's my weapon; but I'm too discreet,
> To run a-muck and tilt at all I meet:
>
>   POPE

Despite the oblique mode of attack, Wooler identified himself as the Editor and had to take the consequences of this like the other radical journalists of the time, being prosecuted in 1817 shortly after the first appearance of the paper. One polemic address, the 'Address to the Unrepresented Part of the Community', makes clear both the constituency his paper was aimed at as well as stressing the fact that in order to change society, this community had to become more actively aware of their current situation:

> You are *something*, you are indeed; and although few dare tell you what you are, you must perceive yourselves to be '*slaves, on whose chains are inscribed the words liberty and freedom!*' SLAVES? Englishmen Slaves? You are startled, and well you may be, but it should be at your *condition*, and not at the proclamation of it. Look around you. Do, I beseech you, make use of your eyes. (*Black Dwarf:* 8 July 1818)

Wooler printed news of the meetings of the Reform movement and signed letters protesting against ARBITRARY IMPRISONMENTS. He included provocative accounts from correspondents of miscarriages of justice:

> INSTANCE OF WANTON AND EXCESSIVE PUNISHMENT
> SIR ... two individuals of the 'Lower Orders,' for carrying coals ashore, which appears to have been scraped from a lighter alongside a collier. The quantity was about a bushel ... *seven years transportation!* (3 March 1819)

In 1819 he printed an elegiac tribute to the memory of those killed in Manchester at Peterloo. Gilmartin points out the importance of the cumulative effect of this journalism to alternative political movements, writing: 'Indeed, radical weeklies like the *Black Dwarf* served the reform movement in something like the capacity that parliamentary reporting served the state, linking leadership and constituency through reports of public meetings and assemblies' (1996: 30). In addition, most regular features of conventional newspapers were inverted in a set of parodies which were designed to entertain but at the same time undercut the credibility of his political enemies. For instance, he had regular sections of news narrated from a mischievous and subversive perspective, such as: 'NEWS FROM THE CITY ...' which signed off: 'Your's, A CITY IMP'.

His most renowned exercise in textual disruption was his 'cross Readings in a Newspaper'. These were a political version of an old game of reading across rather than down columns of print to produce unexpected juxtapositions:

CROSS READINGS
The Ministers are quite shocked to hear – all nuisances will be speedily removed.
   A certain political assembly, it is said will receive an accession of – many notorious swindlers. (*Black Dwarf*, 3 December 1817)

This was supplemented with other word play designed to disrupt conventional associations and formats such as:

VARIOUS SIGNIFICATIONS OF M.P.
Clio Rickamn

... Murderous Plotters ... Monstrous Profligates ... Much Palaver ... Ministerial puppets ... Mighty Promises ... Misled People ... Matchless Poultroons. (ibid.: 13 May 1818)

He was able to include poetic contributions from his readers including an interesting take on a radical's version of press history on 24 December 1817:

THE PRESS
When first gigantic Power awoke
And bound the world in Slavery's yoke
Fair Freedom to repress;
The orators of old withstood
His frantic rage and thirst of blood.
Tho' then there was no Press! ...

But when the sacred art arose,
To tyranny the worst of foes,
To Ignorance no less;
Each Despot, whose unhallow'd hand
Had filled with blood a groaning land
Turn'd pale amid his high command,
And trembled at the press! ...

Rise, Britain, rise! withstand their power,
Now is the dread, the fated hour,
To curse mankind or bless.
The wolves, to make their sheep their prey

Would lure the guardian dogs away,
Whose barking kept the thieves at bay,
O! guard the sacred Press!
R GILMOUR

24 November 1817

Surely the most sardonic example of news reporting and commentary on current events comes in one of *Black Dwarf*'s poems on the death of Queen Caroline:

ON HEARING OF THE DEATH OF HER MAJESTY
Ah Me! what news is this I hear?
Alas? They say the *Queen* is dead!
Bless me! the *onions* will be dear;
For *tears* of *fashion* must be shed!

(*Black Dwarf*, 2 December 1818)

Very similar to the critical analysis of the 'old corruption', Wooler used his paper to support a similar position to Cobbett on the new economic paradigm which was emerging:

DECEPTION OF SAVINGS BANKS
To the Tradesmen, Mechanics, and Labourers.

I have long and ardently, yet hitherto waited in vain, for the appearance of some able production, as a means of inducing some of my deluded countrymen to be on their guard, and to beware of *the cheat*, held out to them, under the name of Savings Banks. T.R. (*Black Dwarf*, 18 August 1819)

Most often Wooler saved his most withering satire for the exchanges between himself as the *Black Dwarf* and his correspondent, the Yellow Bonze, in Japan. In a high parody of the exchanges common in the respectable press and journals of the time, we are offered a radical satire based on cross-cultural commentary between the two:

LETTERS OF THE BLACK DWARF
From the Black Dwarf in London, to the Yellow Bonze at Japan
DANGER OF REASON TO THE POOR AND MIDDLING CLASSES
But alas! high birth is no security for reason. That uncertain gift is not always *found* where it is *most wanted*; kings often lack it; and princes and princesses go without. We can but lament that heaven should so often have suffered common sense to wander among the *lower orders*, where it can be comparatively of no value. Why should the poor possess so *dangerous a quality* as *reason*? They were not born to *reason*, but to *labour*! Why then has providence given them reason to discern the faults and follies of those who were born above them? ... Were I a senator, I would endeavour to remedy this evil. I would enact that no peasant should be

born with the power of thought. I would levy a severe penalty upon every rational expression, uttered by one who had not at least five hundred a year, or a sinecure place. (*Black Dwarf*, 18 February 1818)

Even the heroic efforts of Wooler to invigorate the cause of reform had been exhausted by the declining fortune of radical papers in the wake of the increased taxes on and surveillance of the radical press after 1819. He is writing from an apparent trough of despondency in the last copy of his paper in 1824 in his 'Final Address':

In ceasing his political labours, the Black Dwarf has to regret one mistake, and that a serious one. He commenced writing under the idea that there was a PUBLIC in Britain, and that public devotedly attached to the cause of parliamentary reform. This, it is but candid to admit, was an error.

His despair is based on a recognition that, in order to succeed, any radical journalism needs to be able to depend on the support and political conviction of a radical readership. Without this political commitment of the people, radical journalism only holds half a weapon.

John Wade provided another variation on the radical journalism of the time with his *Gorgon*. Wade was from a manual agricultural background. Self-taught, he had become an advocate of radical reform which sought to overthrow the established economic and parliamentary system. His focus was corruption, as he made clear in his opening paper:

Corruption has not yet encountered a more formidable and dangerous enemy, than in the circulation of cheap, weekly publications; and the malignant, but abortive attempts, that have been made to suppress these lights and guides to the poor, prove with what detestation and alarm their progress has been viewed by the tools of power. (The *Gorgon*, Introductory Essay, 23 May 1818)

He exhorted and orchestrated boycotts of taxed commodities which supported the corruption of the contemporary system of political representation, claiming this would expose the true location of power: 'The more taxes the people of any country pay, the greater is the power they possess over their Rulers'(The *Gorgon*, 8 August 1818).

This journalism provided an organic link to the readerships it was targeting. Public meetings, subscriptions, boycotts of commodity goods, all encouraged an interactivity with an engaged and active readership. The public sphere that the radical unstamped press provided was much more than a space for the polite exchange of political and aesthetic views, it was a crucible in which people could become aware of a range of alternative strategies for understanding and changing the world as they found it. This was far from the paradigm of journalism as an objective practice but very close to an ideal of journalism which offers an active community of readership in which politics and public communication combine with radical intent. Yet as this radical community becomes placated and the press which helped structure and articulate it is swept by legislation and prosecution from the stage, the journalism which had given it expression withers to become merely an echo of its potent voice.

The Six Acts and Radicalism Broken

The response in the radical press to the massacre of Peterloo was the final demonstration to the government of the need to introduce harsher penalties for sedition in order to suppress the considerable influence of these publications. This was achieved through the 1819 'Six Acts'. These made it necessary for bonds of £200–£300 to be paid over to the authorities before a paper could be published, to ensure that the press remained in the hands of respectable, politically acceptable owners. The Acts included a Blasphemous and Seditious Libels Act which was often invoked to curb the perceived excesses of the unstamped at this time. The definition of a newspaper was broadened so as to bring the radical essay-style of paper into a more efficient and repressive jurisdiction and a Newspaper Stamp Duties Act put the price of any papers able to survive this onslaught out of reach of their natural working-class readership. Taxation would now be levied on: 'any paper which contained public news, intelligence, or occurrences, any comments thereon or on matters of Church or State; and which was printed for sale and published periodically within twenty-six days; and which was no larger than two sheets and sold for less than 6d. exclusive of duty' (Hollis, 1970: 156).

The Seditious Meetings Preventions Act also passed at this time was an effective preventative measure which succeeded to a large extent in breaking the link between the radical press and public assembly. Fines, voluntary exile, imprisonment and damages awarded to aggrieved parties – all combined to shatter the first phase of the radical press. They were rationalized in the following way by Lord Ellenborough in a speech to the House of Lords:

> It was not against the respectable Press that this bill was directed, but against a pauper Press, which, administering to the prejudices and the passions of a mob, was converted to the basest purposes, which was an utter stranger to truth, and only sent forth a continual stream of falsehood and malignity, its virulence and mischief heightening as it proceeded. If he was asked whether he would deprive the lowest classes of society of all political information? he would say, that he saw no possible good to be derived to the country from having statesmen at the loom and politicians at the spinning jenny. (29 December 1819, *Hansard*, 1st ser., xli, col. 1591)

Overt political radicalism declined and disappeared during the 1820s. This can be attributed to the draconian anti-radical repression of 1819–22, including the execution of the Cato Street conspirators in 1820, but also to the improvement in economic conditions in the early and middle portion of the decade, to the more liberal reforming disposition of the Tory government and to the widespead popular diffusion of the values of respectability and self-improvement (McCalman, 1998: 181).

There were continued attempts to provide the working classes with material which was designed to provide them with wholesome and uncontentious reading matter in the wake of the suppression of the radical press from 1819. Brougham tried a variation of this with the formation of the Society for the Diffusion of Useful Knowledge (SDUK) in 1826 to help in the creation of a more content and better informed worker. From 1827 this was complemented by a *Library of Useful Knowledge* as a fortnightly collection of pieces on a range of topics from Greek literature to popular science. Charles Knight's *Penny Magazine* was launched in 1832 in an attempt to reach the lower orders with useful knowledge and thereby rescue them from sedition and political corruption. This periodical followed the tradition started in tract form by Hannah More. *Chamber's Edinburgh Journal*, the *Penny Magazine of the Society for the Diffusion of Useful Knowledge* and *The Saturday Magazine* all appeared in 1832 and attempted to tap into the demand for instruction and entertainment evinced by the success of the Sunday papers among the working classes but in more wholesome ways. The latter two were illustrated.

The suppression of the market for radical papers led some publishers to try other more conventional areas of popular taste less troubling to the authorities. Benbow's *Rambler's Magazine* (1822–24) was the most successful and influential with its tales and scandals of sexual licence in high places. McCalman points out that as part of this long tradition II.D. Symonds, one of the Quaker Thomas Paine's earliest publishers, had sold obscene works as a sideline (1988: 205). Benbow also included material drawn from the everyday experiences of his target audience with popular theatre, sport and criminal court reporting. However, in contrast to the political radicalism of the unstamped, this marginal critique of the mores of the ruling classes, although it fits with certain aspects of political critique (Darnton, 1996), was not ultimately anything other than politically opportunistic.

The Second Phase of Radical Journalism

Hollis (1970) has pointed out that there were two distinct phases of the radical press. They both drew on the traditions of radical dissent which emerged out of the print culture of the English Civil War, but whereas the first version was characterized by its desire to expose political corruption, the second was a much more coherent attempt to link the press with an emergent class analysis. The second wave of radical journalism accompanied the generalized push towards parliamentary reform, but was sharpened within the working class by the effects of a renewed period of economic upheaval from 1825 which led many on the left of the Reform movement to further develop radical thinking beyond the limits of a simple change in suffrage.

In the early 1830s the second wave of unstamped papers swept onto the streets. Carlile launched the *Prompter* (1830–31), was prosecuted for seditious libel in 1830 and imprisoned for two years. Along with Carlile's continued presence was Owen's the *Crisis* (1832–34) which acted as a mouthpiece for his political views of common ownership of land, means of production and distribution. Other notable contributions included the *Cosmopolite* (1832), the *Man* (1833), the *Pioneer Magazine of Useful Knowledge and Co-operative Miscellany* (1830–32) and Cleave's *Working Man's Friend* (1832–33).

Radical editors, this time in open defiance of the law, reintroduced the unstamped newspaper, combining news and political comment. They were committed to Reform and spanned the spectrum of radical dissent against the current political establishment from moderate to revolutionary. The veterans of the earlier unstamped press, Cobbett, Carlile and Hunt, who continued to write and circulate their political journalism, were outflanked by more radical and explicitly socialist propagandists such as Hetherington and O'Brien and others more closely allied to the various working-class political organizations such as the National Union of the Working Classes founded in 1831. Chalaby insists that these writers be called 'publicists' rather than journalists for they had no pretence to be objective and explicitly sought to persuade rather than inform (1998: 16–17) This is, however, rather a restricted view of the traditions of journalism which these writers drew upon and also of the contribution they were making to the development of political writing which still has a place, albeit incorporated within the mainstream, by and large, of political journalism. Hollis' perspective seems more appreciative of their historical location within the discourse of journalism and suggests that, for all their ideological commitment and polemic, the unstamped were a 'species of popular journalism' (Hollis, 1970: vii). Radical newspapers were hugely influential in bringing about the Reform Act of 7 June 1832 through their range of agitation and the fears of what they could do to bring about a popular uprising if the demands for Reform were not met. The watered-down version which became law, delivered not universal suffrage but votes for the wealthier sections of the middle class. Even the *Times* had called for mass demonstrations in support of reform in December 1831 (Thompson, 1979: 890). The view of Chalaby also underestimates the specifically journalistic role of the radical press in forming a connection to a whole variety of other sections of radical protest which formed part of a newly invigorated public sphere. If journalism has always had a contribution to make to the formation and transformation of the public sphere, then surely the writing of the radicals during these years made such a contribution in proposing alternatives to the narrow bourgeois version.

Henry Hetherington was the most prominent of the journalists who attempted that radical intervention in the political fabric of the country. His *Penny Papers for the People* first published on 1 October 1830, was first a daily and then a weekly. It was composed in letter style to the people of England or dignitaries such as King, Archbishops or leading politicians: 'It is the cause of the *rabble* we advocate, the poor, the suffering, the industrious, the productive classes … We will teach this rabble their power – we will teach them that they are your master, instead of being your slaves'. Between 1831 and 1835 he produced an eight-page weekly, *The Poor Man's Guardian. A Weekly Newspaper for the People: Established Contrary to 'Law', To Try The Power of 'Might' Against 'Right'*. This was founded with a parody of the small legal stamp on its front page, in black type, of a printing press with 'Knowledge is Power' printed underneath. In announcing that it would cover 'news, intelligence, occurences and remarks and observations thereon …', it clearly set itself against the conditions of the revised Newspaper Act of 1819; eight hundred of its vendors were prosecuted in three and half years, Hetherington was sent to gaol twice, once for six and then for twelve months. These radical papers developed their journalistic credentials more formally in that they did not simply air opinion but also provided a network of information and news, but in the interests of the working-class organizations: 'The papers that served such views, unlike earlier Radical journals, gave news in the government definition of the word, as they reported and commented on each stage in the Reform Bill struggle' (Harrison, 81: 1974).

The difference in political perspective between the first generation and second generation of radical journalism is demonstrated explicitly in this exchange between Carlile and Hetherington. In the *Prompter* on 16 June 1831 Carlile wrote:

> I charge upon the existence of kings and priests, and lords, those useless classes, the common property of the labouring classes of mankind. I charge upon them the common warfare and slaughter of mankind. I charge upon their wicked usurpations, their false pretensions, and their general and tyrannical dishonesty, all the social ills that afflict mankind. I make no exception. The royal family in England is as great an evil … I cry out to all Europe, and more particularly to my own countrymen, DOWN WITH KINGS, PRIESTS, AND LORDS.

This was reprinted in Hetherington's *Poor Man's Guardian* on 18 June 1831 with the addition:

> We perfectly agree with Mr Carlile on the propriety of abolishing Kings, Priests, and Lords … but he does not go far enough – he does not strike at the root of the evil which exists … Were there no property, there would be no Kings, Priests, and Lords … It is property which has made tyrants, and not tyrants property … Down with property.

O'Brien was to become one of the founders of the movement which supported the People's Charter and he edited the *Poor Man's Guardian* from November 1832. In his *Destructive* of 7 June 1834 he provided his own radical interpretation of the useful knowledge he would concentrate on: 'the only knowledge which is of any service to the working people is that which makes them more dissatisfied and makes them worse slaves'.

Between 1836 and 1861 the taxes on knowledge, as they had become known through the years of opposition to them in the radical press, were gradually dismantled, most abruptly in 1836 when the tax on the newspapers themselves, which had risen to 4d, was reduced at one stroke to 1d. This was in many ways a calculated gamble to reduce the power and influence of the radical unstamped but it was not without a secondary aim of reducing the power of the *Times* by introducing cheaper competition. The *Times*, for its part, had indicated its own disinterest by suggesting that the tax would be better removed from soap. Harrison has commented on the extraordinary effectiveness of this form of popular periodical political journalism: 'within about five years they had worn down authority by the collective weight of their mutiny' (91: 1974). With the reduction of the stamp and the increase in the costs of the best in new technology such as the Napier double-cylinder machine, journalism was to find that a blend of news and entertainment was to be the strongest guarantor of the circulation needed to gain a return on investment in an increasingly profit-driven trade. The consequences of press taxation had been to arrest the capitalist development of the press industry, thereby creating the economic conditions that permitted the growth of radical journalism (Curran, 1978: 62). In 1834, the radical Hetherington produced a broadsheet periodical called *Twopenny Dispatch* which promised 'fun and frolic ... Police intelligence ... Murders, Rapes, Suicides, Burnings, Maimings, Theatricals, races, Pugilism', in a last attempt to maintain a foothold for his journalism in an increasingly competitive and commercial newspaper market. Despite their bold experiments in extending the range of their contents to information and entertainment targeted at a specific politicization of its readership, the radical newspapers were drowned in a sea of competition from newspapers, in particular Sunday papers, which produced their miscellany from a perspective which was much more attractive to advertisers. The removal of taxation on papers shifted the onus of control from political to commercial interests and the radical press was the chief victim of this. The Fourth Estate/watchdog tradition which emerges out of this period is one whose journalism, commercially and politically incorporated, acts as a conciliatory, consensual channel between politicians and public opinion, rather than as an inflammatory intervention won on behalf of a radicalized people in pursuit of rights and progress.

The Radical Tradition Continued

The tradition of radical journalism did not disappear completely. To counter the sell-out of the working classes in the Reform Act of 1832, Chartism was born, structured around the six points of the Charter. The *Northern Star*, founded by Feargus O'Connor in 1837, was the most notable contributor to the dissemination of the subtle range of argumentation which the Chartists put forward to support their case and refute the claims of opponents in the other sections of the press:

Every class save the labouring class, has its representatives in the newspaper press ... Why are the working class alone destitute of this mighty auxiliary? The newspaper press, daily and weekly, is the property of capitalists who have embarked on the enterprise upon purely commercial principles, and with the purpose of making it contributory to their own personal and pecuniary interests. It is the course that is profitable and not the course that is just that necessarily secures their preference. (Harrison, 1974: 116)

The *Northern Star* was demonstrably a newspaper rather than a news-sheet or pamphlet with all the generic devices and linkages that had become common for the press. It was started with £690 (Curran and Seaton, 1993: 16), money raised by public subscription in northern cities. It had a network of correspondents who fed it news from across the country. It emphasized class conflict and even played a role in creating a sense of the working class in England (Thompson, 1979). There was a great deal of genuine communal interactivity through the reciprocal support of the paper and its readers in combining to sustain the sense of political solidarity around the paper. Sales, contribution and distribution were all energies ploughed into the broader Chartist movement centred on the missionary zeal of O'Connor as editor. But 1852 saw it close and with its closure came the end of a particular sort of popular and financially successful radical journalism which aimed at informing the people as well as radically restructuring the society which it reported on. Ultimately, it could not survive in the commercial environment which the reduction of stamp duties encouraged. Its political partisanship proved too narrow and its readers drifted towards the more miscellaneous blend of information and entertainment specifically targeted at the working classes by a new generation of Sunday newspapers.

The radical popular press was incorporated and eventually transformed particularly through the economically astute construction of the popular Sunday press. The press had gone from being characterized by low cost, low technology and distributed via an underdeveloped transport infrastructure to become within 40 years hugely more capitalized in terms of production, distribution, advertising revenue and the range of content which all the foregoing could justify.

Radical journalism continues to make brief, if marginal, appearances but always on terms dominated by a capitalized and incorporated industry. This is not to say that it has no place in the history of journalism from the folding of the *Northern Star* but to stress that its power to radically change the shape of society was severely curtailed by the liberal settlement of the mid-nineteenth century, which restructured the market for journalism in favour of the commercial classes whose business it had become. The main gain was in the production of a rhetoric and tradition within which radical journalism still operates. Claud Cockburn, George Orwell and Paul Foot, all belong to this tradition. Perhaps as journalism moves away from its current industrial structures we may see a return to radical pamphleteering, but this time through the more anarchic and de-centred medium of the web. There are still spaces for radical journalism as individual authors and publications form a particular niche in the operations of large conglomerates – John Pilger on the *Mirror* during the Iraq war is a good recent example – but these are commodified spaces within a journalism environment which is institutionally and procedurally balanced towards more conservative positions. This does not close down the potential of such voices and it is certainly better to have them than not to hear them at all – it is just that within such structures, their writing has a more limited chance of effecting significant change to people's opinion and the world in which they live.

6

The Discourse of the Fourth Estate

The Fourth Estate as Political Legitimation

The nineteenth century saw journalism's rise to a political and social legitimacy based on the establishment of its commercial status. The most significant development within this process was the steady consolidation of a style of publication intended to have an influence on the propertied and influential classes. This was linked to the growing profitability which enabled these newspapers to become independent of political control. Their journalism was often hailed as a Fourth Estate, although this was neither a consistent nor absolutely clear set of practices. The claim to constitute a Fourth Estate was, however, an important contribution to the discursive formation of journalism. Despite the fact that it lacked clear substance, it contributed to the establishment of journalism as a mainstream economic and political force and still today provides a touchstone of credibility across the variety of practices which have come to constitute journalism. In the mid-nineteenth century, newspapers in particular were already too dependent on advertising and economic stability to want to seriously consider challenging the political establishment, yet journalism was able through this status as the Fourth Estate to provide an important rhetorical bridge between the interests of the newspapers and those of the newly enfranchised British middle classes. Both sets of activities, middle-class involvement in politics and the establishment of profitable and independent newspapers, claimed legitimacy through this connection and through it forged the dominant discourse of journalism.

The phrase itself is shrouded in all the imprecision of British constitutional history. One could imagine that the three other estates which it complements might refer to the division of medieval society into aristocracy, clergy and common people. Alternatively, it could follow the model of the government composed of the House of Lords (temporal and spiritual) and the House of Commons. In any case, the phrase seems to have been used for the first time in the House of Commons by Macauley who, in 1828, pointing to the press area of the House, referred to them as acting as the Fourth Estate of the realm. From that point, the phrase Fourth Estate has become a commonplace with reference to the news media, particularly to the newspaper in Britain. It is high on emotive value but low on concrete evidence. It implies, at best, an idealistic claim that the press functions as a watchdog of the powerful in society and brings their misdemeanours to the attention of the public. Investigative journalism of all forms is a vital strategy in the claims of the press to act in this fashion. Journalism as 'the institutionalisation of social knowledge' (Boyce, 1978: 13) has come to depend a great deal on a specific set of ideologies concerning this function as a Fourth Estate. It has accompanied the incorporation of journalism into the political and economic status quo and much of the history of journalism narrated from this perspective of the Fourth Estate is paradoxically a history of increasing restriction rather than liberalization, as journalism becomes closer to those centres of power and influence which, in turn, give it their seal of approval. Journalism has done much to establish its credentials by emphasizing this one facet of its operation while downplaying many others as marginal or of secondary importance. The political myth of the press as a conduit between public opinion and the government of the day, journalism as an expression of public opinion flourished from early in the nineteenth century and it began to adopt a style which supported its claims to act in such a watchdog fashion. In addition, it began to claim a greater respectability which was reflected in the growing interdependence of reporters and parliament: 'the upper bench of the strangers' gallery had been devoted to the reporters' exclusive use, with a door in the centre by which they alone were privileged to enter ... But, now, in 1826, they not only retain this bench, but had got a room allotted to them also ... Reporters' Room' (Andrews, 1998, Vol. 2: 166).

Much of the 'ideological baggage' (Boyce, 1978: 19) of the Fourth Estate becomes attached to journalism's descriptions and expectations of itself from this point. Jones argues that they retained a powerful role within journalism throughout the nineteenth century (1996: 12–13). A good example of this comes from the *Times'* leader writer, Reeve, drawing the trajectory of politically interventionist journalism from Junius to the mid-Victorian era: 'Junius ... set the example of that union of accurate and secret political information, consummate ability, daring liberty, and pungent and racy style, which has ever since distinguished the highest organs of the newspaper press' (Reeve, 1855: 472).

Clashes with the political elite of the country were routinely used by newspapers as self-publicity to demonstrate their independence from government control and their duty to provide the best information for the people. Before the 1850s, journalism had sought to define itself in the context of the struggle for a 'free' press. From the mid-century, this freedom was to be increasingly couched in economic terms: 'The main concern of those involved was to throw off the fetters of government control: a purpose which harmonised perfectly with the political ends of an increasingly powerful bourgeoisie ... The next phase of development was one in which economic forces would gradually dominate political ones' (Lee, 1978: 117). The political emancipation of the bourgeoisie had always been an economic issue at heart.

All that had happened in its expression in the history of journalism in the period after the 1850s is that the balance shifted more explicitly to the economic, once the chief political concerns of this class had been addressed by their gaining the right to vote. Professionalization and the discourse of journalism as a Fourth Estate continue to develop as the twin ideologies of the bourgeois press in its pomp in the mid to late nineteenth century and before the impact of the truly popular press with its explicitly mass-market and therefore cross-class orientation towards its public. By the end of the century the place of journalism within the political process was so well established that it could claim for itself: 'a place of power at least equal to half-a-dozen seats in Parliament ... and these free of the Whip, independent of the Speaker, and subject not at all to the gentlemen of the front benches' (Greenwood, 1897: 704).

Advertising and Commercial Independence

In order to consider how journalism became so well established within political life we need to retrace our steps and recall the situation facing the commercial press in the early years of the nineteenth century. At the same time as social and cultural pressures erupted into the radical unstamped press in the first decades of the nineteenth century, a second trajectory for a very different kind of journalism was gathering coherence. The great London dailies of this time were written for an elite governmental and commercial class and were too involved in the struggle for their own economic survival to be much involved in campaigns for reform politics. The increasing impact of advertising revenue which by 1820 was providing the majority of the income of daily newspapers signalled the beginning of the end for the egalitarian potential of the hand-press. A more commercial and more capital-intensive phase of newspaper history was beginning. This journalism increasingly played a part in normalizing the free market and the functioning of capitalism through its advertisements and the need for business capital. It consequently contributed to a rationale for readers to have a stake in this system too.

In addition to the increasing integration of business within journalism, the political will to insist upon pre-publication censorship and state support and subsidy for newspapers had waned by the 1820s. Jones cites two examples of this trend in the Duke of Wellington's 1829 failure to prosecute the *Morning Journal* for libel following the paper's attacks upon him for consenting to Catholic Emancipation, and two years later the decision to acquit Cobbett of a libel charge against government ministers and instead prosecute him on the lesser offence of incitement (1996: 13).

Politicians had hoped that these newspapers would be increasingly accountable to the views of the respectable classes of society through the market and would be less partisan because of their dependence on the business of advertisers and the desire of readers for reliable and impartial information.

These papers were to prove more sensitive to the economic status quo because of pressures from another source – the financial ambitions of their owners. As the radical press was policed and taxed out of the market, a very different form of journalism came to dominate. On the one hand, stamp duties and taxation were perceived by some as keeping newspapers under the control of the wealthy and respectable and also suitable to be read by these classes. On the other hand, more liberal opinion suggested that dropping taxation would make investment more attractive and pave the way for further competition between politically stable newspapers. This was to be the defining debate for the future shape of journalism for this century until the dropping of the taxes on newspapers in the 1850s. It was a time of blossoming confidence of the middle classes in their own power and ability to shape the world in their image. This confidence underpinned the decision to allow a market-inflected normative control of the press to take up the challenge of defeating the radical press not by direct repression but by incorporation. Dropping taxation enabled a form of journalism to predominate which could itself act as a form of social control (Curran, 1978). The discourse of the Fourth Estate was founded within a journalistic landscape which had been largely cleared of alternatives which were not market-based. It created a journalism which was unequivocally a branch of commerce and this was reinforced by the triple pressures of technology, capital and distribution. Technological innovations came at a cost, and newspaper ownership became restricted to those who could invest in equipment and property as well as coordinate the logistical organization required to exploit the growing railway network as a distribution channel. With increasing capitalization came the need to provide more specialist roles within a newspaper as the jobs of reporters, printers, advertising sales people, editors and specialist correspondents became demarcated and fomalized. To support such changes in the structure of journalism, the requirements for large sums of capital investment meant a greater than ever dependence on circulation combined with advertising revenue. The *Times* was the paper which established the most dominant early form of market-orientated independent journalism.

The Reputation of Journalism

The reputation of journalists before the emergence of the ideology of the Fourth Estate was that of either 'hacks or demagogues' (Boyce, 1978: 20). The author of the *History of the Times* tells us:

> The implications of the word 'journalist' in the eighteenth century were not pleasant. A journalist, by common conception, was a writer of paragraphs written in, or against, the interest of a political party or patronage. In the middle of the century Johnson affirmed in the prospectus of the *London Chronicle* that 'Of those Writers that have taken upon themselves the Task

of Intelligence, some have given, and others have sold their Abilities, whether small or great, to one or other of the Parties that divide us'. (*History of the Times*, Vol. I: 16–17)

Journalism had been produced by either pamphleteer or scrivener and there was little in between. In fact, pamphleteers were often the harshest critics of the established press as they saw it: 'If there ever was in the world a thing completely perverted from its original design and tendency, it is the press of England ... It is by the semblance of freedom that men are most effectively enslaved' (Cobbett, *Weekly Political Register*, 11 April 1807).

Some critics concentrated on the inevitable lack of bourgeois lifestyle in men paid to collect and write the news:

> Many of the reporters and editors of this period [early nineteenth century] were 'sad dogs' indeed. The business of their profession keeping them out of their beds half the night, they kept out the remaining half of it of their own choice; and the little hours were consumed in tavern hilarity. (Andrews, Vol. 2, 1998: 32)

There was a social prejudice against people who wrote for a living as opposed to the aristocratic preference for writing as a prestigious recreational form. It was either the mercenary nature of journalists which compromised them or, at the other end of the spectrum of political commitment, the pamphleteers' passionate political convictions which marginalized them. This marginalization is well captured in the following:

> there can be no doubt in the present day the aristocratic prejudice against journalism so survives that if a gentleman with a title allows his irrepressible yearning after lettered distinction to find its outlet in the daily or weekly newspapers, it is whispered by his friends that he has taken to journalism in much the same tone as it might be rumoured that he had taken to drink. (Escott 1875: 49)

The triumph of the market was to even out these polarities and professionalize the practice of journalism as it began to acquire the professionalized norms of balance and objectivity, tailored towards the desires of readerships identified by an awareness of the requirements of advertisers. It is interesting that as the reputation of journalism and newspapers gathered institutional credibility as public servants, the journalists themselves remained dubious figures suspended at the margins of polite society; a situation not much changed today (Sanders, 2002: 1).

The Rise of *The Times*

In the early years of the nineteenth century, newspapers were beginning to free themselves from financial dependence on the government. A great expansion of industry and commerce brought about an increase in the volume of advertising, and once they had built up a good revenue from this source, newspapers no longer required subsidies, either direct or indirect, and could break free from official influence (Herd, 1952: 128).

We will take the development of *The Times* to be paradigmatic of the gravitation of journalism towards mainstream political life, if only for an elite level of the middle classes. *The Times* was not spurred on by abstract concerns for the reputation of good journalism, although it is often narrated as such in retrospect, but by sound commercial considerations of the value of an increasing reputation for independence which flattered the political convictions of its primary readership, the commercial middle classes, and the desire of advertisers to be associated with a newspaper with the ear of such an affluent and influential clientele. It was competition with the other dominant daily newspapers of the era which forced *The Times*, for commercial reasons, to develop the journalism that it did. At the start, John Walter I, the founder of *The Times*, had depended on 'hush money' to make him wealthy (Aspinall, 1945: 225). Its own history acknowledges this contribution to the economic success of the newspaper in its early years which made it very much of its time:

> The Times received for years a subsidy of £300 a year from the Treasury as compensation for its championship of Ministerial policy and its opposition to the party of the Prince of Wales. Three hundred a year 'as a reward for the politics of the Paper' in the words of John Walter I, was a fair sum for a newly founded journal. (*History of the Times*, Vol. I: 213)

Ultimately, subsidies from politicians and fees for the suppression of scandal meant less credibility with an emergent readership and advertisers who wished to be identified with more respectable bourgeois values. Under John Walter I, *The Times* had been simply one part of his publishing and bookselling business which was common among newspaper owners of the time. John Walter II, from 1803, saw the potential to invest specifically in the newspaper and created a better-written product with a much broader scope. Henry Crabb Robinson, for instance, was by 1807 a regular foreign correspondent. In addition to improvements in its content, Walter II took the bold step of introducing steam printing of the paper from 29 November 1814 on a König Bauer Printing Press. The revolutionary nature of this move is highlighted by Andrews:

> A revolution in the history of the newspaper was now approaching, which, whilst it was to add a hundredfold to its importance and influence, and immeasurably to increase its utility, was at one stroke to fix the *Times* in the position which it had recently attained as the leading journal of the world. This was the application of steam power to the printing-press. (Vol. 2, 1998: 77)

Thomas Barnes, a friend of Leigh Hunt and Charles Lamb, who had previously written for the *Examiner*, started as a drama critic and in autumn 1817 was made the editor. Under Barnes it 'was vastly improved as a newspaper, in the sense of a collector and retailer of information' (Fox-Bourne, 1998, Vol. 2: 110). He ensured that it drew on an extensive range of public opinion through a network of nationwide correspondents and was able to channel this astutely into leading articles which took on impressive resonance as reflections on elite opinion among the bourgeoisie. This network was built increasingly without the assistance of government resources which were recognized as a taint to the credibility of the newspaper's claims to independence, and the network extended into the development of international sources to supplement information from domestic informants to turn the newspaper into a much more complete purveyor and processor of news and one which was increasingly able to reflect critically and with authority upon that news. By 16 August 1819 *The Times* could display its newly-minted liberal credentials in its coverage of Peterloo which, incidentally, was one of the first events to be covered live by newspaper reporters in any great number.

The combination of Walter II's business enterprise and Barnes' editorial skills established the newspaper's reputation. Barnes recruited and remunerated the best writers including Edward Sterling, the leader writer who penned the celebrated article which gained the nickname 'The Thunderer' for the paper. On 29 January 1831 he wrote, in support of voting reform proposals for the propertied middle classes, 'unless the people – the people everywhere – come forward and petition, ay thunder for reform, it is they who abandon an honest Minister – it is *not* the Minister who betrays the people'.

Before *The Times'* conversion to the cause of liberal reform, it was the *Morning Chronicle*, a Whig paper, edited from 1817 by John Black, which went further in the articulation of reform and its denunciation of abuses of power and privilege than any other successful paper of the era. This political independence was encapsulated in the range of its political critique. As editor, Black: 'offended the Radicals by demolishing Cobbett's rhetoric and questioning his honesty, and he shocked the Whigs by recognising virtue in Canning and declaring that Wellington was sometimes in the right' (Fox-Bourne, 1998, Vol. 2: 14). In addition, it had led the fight to stop the practices of suppression fees in order to bolster its reputation for independence and therefore reliability and it had gained a reputation for excellent and impartial parliamentary reporting.

The Times, on the other hand, established an early reputation for pragmatism as identified by Hazlitt:

> Stuffed with official documents, with matter-of-fact details, it might be imagined to be composed, as well as printed, with a steam-engine … It sells more, and contains more, than any other paper, and when you have said this you have said all. It takes up no falling cause; fights no uphill battle, advocates no great principle, holds out a helping hand to no oppressed or obscure individual; it is 'ever strong upon the stronger side'; its style is magniloquent, its spirit is not magnanimous … (*Edinburgh Review*, May 1823: 362–4)

It was the exploitation of technological advances and the orchestration of advertising revenues, not its journalism, which enabled it to develop such a scale of operation alluded to by the *Edinburgh Review* and which subsequently gave the paper its ascendancy in the first instance. Its growing reputation and scale as a newspaper of influence assisted the generation of advertising and the wide readership among the affluent classes that advertisers wanted.

By the time of Barnes' death in 1841, its commercial position was established and it was selling more than twice as many copies as its leading rivals the *Chronicle*, *Herald* and *Morning Post* combined. Under his successor, John Delane, the paper developed still further as he built up expertise as a coordinator of the increasingly wide range of talent employed. Delane had started by writing parliamentary reports for *The Times* and then moved to chief editorial assistant to John Walter II. The paper had developed its own authority and voice. It had a rumbustuous style and yet was conservative insofar as it supported the established order. It was selectively critical of government rather than radical in any way in its politics. It switched back to the pre-eminence of foreign reporting to reflect Britain's importance as the centre of a global empire, as the century progressed. It had agents to forward news at Alexandria, Malta, Marseilles and Boulogne and Delane spent as much as £10,000 a year on overland mail costs for these services. John Walter III continued the capital investment to maintain the scale and profitability of the newspaper by introducing the latest printing technology. In 1848 he introduced Applegarth's steam printing machine, which, using eight circular cylinders, could print 10,000 copies in an hour. This was followed (1856) by the Hoe machine which could produce 20,000 per hour and with less labour from compositors.

Francis Williams has commented on the dominance and influence of *The Times*:

> a towering Everest of a newspaper with sales ten times those of any other daily, combining leadership in circulation, in news services especially of the most confidential and exclusive kind – in advertising revenue, commercial profit and political influence to an extent no other newspaper anywhere in the world has ever done before or since. (1957: 100)

Apart from its commercial dominance, *The Times* took on the mantle of spokespiece for this assertive journalism. It was established as the 'Jove of the press' (Andrews, 1998, Vol. 2: 209) when in 1852 it was able to clarify, on its own terms, the respective roles and responsibilities of the press and statesmen, in response to Lord Derby in *The Times* on 6 and 7 February 1852, and outlined its own vision of a fully independent Fourth Estate:

> The press lives by disclosures; whatever passes into its keeping becomes a part of the knowledge and history of our times; it is daily and for ever appealing to the enlightened force of public opinion – anticipating, if possible,

the march of events – standing upon the breach between the present and the future, and extending its survey to the horizon of the world. The statesman's duty is precisely the reverse. He cautiously guards from the public eye the information by which his actions and opinions are regulated; he reserves his judgement on passing events till the latest moment, and then he records it in obscure or conventional language; he strictly confines himself, if he be wise, to the practical interests of his own country, or to those bearing immediately upon it; he hazards no rash surmises as to the future; and he concentrates in his own transactions all that power which the press seeks to diffuse over the world. The duty of the one is to speak; of the other to be silent.

The Times reinforced this statement on the freedom of the press on 6 December 1858, again characteristically in a leading article:

Liberty of thought and speech is the very air which an Englishman breathes from his birth; he could not understand living in another atmosphere. Nor when you once allow this liberty can you restrict the range of its subjects. The principle must have free exercise, or it dies. There is no medium. It would be fatal to say, "Discuss home matters, but not foreign ones." A press so confined would lack the inspiration of that universal sympathy which is necessary to sustain its spirit. Every issue of an English journal speaks to the whole world; that is its strength; it lives by its universality; that idea imparts conscious power, elevates the tone and embraces the will of this great impersonality, invigorates the statement, points the epithet, and nails the argument. It could not speak with half the power it does on domestic subjects if it could not speak of foreign; it could not fly with its wings clipped; it would not be the whole which it is and it would cease to be an epitome of the world.

Given the political and commercial prominence of *The Times*, this was a mighty pronouncement on the role of journalism as a watchdog and guarantor of public interest against the interests of politicians, proclaiming itself, in effect, the true embodiment of the Fourth Estate. Its role in domestic politics was soon to be enhanced by a growing reputation for an ability to convey the latest and best information from abroad, deploying its networks of reporters and agents to bring news back from the war in the Crimea from 1854 quicker than government communications could manage.

William Howard Russell had first come to prominence reporting the Irish potato famine in 1845 and 1846 and was to bring regular, colourful, eyewitness accounts of foreign wars to readers' breakfast tables for the first time and, more importantly, a critical eye able to shift public opinion on the state of the armed forces and the conduct of their leaders in war. He covered the Crimean and subsequently the American Civil War, the Austro-Prussian War in 1866 and the Franco-Prussian war of 1870–71. Delane was able to exploit this coverage to lend increased authority to his leading articles as in this example:

> The noblest army ever sent from these shores has been sacrificed to the grossest mismanagement. Incompetency, lethargy, aristocratic hauteur, official indifference, favour, routine, perverseness, and stupidity reign, revel and riot in the camp before Sebastopol, in the harbour of Balaklava, in the hospital of Scutari, and how much nearer home we do not venture to say. (*The Times*, 23 December 1854)

Among other things it was the achievements of *The Times* during the Crimean War which enabled it to emerge as the champion of enlightened patriotic opinion and this was enhanced by much critical discussion among the influential quarterlies of the era: 'Ministers, even by their own admission, learned the state of affairs in the Crimea sooner, more fully, and more faithfully, through the columns of the daily journals than from their own dispatches' (Reeve, 1855: 483).

The Crimean War was significant for the development of journalism in the way it demonstrated its real political power. *The Times* contributed directly to the fall of a government, the creation of the post of Secretary of State for War, and the intervention of Florence Nightingale which was to alter the perceptions of the rights of wounded combattants to medical support. Russell established that the occupation of a reporter was to go and find out what is happening, which is the basic premise of investigative journalism (De Burgh, 2000: 34). Increasingly, its news was characteristic of a time of great imperial confidence, reflecting: 'the standpoint of the reader was assumed to be that of someone with a serious concern for the affairs of a world power' (Brown, 1985: 111).

The Times had such an ascendancy with its networks of couriers, translators, correspondents, its reputation for influence and impact, its circulation and its quality that it could claim to have established by the mid-century a position of absolute dominance in terms of its effect on bourgeois public opinion and in defining a position for the political role of a newspaper in bourgeois society. Its relationship to its readers and the economic pragmatism of this relationship was succinctly characterized in a letter quoted in the *History of the Times* from Walewski to his patron in exile, Louis Napoleon, 30 January 1852:

> The prosperity of *The Times* is founded on its very large number of readers, who give it more advertisements than to any other newspaper. Moreover, it is an axiom among the founders of this paper that to retain a great number of readers one must anticipate public opinion, keep it alive, animate it, but never break a lance against it and give way every time it declares itself in any direction and even when it changes its attitude to change with it. (*History of the Times*, Vol. II: 151)

The position of *The Times* was further flattered by a steady stream of hyperbole about its influence and function as 'the great potentate in the press' (Fox-Bourne, 1998, Vol. 2: 261). It extended to claims that its sensitivity to the public mood put it at one with the entire nation:

The Times is the one daily newspaper which, having made the national character its scientific study, has completely mastered its idiosyncrasies, has discovered all its prejudices, is intimately acquainted with its follies and its foibles, its virtues and its defects. If the great heart of England wants to know how it beats it must consult the *Times.* (Escott 1875: 42)

This hyperbolic presence also extended to fictional accounts of the time as in Thackeray's *Pendennis* when a newspaper, clearly a fictionalized version of *The Times*, is described in these terms:

There she is – the great engine – she never sleeps. She has her ambassadors in every quarter of the world – her couriers upon every high road. Her officers march along with armies, and her envoys walk into statesmen's cabinets. They are ubiquitous. Yonder journal has an agent at this minute giving bribes at Madrid, and another inspecting the price of potatoes at Covent Garden. (Andrews, 1998, Vol. 2: 329)

The Consequences of Liberalization

Although sometimes related as the most important development in nineteenth-century journalism, *The Times* was far from the whole story. It may well have been the single most important contributor to the establishment of a discourse of the liberal function of journalism as a Fourth Estate and the articulator of independent public opinion, but equally important changes were gathering momentum which, also driven by market awareness and the spread of literacy and political representation, were as important for the longer-term trends of the commercialized journalism of the Fourth Estate. Between the reduction of Stamp Duty in the 1830s and 1840s to their removal in the 1850s, the interests of capitalism and journalism had eventually merged, completing a process which had been in evidence since the demise of the second phase of the radical press in the 1830s as an unattractive commercial proposition. The imperative to fund an increasingly professionalized and capitalized business led newspapers to seek consensual political positions and to continue to broaden their presentation of news away from partisan politics. Political perspectives which naturalized the status quo included more miscellaneous elements in much of the press and a lack of the overarching political analysis which radical journalism had attempted. Brown comments on the consequences of journalism's political and economic incorporation: 'It is a paradox, though an understandable one, that, in proportion as the newspapers grew in social acceptance, being no longer taxed or suspected, so they declined in critical vigour' (1985: 276).

On 5 February 1836, the last conviction of an unstamped paper may have been of a police weekly when John Cleave was fined £500 in the Court of Exchequer for publishing five numbers of a newspaper called the *Weekly Police Gazette* (Andrews, 1998, Vol. 2: 227), but from now on the official publication of crime news and other forms of sensational story began to play a more prominent role in nearly all newspapers as commercialized newspapers provided 'something for most any taste' (Baladasty, 1992: 142).

Curran is more trenchant in his analysis of this discursive shift in journalism from a class perspective and insists that it limits the parameters of all journalistic freedoms henceforth to those conducted in terms of the interests of the commercial classes:

> The freedom conferred by the free market was the freedom of capital to indoctrinate labour ... A tacit model of society which admitted no conflict of class interest, only a conflict between ignorance and enlightenment and between the individual and the state, was the basis on which a free press could be conceived in terms of both watchdog of the government and guard-dog of the people. (1978: 60)

Chalaby (1998) claims that the modern discourse of journalism takes shape at the specific point when market mechanisms begin to dominate the ownership, strategies and competitive practices of public writing after 1855. The period also saw the nature of news become increasingly refined. The establishment in 1851 of Reuter's News Agency began to ensure a regular and more homogeneous supply of routine news. This had the result of easing the chief problem of previous newspapers – the irregular flow of news for a daily press. News had always been a commodity but it was now a more streamlined and capitalized commodity. It was no longer simply an addition to a publisher's portfolio but a valuable product in its own right and an invaluable conduit to the advertisers' revenue. The period saw: 'the growth of news as a commodity, as a commercial product to be shaped, packaged, and marketed with a constant eye to profit' (Baladasty, 1992: 140).

A new form of popular reading for a wider readership was gaining approval and the final abolition of stamp and paper duties saw this accelerate even more. Newspapers gradually began a shift which would witness the incorporation of more of the miscellany of magazines alongside their traditional features and were always keen to pander to larger readerships through livelier, more sensational coverage of events in order to boost their appeal to advertising. In 1853 advertising duty was abolished which added to the commercial revenues upon which the newspapers and magazines were increasingly dependent. In 1855 Stamp duty was abolished and the *Daily Telegraph* was founded, as the *Daily Telegraph and Courier* on 29 June 1855 and heralded its arrival, not without a certain prescience, as, 'the new era of journalism'. The *Daily Telegraph* was the most successful daily experiment on the lifting of taxes. It looked the same as its competitors but at the much reduced price of a penny. It quickly established an identity which distinguished it from the deliberate elitism of *The Times*: 'The Times, the paper for the City merchant, and the *Daily Telegraph*, the paper for the clerk and shopkeeper' (Brown, 1985: 246). It still gave many columns over to leading articles and contained letters to the editor, but it was the ability of Edward Levy to introduce elements of the human interest of American popular journalism to the paper which broadened its appeal and success. As a popularizer, Levy was the forerunner of Stead and Northcliffe. The *Daily Telegraph* produced one of the most important new developments in Victorian journalism in its public campaigning for the concerns of its readers. An example of this is its coverage of one of the great moral dilemmas of the Victorian age, the hitherto taboo subject of the recourse of respectable middle-class men to prostitution as they delayed marriage until they were financially secure to provide for their wives. There was clearly much in this survey which was open to accusations of sensationalism and prurience but it did establish a new form of relationship with its readers beyond these factors. It built on the letters of readers, already an established tradition, but in a novel twist which emphasized contact with this readership and its voice in creating a concerted and large-scale debate. It was credited with the creation of a more participatory journalism, 'moving authority from leaders to Readers' (Robson, 1995: 260). The language of the launch of the campaign indicates something of the rhetorical inclusion of the reader within the paper's project: 'the army of public pity and indignation … a new Crusade … a moral Armada of hope and effort … a vast body of public opinion' (ibid.: 17). The *Daily Telegraph* was within a few years selling more than all other London dailies combined, including the *Times*. It included a growing number of writers, including George Augustus Sala from 1858, who wrote in a livelier fashion than had been the custom in the serious daily papers and reached out to the lower middle classes. Sala claimed impressive interview scalps for the *Daily Telegraph* in Napoleon III in 1865 and Garibaldi in 1866. In its more populist tone and broader social scope and in its pioneering use of interviews, it helped set the scene for the New Journalism of the late nineteenth century. By the 1870s, the use of numerous headlines to lead an important news story was one of the more noticeable innovations in terms of its layout. The invention by the paper of the box number for advertisements is a clear indication of its acumen in exploiting the new economic opportunites for daily newspapers and it had sales of 200,000 by the 1880s. There was, however, resistance to its new brand of journalism. The *Pall Mall Gazette* made frequent disparaging remarks about the *Daily Telegraph*, referring to it on 9 January 1868 as a 'quack journal' because of its association with cheap doctors and patent medicine cures. In the same year, the *Saturday Review*'s two articles of 5 and 12 December on 'Newspaper Sewage' were a clear indictment of the moral values of the *Daily Telegraph* and its nearest competitors, the *Standard* and the *Morning Star*.

Debate and the Discourse of Journalism

After a gestation period of over two hundred years, the word journalism finally entered the English language from French in January 1833 in an article in the *Westminster Review* and launched on its arrival a set of discussions indicative of the tensions which this public and periodical dissemination of information and opinion were provoking. Jones has charted the bearings of the debate:

> Riven by tensions between the memory of persecution and the desire for respectability, between a yearning for 'liberty' and a pious regard for 'responsibility', and caught between the moral and commercial implications of their adherence to concepts of tradition and modernity, the nineteenth-century newspaper was a fascinating but elusive topic for contemporary comment. (Jones, 1996: 9)

The journalism of the nineteenth century was indeed a complex formation which moved to incorporate the impacts of the Reform Acts of 1832, 1867 and 1884 with their implications for the relationship between politics and a widening, enfranchised public. This complexity was added to by rapidly evolving technological, economic and demographic changes which all share intersecting chronologies with that of journalism.

Campbell identifies the chief controversy as lying with the more commercially orientated journalism from the 1830s. She describes how the new word came to signify the yoking of higher and lower cultural forms which was a challenge to existing cultural distinctions (2000: 40). Journalism was therefore taking a distinctly new shape structured around the principles of the commercialization and ultimately the popularization of the information flow. The Victorians became increasingly aware of the implications of this communication revolution. No sooner had the word been minted than it became the hottest topic for intellectual and political debate. Journalism became a very common subject of discussion in reviews (Brown, 1985: 75). Such debates contributed to the discourse of journalism over these years and there was a growing appreciation of its ability to change the direction of social trends and to mould growing public awareness of what it claimed to have achieved: 'That the great changes of recent times have been mainly owing to the influence of the press, is matter of universal observation' (Alison, 1834: 373).

Jones considers that an understanding of this influence by both readers and producers of journalism increasingly came to be deliberately inscribed in journalism's 'mode of address' to the reader (1996: 180). The ways that journalism was debated and written about became more vigorous, from its inclusion in the critical quarterlies of the 1820s and 1830s to Stead's impassioned polemics of the 1880s. This explicit debate forms part of journalism's literal discursive formation yet, paradoxically, this was happening at the same time as a Select Committee of 1851 into the workings of the Newspaper Stamp Act could not establish a working definition of news (Herd, 1952: 151).

The debate on journalism spread into fictional form, most notably in the novels of Thackerey, *History of Pendennis* (1849–50) and Trollope, *The Warden* (1855). There was the first serious attempt at a history of journalism by

Frederick Knight Hunt in 1850 and the growing self-confidence of journalism was captured in the range of metaphorical allusions to what it considered its strengths and contributions to society in the titles of the publications of the time. From the *Telegraph* to the *News of the World*. Light, speed, topicality, integrity, reflections and accuracy were all important in the naming of newspapers and were a barometer of the confident self-image they projected to their readers. With improved technology, distribution and a financial stake in society, journalism came to see itself as an important means of collecting and communicating social information. In its more efficient and profitable representation of social knowledge, it took upon itself a 'specialised role within the social observance of reality' (Smith, 1978: 165).

A social vision of the project of journalism which could be best described as 'advanced Liberalism' (Fox-Bourne, 1998, Vol 2: 141) was often announced in the launch of new newspaper projects such as:

> The principles advocated by 'The Daily News' will be principles of progress and improvement, of education, civil and religious liberty, and equal legislation – principles such as its conductors believe the advancing spirits of the time requires, the condition of the country demands, and justice, reason, and experience legitimately sanction. (*Daily News*, Wednesday, 21 January 1846)

As debate about the worth and status of the new profession of journalism developed in the nineteenth-century magazines and periodicals, there were still those who saw it as a venal and depraved occupation, a 'fugitive literature' (Dallas, 1859: 97) condemned as much by its content as by the circumstances of its consumption. John Stuart Mill's opinion is notable for its lack of restraint:

> In France the best thinkers and writers of the nation write in the journals and direct public opinion; but our daily and weekly writers are the lowest hacks of literature which, when it is a trade, is the vilest and most degrading of all trades because more of affectation and hypocrisy and more subservience to the basest feelings of others are necessary for carrying it on, than for any other trade, from that of a brothel-keeper up. (Elliott, 1978: 176)

The Reviews as Intellectual Community

In a very different but equally authoritative way to the daily press, the reviews of the nineteenth century also contributed to the reputation of journalism as a Fourth Estate. They have been assessed as being 'the mandarin periodical form of the nineteenth century' (Shattock, 1989: 5). They were very much formative of intellectual bourgeois opinion. Much more specifically than newspapers, they were party aligned and did much to retain the political coherence of political factions in public form. The review itself was not a nineteenth-century invention. The non-specialist but serious review of literature and politics which covered a wide range of contemporary interests can be traced to the *Monthly*, founded in 1749, the *Critical* (1756), the *English* (1783), the *Analytical* (1788) and the *British Critic* (1793).

Smith, Jeffrey and Brougham founded the *Edinburgh Review* in 1802 to produce articles on literature and politics. It was a Whig publication and was as conservative in its literary tastes as it was liberal and reformist in its politics. By 1818 it had reached its peak circulation at 14,000. Sir Walter Scott was a regular contributor as was Macauley. The *Quarterly Review* was launched to rival what it saw as the growing influence and prestige of the *Edinburgh* and was based in London . From February 1809 with support from Canning and Scott and edited by William Gifford, it became the leading Tory spokespiece. In April 1817 the *Edinburgh Monthly Magazine,* later to be renamed *Blackwood's Edinburgh Magazine* was first published and 'by its force and startling individuality, easily took first place among Tory monthlies' (Graham, 1930: 230). A radical alternative to these was launched in Jeremy Bentham's *Westminster Review* (1823). Economic, legal, social and political questions as well as much discussion of journalism itself were constant topics of the quarterlies. They began a slow decline from the 1840s onwards 'elbowed out in the political sphere by the newspapers' (Shattock, 1989: 19–20) after they had achieved the height of their influence, although Finkelstein points out that *Blackwood's* continued to perform the most important of journalistic functions in conforming to the particular values and perceived tastes of contemporary readers across the range of its output from the 1860s onwards (2002: 152). They were totally anonymous thereby allowing leading politicians to express controversial views without risking their integrity. This anonymity was eventually broken with in *Macmillan's* from 1859 but persisted far longer in the other quarterlies.

Later in the century the monthlies and then the weeklies took over much of the role of the quarterlies but were aimed at a much broader social readership. They fitted more easily into the commercialized environment of the late nineteenth century than the more high-minded and commercially restricted quarterlies. The *Cornhill Magazine* (1860), an illustrated literary monthly edited by Thackaray, the *Fortnightly Review* (1865), the *Contemporary Review* (1866) and the *Nineteenth Century* (1877) all provided space for topics which needed more reflection and perspective than a daily could at that point offer, together with a wider range of literary discussion for a more extended and enfranchised leisured class which needed aesthetic guidance, political discussion and topical controversy, in a similar way to the newly emerging commercial urban bourgeoisie of the early eighteenth century.

Technology and Professionalization

Journalism became more respectable through the confluence of several factors in the nineteenth century. Increased capital investment, and corresponding increases in profits, enabled advanced technologies to be introduced which in turn enhanced the quality and reliability of the service they provided. This brought about an increasing rationalization and professionalization of journalism. The introduction of steam printing and the increasingly efficient yet expensive equipment which arrived on the scene from the 1830s onwards were to have cumulative effects on the nature of journalism. Technological determinants in combination with political decisions were to have a major role in narrowing the functions of journalism towards a market-driven, lowest common denominator of styles and formats increasingly based on advertisers' and newspapers' constructions of social class.

The combination of news agencies and the invention of the telegraph brought a much more reliable and economical supply of steady information and dictated the emphasis on news which began to dominate the daily press. Reuter set up an office in London in 1851 to provide commercial intelligence and in 1858 extended this service to provide foreign digests of news to London papers. Private news transmission by telegraph began in 1866. This was followed by further developments in printing and telegraphy in the 1860s and 1870s such as the web rotary presses, the private wires and the telephone. Establishing the telegraph under state management from February 1870 enabled information to be systematically and economically transmitted. These innovations allowed the practice of 'double-checking' of sources to become established within journalism and is considered to be one of the essential features of modern journalism (Smith, 1978: 155). The new channels of communication telegraph, railways, penny post, and WH Smith's newsagents with its motto 'All Who Ride May Read', all combined into an impressive network which served the needs of the ambitious news organizations and enhanced the impact and even the reputation of journalism. In addition, local newspapers established the Press Association in 1868 to ensure a cheap supply of London news.

As the capitalization of journalism increased, so too did the need for its functions to become increasingly professionalized and in turn this led to a shift in the aspirations of the profession. Pitman developed a widely adopted system of shorthand in 1840 which added the attraction of mimetic accuracy to the reporting of speech and fitted well with the Victorian epistemological taste for empirical evidence. Reporters were further encouraged within this culture to provide a record of events rather than emotional responses or opinions. Journalism in the daily press was very much news-based. Analysis, discussion and opinion were provided by the evening papers such as the *Pall Mall Gazette*, the *Westminster Gazette* and the *St James's Gazette* (Brown, 1985: 110). Journalism moved from the margins of English society to a more economically lucrative and socially respectable position. It was no longer assumed that it was a medium for political sedition but became the dominant informant of the public as political gatherings, church sermons and other print media waned in significance. The telegraph led increasingly to a systematization of the language of journalism and a more comparable set of practices. The familiar inverted triangle of the story became recognized, as did the slant of papers to particular markets. The telegraph provided more of a verifiable base to much reporting of news so it was to individual angles, interviews or stories that papers turned for claims to the individual strengths of the paper. Yet after the assertive identities of the journalists of the radical unstamped, anonymity was adhered to in most papers on the pattern of *The Times*, implicitly demonstrating that it was the authority of the paper which was paramount, not that of an individual author: 'Defended by some as "the life and soul of journalism", anonymously published articles were held to remove authorial vanity from the newspaper and, in consequence, to enable readers to judge those articles by their contents rather than their signatures' (Jones, 1996: 119–20). It was also a reflection of the varied provenance of much of the news and the process of editing it which was making the identification of a single author more problematic within journalism. Newspapers, under more dominant and influential editors, began to develop what would later be called identifiable house styles and anonymity matched this tendency too. The increased reliability and quantity of news meant that journalism could concentrate more on how material was presented both in terms of the newspaper's identity and in terms of its contextualization with other aspects of contemporary interest. The premium on space, especially under pressure from advertising copy, meant that more stories had to be condensed. Brown notes one particular landmark in journalism's ability to collate and thematize material over a more sustained period of coverage by deploying the new techniques of collation in the 1880s:

> The *Daily Chronicle* was able, without the aid of unemployment figures, to present a picture of labour which was its own creation, and which, by collecting individual scraps of information, offered a new topic for public debate: the columns on the Labour Movement deserve a place in the history of investigative journalism. (1985: 270–1)

The second half of the nineteenth century was the age of the editor in terms of personal biographies and institutional power just as the first half of the twentieth century was the great age of the proprietor. Delane, Levy, Greenwood and Stead are pre-eminent among the names of influential editors of the age. Editors as part owners cemented the increasingly lucid editorial identity of newspapers and the role of editor became more identifiable within the newspaper business as it became more specialized and divided reporting specializations, management, leader column writing, editing and sub-editing. All these divisions of labour within journalism were well established in practice if not in name by the mid-century.

Structural developments within the working world of journalism enabled more consistent networks to be established with a subsequently greater professional identity. Press clubs were established from 1870 for the purposes of socializing and exchange of intelligence among journalists, the National Association of Journalists was founded in 1884 which was to become the Institute of Journalists. It set up a 13-point programme for qualification, assessed any new legislation concerning journalism and was awarded a Charter in 1889. The encroachment of journalism on the intellectual establishment was extended when the British Museum opened a special newspaper reading room in Bloomsbury in 1881 and at the cusp of the nineteenth and twentieth centuries there was a surge in publications on journalism education.

Journalism's role in political life was confirmed when in 1885 the modern Lobby system was introduced and because of the social obligations this implied, it was increasingly likely that leader writers and political correspondents might be expected to be from similar social and educational backgrounds to many politicians.

The Golden Age

Part of the discourse of journalism's rise to respectability was the effusive commentary during the second half of the nineteenth century on its having achieved a golden age: 'that tree of knowledge from which none are forbidden, but all are invited to pick the fruit; that oak of our social and political life, the free press of England' (Andrews, 1998, Vol. 2: 164). Others have rationalized the high-Victorian period as a period of transition between one discursive formation and another: 'The brief hiatus between censorship, corruption and economic controls and the commercialisation associated with publishing for a mass audience has produced a myth of professionalism' (Elliott, 1978: 182).

What is apparent in taking the longer view is that the 'dignified phase of English journalism' (Ensor, 1968) may have been concluded once it began to extend its reach to social classes outside the bourgeoisie which the daily press had concentrated on since 1702, but the discourses which crystallized around the political functions of journalism, in particular its independent role as the Fourth Estate, were incorporated within the wider and certainly less dignified journalism of the modern era. They continue to characterize much of journalism's core practices and the corresponding expectations of its public, even in a multi-media environment. The abilities of journalism to act as a public investigator and a public watchdog may have been increasingly compromised by its commercial success but they remain an essential part of its public legitimacy. For all these were defined in the nineteenth century, they continue to have absolute relevance today.

7

=========
=========

Women's Journalism from Magazines to Mainstream

A Suppressed Voice

Women in journalism are narrated as so often 'hidden from history' (cf. Rowbothom, 1996), often doubly so, as journalism tends to present itself as either being about men, for men and by men or only of relevance to women when dealing with parochial and gender-restricted issues in women's magazines. This chapter will attempt to do something to redress that balance by indicating that women have always contributed more than has been apparent in traditional histories of journalism despite the fact that they have, at worst, been erased from history, sometimes quite literally as in Pebody's *English Journalism and the Men Who Have Made It* or, at best, marginalized within mainstream narratives. This is ironic considering the extent to which the dominant trend of journalism from the middle of the nineteenth century has been to include styles of writing and illustration of greater interest to an idealized woman reader. Including women in the history of journalism constitutes part of what Adburgham has called 'rescue work' (1972: 9). It illustrates how women's journalism, within Bakhtin's (1996) concept of heteroglossia, can be seen as part of a constant power struggle which determines which of the multiple voices of journalism, not all of which are equally valued, will provisionally gain a dominant position. The particular voice of women's journalism becomes integral to claims of social and economic power on behalf of women.

Much of what has developed as women's journalism has come to us out of the complex evolution of the women's magazine as it has evolved both its formats and definitions of the female. Beetham has summarized their complex and mutable relationship between identity and its representation in journalism: 'Just as the meaning of femininity was always being re-made, so was the meaning and the form of the magazine and its conventions' (1996: 5). The journalism of women's magazines has shaped debate around the public and private visualization of the female, constructing a network of imagined communities for their readers. To this extent they constitute an important aspect of the public sphere although one determined by 'biological determinism'

(Ferguson, 1983: 186) and they have also had an important cumulative effect on mainstream newspaper and broadcast journalism as part of a gendered cross-over between popular and quality, personal and political which has been partly due to economic pragmatism as women readers and consumers became more important to the success of news media in general. Despite the fact that early women's periodicals reduced their news content and became predominantly concerned with more 'broadly-defined social needs' (Shevelow, 1989: 47), they have demonstrated the periodical selection of representations of aspects of the world for a clearly defined readership which has always constituted a significant part of what has been understood as journalism. Dancyger makes the point that, in addition to entertaining and informing, women's magazines have played a third role – 'to reassure' (1978: 163), which indicates how they are located within the discourses of journalism, substituting the traditional educational role by reassurance. In this more restrictive way, they have functioned to educate women into their social roles and even determined the borders of acceptable dissent. This chapter will explore the development of women's journalism as it moves, not unproblematically, from magazine to mainstream.

Earliest Developments

Women were identified early in the history of printing as the subjects of specific publications. Some of the first printed publications addressed to women were beauty treatises such as the Jacobean translation of Buoni's *Problems of Beauty* (1606). Early examples of miscellanies specifically addressed to women include the *Ladies Cabinet Opened* from 1639 which explored Physicke, Surgery, Cookery and Huswifery and the *Queen's Closet Opened*, controversial because the Queen it referred to was the wife of Charles I and the date of publication was during the English Civil War in 1655, shortly before the king's execution. Yet there is evidence too of the political engagement of women through the medium of print. Women are often implicitly excluded from discussion in the early public sphere, given its essentially male construction, but women did participate as part of an alternative and competing public sphere through their own print practices (Halasz, 1997). Women of lower and middle rank did contest this public sphere of male letters. The first known woman to make her living from writing was not a journalist but the dramatist Aphra Benn, as early as 1640. After this, women political writers, publishers and printers all threatened the male bourgeoisie's polite discourse of settlement with the *ancien régime*. Women were writers, printers, managers and prominent members of the Stationers' Company until economic and social shifts began to consign them to a restricted public role as the eighteenth century progressed and the Company began to contribute to a generalized male dominance in print culture. Their largest early contribution can be traced in religious/political propaganda pamphlets and through the work of the mercury women selling tracts on the streets of London and other large towns. Women, especially old women who were often itinerant, with names such as Blind Fanny, Irish Nan, Lame Cassie, worked as hawkers and balladeers of political material. Much of this early women's writing was in the form of prophecies or dealt with political questions such as religious tolerance, the tithe system and the relationship of the state to organized religion. Quakers were particularly prominent in this liminal print/oral culture. There were several notable women printers and authors throughout the seventeenth century as print culture became established as a political and commercial vehicle.

Elinor James (*c.* 1645–1719) was an Anglican polemicist who published her opinions on the politics of the age from the perspective of her religious convictions, chiefly and most potently in the form of broadsides bearing her name. John Dunton in his *Life and Errors* paid her a back-handed compliment when he referred to Mr James as 'something the better known for being husband to that *She-State Politician* Mrs *Elianor James*' (McDowell, 1998: 83). Anne Docwra (1624–1710) was a Quaker writer as well as a successful publisher and printer. Her printed tracts dealt principally with religious questions and women's much contested right to prophesy in public. Tace Sowle managed the Quaker press of her family for 50 years and was a member of the Stationers' Company from 1693. She was also notorious for her vitriolic broadsides against public figures. There were even women proprietors such as Sarah Popping who owned *The Dunciad* and was co-proprietor of *The Protestant Post-Boy.*

Joan Whitrowe's publications are illuminating examples of the radical reach of political opinion of the seventeenth century. They amounted to a sustained attack on the privileges of the upper classes and she extended her solidarity and sympathy with the working poor by an understanding of the consequences of early colonialism:

> She criticized the upper ranks' excessive attention to things of the flesh, especially fine food and apparel, and she consistently referred to élites rather than to working people as 'the drunkards, the feasters, the swearers, gamesters, whoremongers, the proud'. ... Above all, she argued that the endless accumulation of capital in the hands of a few must be curbed. (McDowell, 1998: 165)

As women began taking an active part in print culture in the seventeenth century, they were already beginning to be closed down. New controls of the press favoured the capital of groups of established printers and men of property, thus isolating individual women printers. McDowell argues that women had been pivotal to print and literary culture until they became socially and politically marginalized by transformations in the sex-roles into the eighteenth century (ibid.: 5).

Another prominent early woman journalist who challenged male hegemony was Elizabeth Powell who on 7 April 1716 published the *Charitable*

Mercury and Female Intelligence for which she was imprisoned. Her husband had been charged with treason for his publishing activities and went into exile for his Jacobite views. He died in exile in 1716. For the first issue of the *Orphan*, she was sent to Newgate prison in 1716. On her release she produced the *Charitable Mercury and Female Intelligence*. For this she was also imprisoned. On the front page was a translated Italian proverb which testified to her view of patriarchal power relations: 'To speak ill of Grandees, is to run ones self into Danger; but whoever will speak well of 'em must tell Many a Lye'. She, however, returned with the *Orphan Reviv'd – The State of Europe, Embellish'd and Intermixed with Observations, Historical, Political, and Philosophical, concluding with the 'Tea-table tatler or the Ladies' Delight'* from 1719.

The Discovery of Women as a Market

It was not these political interventions by women radicals which attracted male publishers to appreciate the potential in publishing for a female readership. John Dunton was one of the first to begin to probe sustained commercial engagement within this market. Like many innovators in journalism, he was prolific in his publishing projects in general and was referred to as 'lunatick' (Adburgham, 1972: 25) by a contemporary on account of his seemingly eccentric ambitions in the field. After a year of his *Athenian*, it was 'supplied with queries from the Fair Sex', a question and answer exchange for women. Dunton progressively introduced more material for women in his periodical until he became persuaded that there was demand enough for a magazine exclusively for women. This market was growing as leisure and literacy increased for upper middle-class women, not to mention the increased opportunity for their domestic help to also peruse magazines as they went about their domestic chores. This unintended and peripheral audience of domestic helpers must have assisted in the general spread of print culture. The success of Dunton's experiment became translated into the first specialist women's publication, the *Ladies' Mercury*, as a monthly from 1693, which promised to respond to 'all the most nice and curious Questions concerning Love, Marriage, Behaviour, Dress and Humour of the Female Sex, whether Virgins, Wives, or Widows' (Adburgham, 1972: 26). Although Dunton was its driving force, it employed mainly women writers who were selected for their ability to write for their targeted readership, the leisured and literate female bourgeoisie. The *Ladies' Mercury* introduced the tradition of the female confidante in periodical form with 'All questions relating to love' to be sent to 'the Ladies' Society' at the 'Latine Coffee House in Ave-Mary-Lanes' (Ballaster et al., 1991: 470).

Dunton's contribution to the history of journalism was to develop the content of periodical publications to include subjects other than news and politics. This was an extension of periodical miscellany into a different format from that of the mercuries, as it now linked with the myriad interests of an affluent bourgeoisie. Dunton was also not averse to experimenting with a different form of exploitation of women in his *Night Walker; or, Evening Rambles in search of Lewd Women, with the Conferences Held with them, etc, to Be published monthly, 'till a Discovery be made of all the chief Prostitutes in England from the Pensionary Miss down to the Common Strumpet* (1696–7). This was presented under the pretext of 'publick Reformation' but, with its woman-on-the-street interviews with prostitutes, it was little more than an example of early prurient sensationalism for a largely male audience.

By the end of the seventeenth century the growth in the middle classes had precipitated a need for an education for their daughters, if they were to be married into aristocratic families, bringing together wealth and rank. Many of the periodicals aimed at women were designed to contribute to this process of class consolidation and contributed much to the extension of the idealized polite society of the bourgeois public sphere. They indicate something of the plurality of the public sphere which was taking shape and the variety of contributions to its textual construction. The *Ladies' Diary the Woman's Almanac*, which was first published in 1703 for the following year, included complex mathematical, literary and astronomical puzzles and demanded an extensive education of any potential reader. It was published by John Tipper and its success led him to launch *Delights for the Ingenious, or A Monthly Entertainment for both Sexes* in January 1711.

Richard Steele was a great supporter of women's involvement in intellectual and social life and his *Tatler* engaged with women's issues as important aspects of public discourse. Early on, he included as a regular feature a 'Poetical Tale for Ladies' and later he invented Jenny Distaff as a spokeswomen for women. Addison later supported Steele's inclusion of women in public debate characterized by his aim expressed in the *Spectator* 'to establish among us a Taste of polite Writing' which was designed to appeal to their female readership.

However, women writers continued to disrupt notions of polite discourse in their own work. The *Female Tatler* was the most famous respondent to the periodical writing developed in the *Tatler* and the *Spectator*. Its most notable contributor was the coarse and scurrilous Mrs Crackenthorpe, the *nom de plume* of Mrs Mary Delarivier Manley who demonstrated the potential of transforming personal gossip about public affairs into political polemic of a satirical and entertaining nature. The paper's sub-title was *Remarks upon Events and Occurrences* and it had a clear relationship to the reporting of events and opinion formation. From 8 July 1709 it appeared three times weekly and acted as a virulent organ of Tory propaganda in opposition to the Whigs, Steele and Addison. She was also employed as a Tory pamphleteer by Swift and from June 1711 took over the editorship of the *Examiner* when Swift stepped down, editing issues 46–52 herself. Such was the impact of her polemic that one contemporary writer felt moved to complain: 'the present Gain from recent Progress in political Journalism is marred by the outrageous Coarseness indulged in by those who make it their trade' (Adburgham, 1972: 62).

The founder of the first named magazine, Cave, soon saw the opportunity in addressing a magazine exclusively to women. He had already included many features intended for women, including recipes and domestic features, in his *Gentleman's Magazine* on a regular basis, so he felt confident a readership existed for a women's edition. *The Lady's Magazine*, a shilling monthly, could be best described as the *Gentleman's Magazine* without the politics and included contributions from prominent writers, Jane Hughes, Catherine Cockburn and Elizabeth Carter. It was successful enough to be followed by the identical sounding *The Ladies' Magazine* from 1749, published by Jasper Goodwill as a twopenny fortnightly. In his introduction, Jasper Goodwill offered it as:

> a most agreeable Amusement, either in the Parlour, the Shop, or the Compting-house, and a delightful Companion in Retirement; as it will contain an agreeable Variety of Subjects in the Circle of Wit, Gallantry, Love, History, Trade, Science and News; and will be a most innocent, diverting, and profitable Entertainment for young Masters and Misses, by giving them an Early View of the polite and busy World. (Adburgham, 1972: 106)

It was, in fact, more distinguished by its lurid eye-witness accounts of contemporary crime and punishment. It contributed much to the developing range of journalism from outside the newspaper format. It contained a diary of events at home and abroad, letters, advice, pieces of contemporary interest concerning female morality and education, some puzzles and poetry but in general, like Cave's magazine, little original material apart from its sensational reporting. In many of its features such as the announcements of births, deaths and marriages and digests of news, it indicated how the technologies of communication were still restricted enough for both magazines and newspapers to share many elements until two very distinct vehicles diverged one hundred years later.

Certain of the early women's journals resisted the lucrative pull of the miscellanies. From 16 December 1737 until 14 March 1738, Lady Mary Wortley Montagu published the *Nonsense of Commonsense* as a Tory political riposte to the Opposition paper *Commonsense*. The centrepieces were Lady Mary's essays. In addition, it included a few columns of news items, statistics and stock reports written by hired journalists. She was a great champion of education for women and a staunch opponent of frivolity and immorality. She was an admirer of both Steele and feminist pioneer Mary Astell, but there was a class perspective to all of this as she wanted those things she approved of for women to be the exclusive domain of the upper classes.

Modelled on the format of Addison and Steele's periodical, Eliza Haywood, as editor and contributor, produced the *Female Spectator*, a monthly paper in the moral-essay tradition, from 1744 to 1746. The editorial staff were introduced as a Lady, A Widow of Quality and the Daughter of a Merchant. These were supplemented by a wide range of social reporters who provided gossip, libel and scandal from all the major towns and cities of England and the Continent. It developed a correspondence column in which opinions, advice and caution on fashions and morals of the time were discussed. Shevelov considers that this, the first magazine by a woman exclusively for women, graphically represents the process of inclusion and restriction of women's social position through the textual construction of their difference (1989: 167).

Charlotte Lennox, already a renowned novelist, in 1760 began her own magazine, the *Lady's Museum*, 'Consisting of a Course of Female Education and Variety of other Particulars for the Information and Amusement of Ladies'. It was to be the last of the generation of women's essay-periodicals and the fullest expression of women readers' engagement with knowledge (Shevelow, 1989: 188). When this period came to a close, women's journalism was confined to a narrower set of discourses for women – domestic, sentimental and escapist. After 1760 the magazine format began to dominate over the essay periodical and attitudes to women had changed so much that White observes: 'The eighteenth century began with an intellectual revival in which women participated but it ended with Mary Wollstonecraft's impassioned denunciation of sexual discrimination showing that the intervening years had witnessed a marked change in social attitudes' (1970: 33).

The first and most successful exponent of the new and limiting women's journalism was the *Lady's Magazine or Entertaining Companion for the Fair Sex*. It was launched in August 1770 as a sixpenny monthly of literary miscellany for women and ran for 80 years. This publication echoed the emergence of literary salons for bourgeois women in the late eighteenth century in which characters like Hannah More were very prominent. The *Lady's Magazine* produced:

> [a] formula that magazine editors were to follow for nearly two centuries: a little instruction, a little fashion, beauty, health, cookery; some free offers such as the embroidery patterns and music sheets of songs; a good serial story, some shorter romantic tales, some charming romantic pictures; a little sentimental verse. And, of course, the answers to readers' letters, the heart-throb column. (Adburgham, 1972: 150–1)

The *New Lady's Magazine, or Polite, Entertaining, and fashionable Companion for the Fair Sex: A Work Entirely Devoted to their Use and Amusement* was published by the Rev. Mr Charles Stanhope from February 1786 and ran for nine years along almost identical lines as the *Lady's Magazine*, proving that there was a substantial market for such publications. There were engravings of foreign and domestic beauty spots, fashions and the fashionably famous, recipes, songs, accounts of duels and poetical essays. At this point, women's magazines still offered short news bulletins from home and abroad – in 1796, for instance *the Ladies' Magazine* produced a startlingly vivid account of 'The Sufferings of the British Troops in the Retreat through Holland, 1795–6' and a digest of annual occurrences. These magazines acted as the embodiment of imaginary communities for female readers, since they were prevented by social convention and economic practice from having a material space in which they could meet if they did not belong to the social elite who frequented the salons. The middle classes and the provincial women's reading public craved the style of community that these magazines offered and therefore their success was hardly surprising.

Hannah More and Other Women Journalists

Hannah More was not the first to publish sentential tracts for the poor to save them from the temptations of despair or radical thought. From 1788 *The Family Magazine* had been produced by Mrs Sarah Trimmer including sermons, instruction and morality tales for the poor from the fictitious Squire and his Lady in their exemplary village, like a popularized version of the characters in the *Spectator*. There were descriptions of foreign lands, largely intended to make the lowly reader aware of the benefits of their lot in England. Taking her lead from the austere traditions of the Society for the Propagation of Christian Knowledge founded in 1696, Hannah More provided another sterner contribution to the archive of periodical publication by women. From 1795 she published monthly tracts called the Cheap Repository Tracts, consisting of stories, sermons and ballads. They astutely exploited the format of cheaper popular publications such as ballads and chapbooks with woodcuts and large print. Between 1795 and 1798 she produced 114 of them, writing at least 50 herself. They were politically conservative and populist, written in clear and simple language with an overall bias against the French Revolution and radicalism in general. Like many of her generation, she blamed the French Revolution for a generalized crisis in English society and morals. Her publishing and her missionary zeal were prompted by widespread fear of the impact of revolutionary material on the impressionable working classes. They were enormously successful in terms of sales, selling 2,000,000 copies in under two years.

The start of the nineteenth century saw struggles to identify a more specific place for women in periodical publishing. The family magazine market, for instance, expanded significantly. Although social expectations restricted women's role to a domestic and subservient one, women's magazines still strove within these limitations to find ways of extending the relevance and impact of their designated discourse in a form which was to play a significant part in how women's journalism itself was to encroach upon the mainstream discourse of journalism. As owners of magazines sought to avoid the taxation on newspapers and as the newspapers became better equipped to collect and distribute news on a reliable basis, news slowly disappeared from women's magazines as they became more oriented towards domestic entertainment and consumption. The gradual erosion of news from their pages meant that women were being marginalized in terms of involvement from the political issues of the day. Furthermore, it had the effect of institutionalizing the absence of news from women's reading, thereby defining 'femininity as incompatible with engagement in public affairs' (Beetham, 1996: 26). Throughout the nineteenth century the trend was for women's magazines to become more focused on domestic issues. Adburgham sees this as prompted by, first, a reaction to the permissiveness of the regency period and, second, because of the increasing influence of the narrow-minded, newly-rich industrialists and their families from the North, many of whom belonged to evangelical sects (1972: 271). This removal of women and female discourse from the public/political into the domestic/private was captured in the launch issue of *The Lady's Magazine*:

> The times are changed ... women have completely abandoned all attempts to shine in the political horizon, and now seek only to exercise their virtues in domestic retirement. The wise (who happily form the majority) perceiving the bad taste manifested in striving for mastery with man, are contented with truly feminine occupations, but in discarding their follies, and in endeavouring to become the rational companions instead of the toys and tyrants of men have fallen from their high estate and dwindled into comparative insignificance ... the proud lords used to acknowledge the equality of the sexes – but now if a lady should dare to aspire to literary distinction, she meets with little encouragement. Magazines, journals and reviews abound with sarcastic comments upon the blue-stockings and their productions. Intellectual acquirement, when applied to a woman is used as a term of reproach. Writers ... proclaim the mental as well as the bodily inferiority of the weaker sex. (Launch Issue, 1825)

Women journalists remained restricted. Most had subservient roles on newspapers and produced the tedious stock reports characteristic of what had become known as the 'penny-a-liners' – deskilled and unprofessional. Even those with more to offer had to conform to the traditional anonymity of journalists and were therefore invisible as women. The expansion of printed periodicals and newspapers of the 1830s and 1840s produced no cheap women's publications. The magazine continued to be aimed at the affluent and leisured upper middle classes, in particular, the new class of wealthy industrialists, who craved social respectability and an education in the ways of the world of the bourgeoisie for their wives and daughters. Women's journalism was alert to the attractions of this ready-made market. The magazines which were tailored to it continued to exclude politics and consequently the areas they did deal with such as leisure, entertainment and fashionable culture became entirely feminized, a trend which was to have lasting consequences for all journalism. However, there were renewed attempts to ensure that women took control of this area of journalism even within its narrow remit: 'After generations of carping male editors, the publication of *The Ladies Cabinet* (1832), edited by a mother and daughter, Beatrice and Margaret de Courcy, claiming "that none but women can speak or write for women" promised greater enlightenment' (Dancyger, 1978: 45).

This may have brought more editorial insight to women's magazines but it did not alter the dominant discourses which restricted women to representations of their world which centred upon domestic identities or sentimental escapism. This was also true of broadly family papers such as *Eliza Cook's Journal* (1849–54). Its contents were either sentimental or moral but always determinedly 'unpolitical' in their exposition. It deployed an extended metaphor of a dinner party to describe its conduct and content:

> a plain feast where the viands will all be of my own choosing, and some of my own dressing, hoping that if what I provide be wholesome and relishing, I shall have a host of friends at my board, whose kind words and cheerful encouragement will keep me in a proud and honourable place at the head of the table. (Opening Preface to the journal, Mountjoy, 1978: 273)

After the lifting of the taxes on knowledge, there was a boom in capital and technical investment in both newspapers and magazines as they became progressively more industrialized. The great capitalist expansion of the mid-nineteenth century came at the same time as an increased need to monitor and discipline leisure among classes hitherto unused to it. The magazine and the Sunday newspaper are part of this twin development. As earlier magazines had been crucial contributors to the public sphere in a diffuse and diverse way, they were now becoming crucial to the formation of commodity and leisure culture as an extension of that sphere in print.

Women Journalists and Journalism

As we have seen, although the market for women's magazines was strong, they were often owned and sometimes even written by men. Hunter's research into the *Lady's Magazine* indicates that as little as a fifth of its content was contributed by women in its early years, despite claims that it was for and by ladies (1977: 109). During the first half of the nineteenth century, women continued as contributors and writers on magazines in particular but were excluded from the masculine world of full-time journalism on newspapers. Sebba writes of the steady opening of journalism to women in the nineteenth century: 'Becoming a journalist in Victorian times was one of the very few routes open to intelligent women with some education to rise beyond humble origins or out of a failed marriage' (1994: 3). The inclusion of women in the increasingly professionalized arena of newspaper journalism was extremely problematic for the whole notion of mid-Victorian professionalization as: 'The nineteenth-century creation of professions – whether journalism, medicine or engineering – was always predicated upon the exclusion of women and others deemed unsuitable for the job. The presence of women in journalism threatened its status as a profession' (Beetham, 1996: 43). Writing for magazines allowed women to work from home anonymously, efficiently and respectably, remaining confined to their designated domestic space while enabling them to earn some irregular income and contribute to the household economy through the fruits of their education. Christian Johnstone, for example, as editor of *Tait's Edinburgh Magazine* between 1834 and 1846, felt she never received the recognition she deserved because, in her own words, 'the woman who turns her talents to any profitable use is, in some occult sense – I own I do not comprehend it – but she is in our Society *degraded*' (Houghton et al., 1987: 479–80).

One advantage of journalism for women was that it allowed, through its convention of anonymity, resourceful women to smuggle themselves into print even if it meant that they often wrote in 'drag' (Easley, 2000: 154) for Victorian periodicals and even newspapers. One such author was Harriet Martineau who began her career in journalism in 1821 by publishing her first anonymous essay in *The Monthly Repository*. She signed the piece with the letter 'V'. She wrote on a range of topics throughout her career, from slavery and political economy to hypnotism and mesmerism, in a variety of influential reviews and magazines. Moving beyond these and into newspapers, she wrote her first anonymous leaders which appeared in the *Daily News* in 1852. One of the techniques which she perfected was the biographical sketch, which she contributed to both the *Daily News* and *Once a Week* in a column entitled 'Representative Men' and its advantage for a domestically located journalist was that it did not require any personal contact with the subject and relied more on an ingenious compilation of details from any number of sources. Yet she was still compelled by the conventions within journalism at the time to contribute as a man when writing on such important and political issues as in this extract where she clearly writes as a male author expressing solidarity with others who have wives:

> We must have a release from the ragged edges, loose buttons, galling shirt-collars, and unravelled seams and corners which have come up as the quality of needlewomen has gone down. Let our wives undertake the case of the remnant of the poor sempstresses – the last, we hope, of their sort. (Martineau, 1859: 328)

Margaret Oliphant was another prolific woman journalist of the time who wrote to Blackwood self-deprecatingly of herself as, 'a womanish story-teller like myself' (Shattock, 2000: 168). She wrote for a wide range of influential and male-orientated magazines and reviews – the *Edinburgh* and the *Fortnightly*, the *Contemporary Review*, *Longman's Magazine*, *Macmillan's*, the *Cornhill*, the *Spectator*, the *St James's Gazette* and was best known for her long association with *Blackwood's*. She was no radical on women's issues, being conservative on votes for women, divorce and the maintenance of separate spheres and this was reflected in her writing, making it acceptable to the publications she wrote for and accentuating her male-identity in print.

Eliza Lynn Linton was the first full-time Fleet Street journalist who was from 1848 on the payroll of the *Morning Chronicle,* most notably as a Paris correspondent. She was not employed in the casual, freelance way which had become common for women journalists at the time and was respected for the reporting she did as a woman, not needing to hide behind the convention of anonymity. Lady Florence Dixie was another pioneer in women's journalism, first providing reports on life and politics in South Africa from 1881 to 1882 for the *Morning Post* and then, on her return to England, contributing articles on a range of topical issues from Irish Nationalism to the Women's Suffrage movement. With the New Journalism of the 1880s and its increased emphasis on personal tone, interviews and sensation targetted increasingly at a female newspaper reader, women journalists were more in demand than ever to provide the prerequisite writing. Flora Shaw was notable for her work on the *Pall Mall Gazette* from 1887 and her reports from Gibraltar before she moved to the *Manchester Guardian*. Hilda Friedrichs was the journalist who provided many of the interviews on the *Pall Mall Gazette* which Stead deployed as a marker of the new style of public journalism.

An Expanding Range

The woman's magazine had continued to target the bourgeoisie into the middle years of the nineteenth century until in 1852, Samuel and Isabelle Beeton produced the *Englishwoman's Domestic Magazine* for the lower middle classes. While Samuel was the entrepreneurial publisher, Isabella Beeton was a contributing journalist and its editor until her death at 28. It was monthly and priced, as an indication of its preferred readership at the cheap end of the market, at twopence, down from the customary price for magazines of one shilling. Such a new magazine could be profitably sold at such a price because of the increased revenue available from more extensive advertising and from the increasingly affluent lower middle classes. It was an immediate success because its readers were a new female reading public. It was claimed that it was selling 50,000 copies per month very shortly after its launch and quickly cultivated a bond of community with its audience. It organized readers' essay competitions, most remarkably on Women's Rights and other controversial topics of the day. This stance, radical for its time on a popular magazine, was complemented by editorials supporting progressive positions towards women's isses by Samuel Beeton. It was also practical, offering tips and help on everything from child-care to pets. To capitalize on this success in 1861 Beeton launched a weekly newspaper for women, the *Queen*, which was based on the successful format of the *Illustrated London News* with a 'news journalism centred on the visual'. It had a clear view of the range suitable for such a publication:

> When we write for women, we write for home. We shall offend very few when we say that women have neither heart nor head for abstract political speculation; while as for our liberties, or our political principles, they may safely be left to men bred in the honest independence of English homes. (*Queen* 1, 1861: 1)

Such was its success that it was able in 1863 to incorporate the earlier experiment in women's newspapers, the *Lady's Newspaper* (incorporating the *Pictorial Times*), which had been launched in January 1847. It covered tragic accidents, royal and society news, gossip and short summaries of a variety of news, all lavishly illustrated wherever possible (Beetham, 1996: 90).

The female-oriented magazine was having an impact in other more general areas of journalism. *Macmillan's Magazine* and the *Cornhill*, launched in 1859 and 1860 respectively, endorsed the increasingly feminized magazine tradition by addressing women readers specifically as part of their readership. The trend to include women as audience by concentrating on areas which had become feminized, such as illustration, leisure and consumer items, was becoming established as an economic prerequisite for owners who wanted to reach as broad a market as possible and thereby good standing with advertisers. It was to become extended to more general newspapers at the popular end of the market by the end of the century.

It is easy to underestimate the radical break with traditional magazine politics of the Victorian era ushered in by the Beetons. As late as the 1840s, despite the fact that women had edited radical, unstamped newspapers in the 1830s, such as Eliza Sharples on the *Isis* of 1832, women were systematically excluded from the discourses of radical politics. The Chartists' demand for 'universal' voting rights meant votes for men. Slowly a discourse began to return which recalled an earlier era of women's journalism which included radical social critique but this time for a wider audience. White sees this era heralded by the appearance in 1846 of *The Female's Friend*, a magazine which dedicated itself to 'elevating the character and condition of women' (1970: 47). From the 1860s, magazines and periodicals dedicated to issues of women's rights flourished across the United States and Western Europe. As part of this growing trend in England we see the *Englishwoman's Journal*, edited by Bessie Rayner Parkes from 1858. This was followed by *The Lady's Review* in 1860 which was the latest attempt to incorporate discussion of the social changes affecting women into a women's magazine. It was not a commercial success and folded within the year. The *Alexandra Magazine* (1846–65) and the *Victoria Magazine* (1863–80) both made a serious contribution to the cause of women's emancipation and suffrage. The *English Woman's Journal* (1858–64), edited by Jessie Boucherett, was influential but had a limited circulation and pronounced polemically in favour of women's rights. The *Woman's Suffrage Journal,* edited by Lydia E. Becker from 1870 to 1890, was one of the longest surviving and most prominent attempts to secure a specifically radical form of women's journalism campaigning on women's issues. They all suffered, like the more broadly defined radical press of the early nineteenth century, from the irreconcilable tension between the necessity for commercial success in the commodified field of journalism and a desire to promote radical alternatives to contemporary problems. Yet they succeeded in setting the terms of the debate on women's rights which were to become influential in mainstream political debate and its coverage in the journalism as a whole.

Specific fashion magazines and the general inclusion of items on fashion in magazines aimed at women really took off in the 1830s but even before this, fashion journalism had already contributed some very specific features to women's journalism. The most renowed pioneers were the *Gallery of Fashion* in 1794 which was the first English magazine covering fashion exclusively with colour plates as an innovative attraction and the *Magazine of Female Fashions of London and Paris* in 1798. Fashion magazines were always London-based as consumption and shopping were always their driving forces and these were located centrally where the prestige shops were. The location of the editorial offices of the women's magazines in the capital assisted in creating a commodity culture for the affluent metropolitan middle classes. *La Belle Assemblée, or Bell's Court and fashionable magazine, Addressed Particularly to the Ladies* was launched in 1806. In its elegant style and sumptious illustration it was the ancestor of the glossy magazines of today and boasted a wide range of editorial content. By the early 1830s it had become the dominant London fashion publication and had expanded to include an even broader diet of journalism including A Monthly Review of New Publications, Music, Drama, and the Fine Arts, Tales of a Physician, The Animal Kingdom, A Country Album, and a list of births, marriages and deaths.

The Late Victorian Era

Following the Compulsory Education Act of 1870, there was an expansion of women's magazines with 48 new titles entering the field between 1880 and 1900 (White, 1970: 58). They were aimed at the lower ends of the social spectrum, at the increasing numbers of women employed outside the home in service, factories, offices and shops, as well as working-class housewives intrigued by a diet of escapism and entertainment. These magazines 'provided a glamour later supplied by the cinema' (Dancyger, 1978: 94). There were also technological innovations which ensured the new readership could be better provided for in terms of quality and an increasingly important visual appeal. In the 1880s wood-pulp paper was introduced, replacing rags, dramatically cutting the cost and improving the quality of paper at the cheaper end of the market, making it more suitable for illustration. By 1882 the half-tone process had been introduced which assisted in raising the presentational standards of advertisements in women's magazines. This in turn demanded more sophistication from advertising in general than it had been providing for newspapers where it had acquired a rather unsavoury and boastful reputation. Advertisements and, in particular, brand names became an increasing part of the landscape of periodical publications from this point onwards.

By the end of the Victorian era, inflation and changing employment patterns meant that many women, especially the middle classes, had to be more involved in running their own households and in economizing. The last twenty years of the nineteenth century witnessed the arrival of, among many others, the *Housewife* (1886), *The Mother's Companion* (1887), *The Ladies' Home Journal* (1890), *Woman at Home* (1893), *Home Notes* (1894) and *Home Companion* (1897). These sixpenny monthlies were typified by *Woman at Home* (1893–1920). It had less news than *Queen* indicating the more domestic emphasis of these publications; fiction, fashion, domestic hints, celebrity interviews, tips on beauty and hygiene and most significantly the letter-columns of Annie Swann 'Over the Teacups' and 'Love, Courtship and Marriage', which developed the intimate tone of confessional dialogue, building up a public idiom for the magazine. Across the miscellany of these magazines the female public sphere was being further consolidated within a particular domestic economy and rhetoric.

In terms of true mass markets for woman's magazines there was a further development which was the introduction of the penny weekly. *Home Chat*, published by Harmsworth from 1895, claimed that the 200,000 copies of its first print needed to be supplemented by 35,000 additional copies to meet demand. It was lively and entertaining as was the Harmsworth aim for all his publications, previewing his ambitions for the *Daily Mail*: 'providing a weekly woman's journal for a penny which should be the equal in the quality of its contributions both editorial and pictorial to any of the sixpenny journals' (White, 1970: 76).

All the major publishing players joined in this lucrative market. This kind of journalism built upon the patterns of the previous sixpenny month-lies and extended its reach to a larger readership. It was characterized by the breaking up of information into short and memorable fragments and the intimacy of its tone, both of which moved it closer to the lived oral experience of many of its readers in how they exchanged information themselves in their social lives. This reinvigoration of the oral tradition of news exchange was one of the key shifts in journalism at a popular level at this time and was to become more pervasive across the twentieth century. It formed an intrinsic part of the New Journalism.

The Return of the Suppressed

Women were identified by the new popular press as commercially essential to wide-scale success since they took significant economic decisions within the domestic economy and were more affluent, as social and economic changes meant that it had become more common for women to be working outside the home in paid employment. The New Journalism took on many attributes that had been associated with women's journalism for over a century and made them commercially attractive to a wider and more general readership through the inclusion of more personal detail and human interest in its news. Furthermore, it borrowed from the magazine the conversational tone and incorporated it more than newspaper journalism had done in its reporting. This was made explicit by Northcliffe who identified 'woman appeal' as crucial to the New Journalism (Friederichs, 1911: 55).

In his accusation that the New Journalism was 'feather-brained', Arnold's (1887) criticism was not only based upon cultural elitism, it was also implicitly critical of its engagement with these hitherto feminized characteristics. Beetham has pointed out that: 'the opposition of "reasonable" against "featherbrained" implicitly mobilised the vocabulary of gendered identity' (1996: 119). The New Journalism also drew on the visual character of the periodical which Beetham characterizes as a further 'feminization', as femininity had been located in and defined by appearance as masculinity had not (ibid.: 126). This visual aspect of not only the popular newspaper but the whole of print and television journalism becomes increasingly dominant through Christiansen's *Daily Express* of 1933 to the layout of all contemporary newspapers and the visually dynamic television broadcasting of the present day, as they are all enormously aestheticized. Yet this incorporation of 'feminized' discourse and representational modes was not designed to empower women, it merely allowed profit to be better extracted from their custom. Increasingly, feminized modes of representation in journalism brought more women into journalism. Women journalists were becoming more visible as by-lines increased in newspapers and magazines and consequently journalism began to appear more often as an employment option for women, although their role was too often restricted by gender stereotyping, as illustrated by Arnold Bennett who, while he was editor of *Woman*, wrote a little book called *Journalism for Women* (1898) in which he made his opinion quite plain: 'In Fleet Street there are not two sexes, but two species – journalists and women journalists, and we treat the species very differently. Women are not expected to suffer the same discipline, nor are they judged by the same standards. In Fleet Street femininity is an absolution, not an accident' (Adburgham, 1972: 272). Women were prominent enough in journalism for the Institute of Women Journalists to be founded in 1895 and by 1898 the issue of women in journalism was becoming pressing enough for *The Woman at Home* to run a symposium entitled 'Is Journalism a Good Profession for Women?'.

The Twentieth Century – Infiltration/ Incorporation

Building on the intimacy of tone of the New Journalism, a community in print based on increasing reader identification was key to the expanding market for all types of journalism in the twentieth century. This was most obviously expressed in women's magazines on the problem pages which served as a barometer of changing social and cultural trends. Yet there was little overt political debate in these magazines, despite the rise of the suffrage movement. They seemed to pre-empt the slogan of *Woman* 'Forward! But Not too Fast' in their measured and cautious embrace of change. They chose to follow rather than lead public opinion like much journalism of the time, acutely aware of the commercial pragmatism required within mass markets. There were attempts to provide more politicized interventions into the sphere of women's journalism. These included from August 1907 the Women's Trade Union League paper, aimed at a proletarian readership and edited by Mary Macarthur, *The Woman Worker* priced 1d. and from 1914 the *Women's Dreadnought* was launched as the Suffragettes' official organ. By and large though, the working class was appellated as a commercially located readership within an individualized tone of address. *My Weekly* was launched in 1910 for working-class women with the following editorial:

> My editorial experience has left me impressed with one thing in particular and that is the need for what is called the 'personal note' in journalism ... I will try to appeal to readers through their human nature and their understanding of everyday joys and sorrows. For I know well that, in order to get into active and intimate relationship with the great public, one must prove oneself fully acquainted with its affections, sentiments and work ... I understand, too, that human nature is strangely and pathetically eager for friendship. I mean willingly to become the confidante of readers, young and old, rich and poor, who can safely trust me with their ideas and difficulties. (White, 1970: 87–8)

Commenting on the traditional address of these magazines to a commercially orientated sense of commonality with the reader, Mary Grieve has observed: 'This close contact with the reader has been our gold-mine since the first journals made their genteel début to the present day' (1964: 96).

Ｗoman was relaunched on 1 June 1937 as a 2d weekly and changed the woman's press in Britain completely (Reed, 1997: 189) by extending its brief to include a more broadly defined social conscience for a middle-class women's magazine. In market terms, it saw a drop in circulation of 30 per cent but it encouraged other magazines to develop this part of their appeal (White, 1970: 11). In extending the range of journalism in these popular women's magazines to include topical issues such as divorce, social issues, birth control, parenting and women at work through the war years and beyond, the women's press was seen as entering something approaching its own golden age, as indicated in this extract from *World's Press News*, 7 October 1943:

> Only some forty years ago the woman's magazine was an inconsiderable factor in journalism. Today it has won a dominant and very adult place in the periodical field, and is rivalled in sales and social influence only by the newspapers. This phenomenal growth of the woman's magazine is directly due to – and has been largely commensurate with – the advance of woman herself as a political, economic and moral force in the life of the nation. (Ferguson, 1983: 19–21)

Good Housekeeping which had been part of the landscape of women's magazines since 1922, took on the mantle of social responsibility for middle-class debate on the sort of women's issues launched by *Woman*. In May 1946 it made the following stalwart call to women to play their part in the post-war reconstruction which could have appeared in the popular daily newspaper the *Daily Mirror* of the same era, illustrating the extent of the interpenetration of writing about women within popular news media at this point:

> if we are to survive as a nation, Britain will have to allow our women as well as our men to use their energy and ability ...
>
> Yet now the war is over, some people seem to think that women should go back to just the kind of jobs they did before the war and accept once more the same old artificial reasons and limitations. To my mind that would be disastrous ... We women must assume the responsibility of making our full contribution in the field for which our personal capacity fits us. Many women will rightly choose marriage and motherhood and feel that under present conditions the making of a home and bringing up young children is a job to which they *wish* to give the whole of their time. Others, many of whom are professional women, wish to combine marriage and motherhood with at least a part-time career ... we do need an adequate supply of women with first-class qualifications to serve on policy-forming bodies ... If we can carry forward into the future the spirit of individual efficiency shown by British women in the war years, then we need not fear the problems of tomorrow. (White, 1970: 136–7)

From the 1960s, we see increasingly a trend towards a much more commercialized version of a lifestyle publication which uses advertising and editorial to position readerships as consumers and as lucid participants in the selection and maintenance of specifically gendered lifestyles. *Flair* (1960) and *Honey* (1961),were two early examples of this development. In addition, the growth of disposable income and the virtual invention of a new consumer category of youth culture saw the creation of more niche markets for women's journalism. These exhibited a similar intensified linkage of writing, editorial and consumption. Such specialization meant a reduction in general interest articles and a newly configured retreat of women's journalism from more broadly social themes. *Cosmopolitan*, launched in Britain in March 1972, was the high point of this modern trend and the paradigm for subsequent women's magazines aimed at and constructing at the same time the newly 'liberated' sexual and economic woman. Helen Gurley Brown was quoted in the *Guardian*, 20 June 1977:

> *Cosmopolitan* is every girl's sophisticated older sister ... *Cosmopolitan* says you can get anything if you really try, if you don't just sit on your backside and gaze in on life with your nose pressed to the glass ... we carry our profile, one piece on health, one on sex, two on emotions – we had a good one the other day on the Good Luck Factor – one on man/woman relationships, one on careers, one short story and one part of a major work of fiction, as well as our regular columns. (Ferguson, 1983: 37)

Cosmopolitan is still the market leader with a British circulation of 460,000 in 2002. It is produced in 48 editions which are translated into 25 different languages, incorporating values of an anglophone culture into local vernacular cultures.

Against the rising tide of increasingly commodified women's magazines, there were influential minority publications which offered radical alternative critiques to mainstream commercialized views of women. The most significant of these was *Spare Rib* from 1972.

Women's magazines have retreated, in the main, from engaging with broader social issues to concentrate on the increasingly lucrative combination of advertorial journalism supporting the commodity lifestyles at their core. In the popular press, incorporating features of woman's magazines earlier than their broadsheet cousins, Marjorie Proops on the *Daily Mirror* gave advice in an agony aunt column which became an influential commentary on the changing mores of British women in a daily newspaper which had long been part of the magazine agenda. Certain of the most powerful of newspaper columnists were women, such as Jean Rook on the *Daily Express* and Lynda Lee-Potter on the *Daily Mail,* both of whom made powerful contributions to the 'public idiom' of their newspapers in their interviews and opinion columns – defining the place and role of a women's voice in a middle-brow national identity. Women's journalism has developed alongside lifestyle features more generally in the broadsheet press from the 1990s. Before this, Mary Stott, as women's editor of the *Guardian* (1957–71), pioneered feature writing that was a step forward from the agony aunts and problem pages of magazines and popular press in attempting to widen the resonance and reach of journalism aimed at women. As the world began to open up to women, she gave space to writing about balancing work and child-raising, depression, physical problems relating to women, and also included letters from readers who were allowed to play their part in opening up a new public sphere of women's discussion. Newspapers, especially broadsheets, have moved commercially to include more of interest to increasingly affluent and socially engaged professional women readers.

We may broaden out from this analysis of magazines to women's journalism in general. Van Zoonen (1994) has indicated that the problems surrounding women's journalism are not simply in representation or of personnel, but are embedded within the 'gendered structure of media production'. Some of this structural bias has to do with the male traditions of the work but in more invisible ways it has to do with the very patterns of what has become valued as good journalism within institutions, particularly with regard to hard news. Creedon (1989) has argued that consequently women, even within mainstream journalism, have been confined to 'velvet ghettos'. Stuart Allen has blamed this on the embedded masculinist bias within traditions of 'objective' reporting (1999: 136). Even while some successful journalists such as Kate Adie can be quoted as saying: 'things have changed radically in the last 15 years for women reporters', in terms of the powerful managers and decision-makers within journalism, little has changed to the benefit of women. Research results from different Western countries, according to Van Zoonen, have demonstrated the minority position of women in traditional news journalism (1998: 45).

The increasing presence of women in journalism is made problematic by the changes occurring in the status of market-driven journalism. This returns us to the anxieties which have haunted women's journalism since before the arrival of the New Journalism. The politicization of the personal, such a sloganized aspect of the feminist generation of the 1960s and 1970s, may well have its progressive agenda but it is also, within commercialized journalism, exploited as a strategy to incorporate more populist approaches within an entertainment-driven culture. Sebba points this out graphically in an incisive analysis of the attraction of the report that brought television reporter Kate Adie to prominence during the 1980 Iranian Embassy siege:

> As the Embassy shook with the sound of gunfire, Kate was to be seen crawling along the pavement yelling for a microphone. She recognises today that the disturbing element in this kind of reporting is that 'it is just like the movies'. Inevitably, viewers come to expect their news increasingly to be served up as entertainment and a woman television personality – especially a pretty one – witnessing the danger is particularly effective in lending to the excitement an additional frisson. (1994: 266)

In light of this it seems ironic that the same journalist, Kate Adie, was accused of referring to the current generation of television journalists as 'bimbos' at Cheltenham Festival of Literature in October 2001. However, it is interesting to note that while women foreign reporters on televison and in print continue to break down the barriers, they are still working within a paradigm established by Lady Florence Dixie. In other areas of journalism they are still remarkably rare. Julia Langdon was the first woman to be appointed as a political editor, on Maxwell's *Daily Mirror*, as late as 1984. Women political editors and editors have been seen on national newspapers; Eve Pollard at both the *Sunday Mirror* and the *Sunday Express*, Patsy Chapman at the *News of the World*, Wendy Henry and Bridget Rowe at the *People* and most recently Rebekah Wade became, in January 2003, the first woman editor of a national popular daily newspaper when she took over at the *Sun* in what may appear to be a rather pyrrhic victory for women. Nonetheless, women broadsheet editors and chief political correspondents are few and far between.

There is still a marked tendency within radio journalism for a partitioning of jobs for women. Writing of her experience in radio, prominent broadcaster Sue MacGregor recalls:

> Eighteen years and four general elections on from the time I first joined *Today*, there are still remarkably few women fronting current affairs programmes. As programme producers and editors women are now universally accepted ... [from Afghanistan] Kate Clark, Jacky Rowland, Susannah Price and Catherine Davis from the BBC World Sevice all distinguished

themselves with daily accounts of the battle, and their names became almost as familiar as John Simpson's. But the number of women as front-line political interviewers is still lamentably low.

Perhaps it is partly a matter of style: interviews are expected to be more confrontational these days, and confrontation is an approach with which men are generally more comfortable. (2002: 326–7)

A more positive aspect of women's experience on radio has been the tradition of an exclusively women-oriented journalism which has been characterized by the survival and evolution of the *Woman's Hour* format.

The ambivalence of the role of the magazine in the articulation of the fragmented and increasingly commodified experiences of women reflects the Janus-faced aspect of journalism towards their participation. Certain accounts of journalism might privilege the increasing profile of women in mainstream journalism from the middle of the nineteenth century as evidence that journalism was changing in ways which enabled a fuller representation of the world from a perspective which allowed women more than a narrowly defined domestic role within patriarchal society, that journalism was becoming more inclusive. The increasing feminization of mainstream journalism has all the characteristics of a hegemonic compromise, allowing female voices into the discourse of journalism while doing so on the terms of the dominant male perspective, particularly when they have the potential to improve profitability. The danger for the dominant perspective and the optimistic perspective for women's journalism is that once inside, no matter how compromised by the existing structures, women are potentially able to rearrange the existing patterns and reshape this discourse, however slowly. Incorporation is not one-way traffic. The ambivalent potential of women's periodicals within journalism has been well expressed by Shevelow:

> But in looking at the periodical, which was then and remains now one of women's principal – and for many women, the only – means of engagement with print culture, we are reminded that the tools of liberation are not in themselves liberating. Print culture can provide the bricks and mortar for constructing a prison – or the dynamite for shattering its walls. (1989: 198)

We can surely generalize that point from print culture to journalism of all styles and formats. The commodification of journalism has seen a tendency to include more lifestyle-oriented features including more and more personalized accounts of experiences from both male and female writers. This forms part of a blurring of hard and soft news which has been a constant in the process of magazinification. Overall, women's journalism is a contentious, ambivalent and hugely interesting set of practices which continue to shape a diverse public sphere but much more within the mainstream of journalism than previously, as a commodified settlement within the predominantly patriarchal discourses which still structure women's contribution to that mainstream.

8

Popular and Consumer Periodicals

The Most Influential Format

In the previous chapter, magazines for women were explored as part of the history of women's journalism as it moved from its 'velvet ghetto' to more prominence in the mainstream of journalism. This chapter will look more broadly at the history of periodical publications which have not seen the provision of the latest news as their primary objective. These cover a wide range of formats, from essay sheet to lifestyle magazine, from generalist to specialist. This history will touch again on some of the more important moments in the development of journalism, drawing these strands together to underline how the miscellany and general reach foregrounded in many periodicals have always played a part in its discursive formation. It will take a broad view of this journalism across historical periods and between specialist magazines and broad-based Sunday newspapers in order to explore the flux between the types of primary public information traditionally provided by newspapers and those media which deal in the wider range of secondary social information. It will concentrate on the contribution of this journalism to other ways of knowing about the world other than the narrowly political. Across periods of great disparity in terms of technology, politics and economy the periodical has provided many of the crucial debates around which the discourse of journalism has been constructed. Perhaps to make an extravagant claim, the periodical and the magazine have been the most fertile and influential journalism formats.

This chapter will not consider journalism as constituted by the rise and fall of one particular form of public discourse, namely politics, as in some narratives of journalism, but as a more complex relationship involving the ebb and flow of influences between periodical and other journalism formats as they have been, in their turn, shaped by economic and social circumstances. This study considers that it is monologic, even restrictive, to attempt to close down journalism to a narrow set of explicitly political functions while ignoring the longevity of its ability to engage with the wider cultural discourses of pleasure and profitability. Tendencies to close down journalism's main function to a restricted engagement with didactic, instructional forms of political information and opinion are exposed as inadequate in describing journalism's true range at several historical junctures. The newsbooks of the Civil War were increasingly encroached upon by the miscellany of more varied material in many of the mercuries, particularly the satirical ones. The dullness of official post-Revolutionary newspapers witnessed the reaction of a burgeoning experimentation in format and content as soon as the Licensing Act expired and the first periodical gazettes appeared. It was the first named magazine, the *Gentleman's Magazine*, which fought the battle to provide the reading public with accounts of Parliament in peace time. The restricted diet of political polemic of the radical unstamped finally was forced out of the market by periodicals and Sunday newspapers which could provide for a wider audience with a more limited engagement with radical political positions and greater appeal to advertisers. The market forces of mass consumption also meant that the newspapers, including the broadsheet quality newspapers, have been obliged to move closer to the format and variety of the general magazine – a process which begins with Newnes's *Tit-Bits* and is accelerating still in today's print media. It is also significant that popular broadcast formats within journalism have also borrowed the term magazine to describe their content and approach, from the *Today* programme on radio to breakfast television.

The inclusion of a wide range of cultural experience for the general reader has a long history in print journalism. News blended with entertainment, often of the most scurrilous kind, had erupted into periodical form in the English Civil War with publications such as *Mercurius Fumigosus* and *Mercurius Jocasus* (1654). At the Restoration, periodicals with a more serious, even self-conscious awareness of their contribution to print culture quickly followed, indicating the potential of such publications to contribute to the field of journalism by disseminating general information and debate among the learned classes of society. The *Journal des Savans* was published from January 1665 as a 12-page weekly review of literature and ran for 250 years. A similarly highbrow venture emerged the same year from March, with the *Acta Philosophica Societa Anglia*, published by Henry Oldenburg, later renamed the *Philosophical Transactions of the Royal Society* and concentrating on a monthly digest of scientific articles. Other experiments in periodical form continued. From 1691 to 1696 John Dunton produced the *Athenian Gazette or Causistical Mercury* (soon shortened to the *Athenian Mercury*), a twice weekly which included poetry and, most interestingly in terms of the evolution of periodical writing, printed answers to readers' questions on the topics covered in its pages. The *Athenian Mercury* announced itself as a 'popularizer' of useful information in its first number and sought to 'communicate knowledge more generally and easily than has been formerly done'. It provided a wide range of information in digestible form for an educated readership. John Dunton's *Pegasus* (1696), provided, with 'News and a Jacobite Courant', what he called an Observator – a dissertation or serialized instruction upon some moral, political, or historical subject of topical interest. In 1692 came the *Gentleman's Journal* from a French Huguenot, Peter

Motteux, which was modelled on his successful *Le Mercure Galant* from Paris where it had been first published in 1672 and which continued the provision of court gossip for the fashionable and wealthy, indicating that even for such an educated readership, information was still best served blended with a carefully targeted form of entertainment. These periodicals were preparing the ground culturally for the full development of the bourgeois public sphere in the literary journals and essay sheets of the early eighteenth century. The newspaper was simply not broad enough in its social and political ambition to be seen as serving this purpose at this time.

The successful periodicals were copied and proliferated as a type. They provided an opportunity for writers with the flair and ambition to earn their living. Daniel Defoe, for example, worked briefly for the *Athenian*. On starting his *Review* he contributed a weekly feature entitled, 'Advice from the Scandalous Club', the essay style of which was to gain huge influence and popularity at the start of the eighteenth century as the most admired form of periodical output. It was most successfully exploited in the *Tatler* and its successor the *Spectator*. Adburgham claims that together they 'created a new kind of journalism' (1972: 55).

It was in periodical form, indeed in the first named 'magazine', that attempts to cover parliamentary debate were renewed, not in the daily or thrice-weekly newspapers which retained a relatively cautious approach to public affairs. Cave was the first to use the term 'magazine' for his *Gentleman's Magazine* and the name quickly became widely copied. It was a mixture of miscellaneous elements collected from elsewhere, literature, political writing and criticism, leaving the more ephemeral business of current news to the newspapers themselves. Johnson wrote for it from 1738 and was its parliamentary editor (1740–44) working on the reports from the Parliament of Lilliput. Cave also produced the first 'magazine' aimed at women in his *Ladies' Magazine or Monthly Intelligence*. As newspapers began to concentrate more on political and financial news and attempted to incorporate some of the features of the essay sheet, literary magazines continued to flourish as the medium for discussions of contemporary tastes and ideas. Johnson's *Rambler* and *Idler* are two of the most famous examples of this continuing tradition into the middle of the eighteenth century.

Miscellanies of Useful Knowledge

As literacy spread during the Victorian period, there was more reading matter for lower social classes. Since newspapers aimed high, periodicals were often where the tastes of the poor were determined. In fact, Shattock and Wolff claim that it was predominantly in the periodical form that social experience of the period was embedded: 'The periodical press is neither a mirror *reflecting* Victorian culture, nor a means of *expressing* Victorian culture but an inescapable ideological and subliminal environment, a (or perhaps *the*) constitutive medium of a Victorian culture' (1982: xiv–xv).

In the Victorian period, magazine and periodical journalism provided the bulk of the reading matter directed at working-class readerships. Most of it had the explicit goal of marginalizing radical political debate by foregrounding entertainment and domestic contentment and thereby played an important normative role in the shaping of a particularly docile form of popular proletarian public sphere. The *Cottager's Monthly Visitor* (1821–56) is a good early example which offered a self-recognition of dignity and acceptance of social status for the lower classes as a counter to the influence of radical unstamped papers. In 1832, it was the arrival of three cheap magazines which ushered in journalism for the lower middle classes. They were *Chambers's Edinburgh Journal*, the *Penny Magazine* and the *Saturday Magazine*. These differed in appearance, formula and commercial strategy but they all cost a penny, sold in their tens or even hundreds of thousands and aimed to provide 'wholesome' reading for the working man (Beetham, 1996: 45). They all sought to combine the containment of political ambition with the education and entertainment of lower classes. They were often under the explicit influence of societies dedicated to specific social goals. The Society for the Propagation of Christian Knowledge, for instance, supported *The Saturday Magazine* (1832–44) and the Society for the Diffusion of Useful Knowledge lent its influence to the *Penny Magazine* (1832–45). The most successful, however, *Chamber's Journal* from Edinburgh (1832–1956), was a combination of entertainment and instruction which had a more commercial drive and was marketed across Britain, having English and Irish editions as well as its original Scottish imprint.

It will be sufficient to briefly highlight one of these magazines. Charles Knight made an important contribution to the journalism of moral reform so central to the ethos of the age through his popular periodical the *Penny Magazine,* which he began in 1832, six years after the establishment of its chief sponsor, the Society for the Diffusion of Useful Knowledge (SDUK). Under the law of 1819, it could not be classified as a newspaper and could therefore compete with the unstamped weeklies at their own price level. It has been described as 'realistic' and 'socially conscious' (Dancyger, 1978: 109, 134) and owed its credibility with its readers to this aspect of its content. It soon reached a circulation of 200,000, three times that of the Society for the Diffusion of Christian Knowledge's *Saturday Magazine*, and more than ten times that of the radical *Poor Man's Guardian* (Jones, 1996: 105). It was carefully constructed to appeal to all classes, supported liberal versions of Reform, the dignity of labour and the working classes, praised the economic status quo and the efficiency of the political economy as a means of gradual social improvement, and illustrated the evils of drunkenness. It contained aspects of encyclopaedia knowledge, combined with extracts from literature it considered uplifting to its readership. It made journalistic forays into museums and factories and was heavily illustrated. It was a model of paternalistic, periodical journalism designed to contribute to the liberal education of the working classes as associates of a public sphere but not as participants in this forum on anything like an even footing with the bourgeoisie. It was nevertheless popular and even after the demise of the SDUK in 1846 and the lifting of taxes on newspapers, this readership continued to support magazines aimed at 'conservative meliorism' (Mountjoy, 1978: 277), encouraging the lower classes to accept and work within the restrictions of their social status to better themselves. T.B. Smithies' *British Workman and Friend of the Sons of Toil* (1855–1921) was widely imitated and very successful in this tradition.

Extending Opinion and Debate

Periodicals also contributed throughout the nineteenth century to stimulate and form a wider bourgeois intelligensia. In addition to the battle for the pockets and minds of the working and lower middle classes, the first half of the nineteenth century also saw the rise of a select range of literary periodicals which made a distinct contribution to the formation of a high culture of journalism which in part paved the way for the improving reputation of the practice at least at the top of the trade! The *Edinburgh Review* (1802), the *Quarterly Review* (1809), the *Edinburgh Monthly Magazine* (1817), later to be renamed *Blackwood's Edinburgh Magazine* and the *Westminster Review* (1824) were targeted at the intellectual and cultural elite of the country. These periodicals provided more in-depth debate than the daily newspaper could, freed as they were from the tyranny of daily deadlines and the insistence on topicality. They were very much an extension within journalism of the practices of the bourgeois public sphere, but one which had become more explicitly politicized.

   In the 1860s, there was a second wave of literary periodical production as the products of wider educational and social opportunities sought to establish reading communities of their own through more frequently published periodicals. The publishing cycle of the quarterlies was to prove too pedestrian to deal with the topicality of discussion now demanded by the readership of the new monthlies. They continued many of the features of the quarterlies but with greater frequency and less overt elitism. The most prominent were *Macmillan's Magazine* (1859), the *Cornhill* (1860), the *Contemporary Review* (1866), the *Nineteenth Century* and the *Fortnightly Review* (1865). The *Fortnightly*, a monthly after its first few issues, provided sympathetic accounts of working-class problems, trade unions and even the struggles of the Paris Commune, in frequent articles by two positivists, F. Harrison and E. Beesly, but these views were editorially balanced by contributors who wrote from the perspective of ther orthodox political economy (Mason, 1978: 285). The *Contemporary Review* (1867) espoused moderate social reform. The *Nineteenth Century* (1877) gave the fullest coverage of socialist viewpoints – Kropotkin, Keir Hardy and Sidney Webb all contributed to its output. One of the major contributions of the monthlies to the changing face of journalism was from the mid-century with their push against anonymous journalism with signed articles. In addition, they extended the cultural and political commentary which had always constituted an important strand of journalism, to an enlarged middle-class readership.

Popular Sunday Newspapers

One of the greatest influences on all journalism has come directly and indirectly through the medium of the popular Sunday newspaper. Around 1780 the first Sunday paper was produced by Mrs E. Johnson, *E. Johnson's British Gazette, and Sunday Monitor,* later to become the *Sunday Monitor*. It was similar in layout and content to any daily paper with the exception that it provided religious instruction (Black, 1991: 251). Such attempts to curry favour with a Sunday readership through concentrating on religious matters were to prove short-lived as the subsequent history of Sunday newspapers would demonstrate. The paper launched in 1796 by John Bell as *Bell's Weekly Messenger* was to provide the first example of what could be recognized as the prototype of this particular form of periodical. It aimed at providing a miscellany of news and entertainment for a cross-section of readers, including specifically women readers. The form of low-brow, social inclusivity aspired to by the paper was to prove hugely successful and have an impact across a whole range of journalism. The Sunday press developed an alternative to the instruction and enlightenment of the journalism of moral reform of Knight and More by trading on the tradition of printed material for the poor which had been the preserve of a plebian print culture for the best part of two centuries – broadsheets, almanacs, chapbooks, last dying speeches and illustrated ballads (Shepard, 1973). The Sunday papers emphasized that the working people could expect entertainment from their periodical reading, not simply political or didactic instruction.

From the 1820s a different kind of Sunday newspaper began to establish itself. McCalman claims that it was the criminal papers and scandal sheets of the late 1820s which were to introduce in periodical form the sensationalist ingredients of the mid-century Sunday papers. They provided the escapism and prurience which in combination were to prove so popular (McCalman, 1988: 236). John Duncombe's *New London Rambler's Magazine* (1828–30) and Benbow's *Rambler's Magazine* (1822–24) were the earliest examples. Cleave's *Weekly Police Gazette* between 1835 and 1841 contributed to these developments in its successful mixture of court reporting, which emphasized the foibles of the rich and the viciousness of the poor, with political analysis which attempted to frame both social extremes in a radical context. Its sales peaked at 20,000 in the mid-1830s (Berridge, 1978: 274).

The generation of Sunday papers which built upon the market established by the criminal and scandal sheets included sex, sensation and sport, intermingled with a wide range of the news of the week from home and abroad, news which stressed human interest and the lived experiences of the working people wherever possible. At the start, they also included a concentration on perspectives which were radical in the espousal of the rights of the poor and the excesses of the rich, but these impulses were held in check by their need to be attractive to advertisers as well as readers and were limited to an 'old corruption' style of reporting. The best combined entertainment with political information and polemic. They became successful as the unstamped began their terminal decline in the mid-1830s, as a pragmatically commercial form of radicalism had found a sustainable market. The popular Sunday press, according to Vincent, played a large part in developing a commercial format for journalism which 'in translating the discrimination of news into a completely new category of popular leisure coincided with the virtual disappearance of working-class politics' (1993: 252). Mass agitation subsided after the passing of the Reform Act in 1832, for instance, the National Union of the Working Classes dissolved in 1834. The working-class tradition in journalism had become limited in scope and too dependent on individual address. The 'razor-sharp rhetoric of class war' (Epstein, 1976: 71) identifiable on the *Northern Star* was pushed out by publications which could appeal, particularly on the day of rest in the working week, to a broader and more escapist range of material which was more commercially attractive. Vincent also emphasizes the negative aspects of the personalization of the radical press tradition which was 'too dependent on the position of its proprietor to escape the negative aspects of the personalisation of address which had been so characteristic of the working class political papers. O'Connor's "My Dear Friends" ... had become "My Dear Children" by ... 1848' (1993: 251).

The title of one Sunday newspaper from 1842 compresses the specialisms of the emergent dominant Sunday paper in its broad popular appeal and targeting of the staples of popular fiction, crime, sex and sport, quite nicely for the purposes of illustration:

> *The Penny Sunday Chronicle*
> *People's Weekly Advertiser*
> *Sporting and Police Gazette and Newspaper of Romance*

The Sunday newspapers were to have a great influence on journalism in general as it underwent an intense process of commercialization and popularization. Yet as journalism became more financially attractive to respectable businessmen as an investment, the journalists on these periodicals were not enjoying any improvement in status despite the commercial success of their product. Bulwer-Lytton described Sunday paper journalists as 'broken-down sharpers, ci-devant markers at gambling houses and the very worse description of uneducated blackguards' (Elliott, 1978: 176).

As with all developments in the history of journalism, those of the magazine and periodical were inextricably linked to the economic and social infrastructure and, in particular with magazines, the growing impact of leisure and consumerism from the mid-nineteenth century. Two determining factors for the magazine and its content were the growing urbanization and increasing advertising from this period which in combination facilitated larger and more homogeneous readerships. In May 1843, *The Family Herald* was launched and became one of the most popular weeklies. It was among the first to exploit the potential of national distribution through the newly extended railway network from the late 1830s and early 1840s. It combined poetry, fiction, questions and answers, statistics, riddles and popular science in a blend of wide generalist appeal to the readers of the lower middle classes and literate working classes. Its layout was limited by its desire to cram as much in as possible and therefore provide visible value for money.

For a more sophisticated visual appeal within popular journalism we can look to the launch by Herbert Ingram in 1842 of the *Illustrated London News* with 32 woodcuts on its 16 pages. This was to show how journalism and illustration could be combined in popular form for a large audience. By 1855 the *Illustrated London News* was selling in excess of 130,000 copies a week which was ten times the daily sale of the *Times*. As an innovative medium, with its combination of features and its lively style and copious illustrations, it could lay claim to be one of the most important news channels of the day and its format and style were widely imitated at home and abroad.

As Stamp Duties and taxes on newspapers were reduced and abolished, it was three new weekly papers, the *News of the World* (1843), *Lloyd's Illustrated London Newspaper* (1842) and *Reynolds' Weekly Newspaper* (1850) which were to refine the popular Sunday market and exert a potent impact on popular journalism in general as it came to dominate in the era of mass readerships and the New Journalism. They all managed a version of radical rhetoric for their target audience combined with continuities in an appeal to older traditions of popular entertainment of stories, illustration, song and sensation. *Lloyd's* and *Reynolds'* in particular were the forerunners of the modern mass media in their combination of large readerships and a broad-based diet of information and entertainment, together with successful advertising and effective distribution. As the lower classes became attracted to their de-politicized, commercially-orientated content, this form of periodical journalism had become 'the effective means of social control which the establishment had always hoped the popular press might be' (Berridge, 1978: 256).

The conundrum for even radical proprietors like George Reynolds, who was himself a Chartist and had links with organizations of the working class, was how to reconcile a commitment to radical politics with the imperative to make money from his business. The solution was to be pragmatic enough to combine a radical position on political matters with individualized attacks on corruption in politicians, aristocrats or ministers and to offer this as part of a miscellany which included entertainment and escapism. He provided a menu which was palatable to a broad combination of working-class and lower middle-class readers. Although Reynolds was accused of opportunism by critics as esteemed as Karl Marx, Curran has posed the pertinent point:

'it is difficult to see what else he could have done if the paper was to survive the transition to an advertising-based system' (Curran and Seaton, 1993: 42).

By the mid-1850s the combination had proved so successful that *Lloyd's* and *Reynolds'* were boasting sales in excess of 100,000. From 1861 and the removal of the Paper Tax, *Lloyd's* and *Reynolds'* could both be sold for a penny: 'The working class paper had become big business' (Berridge, 1978: 264). Mass readerships and cheap products meant an increasingly attractive combination for advertising. This had implications for all of journalism but especially the magazine and periodical market. Over the next 30 years, both *Lloyd's* and *Reynolds'* reduced the amount of hard political news and replaced it with more of the general news and entertainment that were popular with the broadest possible readership. As contributors to journalism, their impact was considerable. Their brand of commercial popularization was to drive change into the twentieth century and indicated the importance of periodical and magazine style to the mainstream of journalism and its altering configuration within the public sphere. It was popular periodical journalism which provided the bridge between the mid-century popular press and the evolution of the recognizable mass circulation daily newspapers of the twentieth century. *Lloyd's* had the first regular circulation of 1 million by the time of the *Daily Mail*. It was more in favour with advertisers because of its less radical politics though *Reynolds'* was also pushing towards half a million.

These papers built up the same close relationship between reader and periodical which had been a feature of the radical unstamped and later Chartist press and this was carried over as part of the cultural tradition which sustained them as profitable enterprises (Berridge, 1978: 251). Such a textual relationship had been a consistent feature of women's magazines and would be a vital component in the success of the New Journalism later in the century. There were other ways in which they drew on traditions of the radical press such as campaigning. *Reynolds'* was heavily involved in the support and organization of radical protest and reform, publishing advice and letters of support from readers. Yet ultimately these papers were run for profit not politics.

A different and, in the long term, even more successful experiment in the Sunday market was the *News of the World*, launched by John Browne Bell in 1843 as an 8-page, threepenny weekly. Its opening number expressed much of the hybrid identity of the new Sunday newspaper and its contribution to commercially astute journalism in its targeting of a range of general contents to a broad market:

> Journalism for the rich man and journalism for the poor have up to this time been as broadly and distinctly marked as the manners, the dress, and the habitations of the rich are from the customs, the squalor, and the dens of the poor. The paper for the wealthy classes is high-priced; it is paid for by them, and it helps to lull them in the security of their prejudices. The paper for the poorer classes is, on the other hand, low-priced, and it is

paid for by them; it feels bound to pander to their passions. Truth, when it offends a prejudice and shows the evil of passion, is frequently excluded from both. The first is often as remarkable for its talent, for its early intelligence, as the other, we regret to say, is for the absence of talent and the staleness of its news. (1 October, 1843)

It continued, admitting that to ensure the success of its mission it had to secure a large circulation:

FEARLESS ADVOCACY OF TRUTH
It is only by a very extensive circulation that the Proprietors can be compensated for the outlay of a Large Capital in this Novel and Original undertaking, but they are confident that Public Patronage will keep pace with desert, and that the numerous attractions – the intrinsic merits, as well as the extraordinary Cheapness – will be duly appreciated: and that, in point of Circulation, this Paper will soon stand first among the most Popular, as no pains will be spared to establish its character as First among the Best of the Weekly Journals.

Posters advertising its launch boasted that it would prove 'The Novelty of Nations and the Wonder of the World – the cheapest, largest and best newspaper'. It was clearly aimed at poorer classes but was also attractive, in terms of advertisements, to the wealthier commercial classes. It soon moved its coverage of court cases to a prominent position in order to secure for itself a growing reputation for reporting all the salacious and sensational details which emerged. Accidents, murders, grotesque discoveries were all sewn into the fabric of the paper. There was legal advice to correspondents and a full news service, including issues slanted towards the political preferences of the poor. It made the most of the goriest details of the 1888 Ripper murders. By late Victorian times, it was heavily advertised nationwide on billboards and exploited the development of a national network of distribution entirely geared towards a Sunday paper.

After the first World War it further developed its difference from the daily press by accentuating a sensational reporting with a moral tone. The *News of the World* has always argued that it was pursuing public morality by publishing details of the punishments of offenders, particularly the moral sermons from judges or magistrates and especially when the guilty parties were prominent figures of the establishment themselves. Vicars, MPs and aristocrats were heavily featured in its sensational reporting on the lapses of the great and good. The paper tended to move its focus from aristocrats to common people after the Judicial Proceedings Act became law in 1926 and restricted reports of divorce cases which had been such easy copy for the newspaper. Afterwards it would have to do a bit more digging to provide its dirt.

Its high point of direct cultural and economic significance was in the 1960s when it reached a circulation of 6,250,000 and brought the world the definitive story of the era. In breaking news of the 1963 Profumo Affair which saw a prominent Conservative Secretary of State, John Profumo, and the Soviet naval attaché, Yevgeny Ivanov, sharing high-class prostitute Christine Keeler as a lover, the *News of the World* juxtaposed sex, spying, cocktails and corruption in high places for its world-record readership. Its scandal-led journalism chimed with the times and in telling the story from the perspective of Christine Keeler, it endorsed much of the type of pseudo-radicalism with which the paper had been associated for over a hundred years. It seemed to capture a whole era in its iconoclasm, declamation of corruption in high places, blended with details of the lives of the glitterati of the swinging sixties. Some years later Rupert Murdoch, the owner from the late 1960s, expressed his commitment to this tradition of sensational exposé when he announced: 'When things go wrong it is in the interest of those in power to conceal and it is in the interest of the press to reveal. The muck-raking tradition in popular journalism is an honourable one' (Bainbridge and Stockdill, 1993: 237).

Popular Sunday newspapers may have always shown less interest in politics and devoted considerably less space to the staple diet of the ideal Fourth Estate newspaper (Negrine, 1994: 45) but they do contribute to populist espousals of campaigns which seem to capture something of the mood of their readership, no matter how reactionary and ill-advised as in the recent case of the policy of the *News of the World* to name and shame paedophiles. Their contribution to the construction of a populist *Zeitgeist* is still a significant social reality, even if it is one restricted to a conservative and moralistic consensus. They are strong on scepticism towards those in authority, particularly politicians, and have their fair share of celebrity gossip. Their iconoclasm reinforces the reputation of much of popular journalism, at least at a superficial level, to be no respecters of rank and status. They continue to provide a successful mixture of entertainment and carefully manufactured empathy with the common people which does not extend to anything like a radical politics in their content. They might well constitute a reasonable survey of the state of the populist nation. Since the 1960s, popular Sunday papers have seen their concentration on sex, sensation, sport and scandal spread to other parts of the news media as part of the process of tabloidization (see Chapter 9).

Narrowcasting and Commercial Incorporation

Other developments within journalism as a whole came from the birth of a wider range of consumer-led magazines from the mid-Victorian period. *Vanity Fair*, launched in 1868 as a 6d weekly, was a society paper full of gossip on the celebrities of the day and included colour lithographs of many of them as collectables. Labouchère's *The Truth* from 1876 provided high society's foibles for the titillation of the lower orders. In the 1870s and 1880s there was a leap in advertising in newspapers and magazines which coincided with a real increase in disposable income among most groups of society. The advertising which fuelled the New Journalism as it expanded into newer readerships also drove the magazine market and Curran claims (Curran and Seaton, 1993: 43) that between 1866 and 1896 numbers leapt from 557 to 2,097, all aimed at specific groups which could be delivered to advertising in terms of their trade, profession or hobby. Magazines targeted at specific areas of society become more prevalent. The *Field* in 1853 was the first hobby magazine and the trend for magazines for specific interest groups flowed from the upper middle classes downwards as consumer trends and affluence enabled mass markets for hobbies to develop. The *Shooting Times* and *Country Magazine* both make their first appearance in 1882, followed by publications such as *Amateur Gardening* and *Horse and Hound* in 1884, *Yachting World* in 1894 and the first British motoring magazine *Autocar and Motor* in 1895. They were made more attractive by the illustrations which were on better paper and took advantage of improved techniques of photo-reproduction. These improvements would begin to force newspapers to increasingly look to their visual content as consumers of journalism became attuned to a wider range of visual sophistication.

With the expansion of advertising, popular magazines tested markets for journalism lower down the social and financial scale and soon began mapping the interests of that market. From the 1880s the market for periodicals was divided very much along what were perceived to be class lines: the penny weekly, the sixpenny monthly, the illustrated social weekly and the penny women's weekly, and each of the major players, Newnes, Harmsworth and Pearson had their own variant in each field. The new generalist magazines which prospered dealt with the domestic issues and consumer news which had been traditionally left to specialist women's magazines. *Tit-Bits* was the herald of the 'new weeklies' of the 1880s. Sold as a penny weekly, it illustrated perfectly how information could be sold as entertainment. It contained no illustrations but plenty of competitions, prizes, jokes on the front page and a considerable amount of news of public affairs, but from a random selection of sources and in no particular order: 'It will be a production of all that is most interesting in the books, periodicals, and newspapers of this and other countries' (Vol. 1, No. 1, 22 October 1881). It quickly spawned rivals in *Pearson's Weekly* and Harmsworth's *Answers to Correspondents*. Of the three rivals, *Answers* was the most developed in terms of its journalism with eye-witness accounts, reports on contemporary events from first-hand, exposés and aspects of criminal news all tackled with a vitality and originality lacking in the other two. It was a world presented in all its fragmentary and lively disorder and was a huge commercial success which galvanized the beginnings of the commercial concentration which became the New Journalism in the daily press. Another of Newnes's successful experiments in periodical form was the *Strand Magazine* from 1891 which was the most successful combination of entertainment and informed debate for a varied and mostly male readership and provided an excellent platform for a wide range of advertising. It was a widely imitated response to American imports at the end of the nineteenth century such as *Harper's Century* and *Atlantic Monthly*. It was handsomely illustrated and aimed at a family readership.

As well as general magazines aimed at a consensual political middle ground, there was one periodical which demonstrated that magazines which targeted a readership in terms of right-wing political commitment could still be commercially successful. *John Bull* by Horatio Bottomley, which was started in 1910, became the first periodical million seller by the middle of the first World War. It was almost entirely devoid of illustration. It was a penny weekly full of patriotism, anti-authoritarian concern over injustice towards the lower ranks of the armed forces, public affairs, social issues, editorial pages, horse racing, very little fiction and much written by Bottomley himself. Because of its popularity and great circulation it was very successful with advertisers.

Bernarr Macfadden brought his *True Story* (1919) and *True Detective* (1924) to Britain from the United States which developed in magazine form the tradition of crime news which had been so firmly embedded in the popular press in Britain for some time. Such was the spread of the market for periodicals in the 1920s a critic could complain of, 'The bewildering heterogeneity of periodical enterprises has now become almost appalling. Every business, industry, sport, trade, profession, artistic leaning, intellectual interest, ethical tendency or religious faith, has its magazines and journals' (Graham, 1930: 391).

There were still attempts to provide magazine journalism with a more traditional social conscience as with *Picture Post* from 1938. This provided information with extensive editorial and was not simply illustration devoid of journalistic context. It was a great propagandist on behalf of social and economic justice in its heyday of 1940 to 1950. *Tit-Bits*, *Pearsons* and *Answers* all powered on into the 1930s supported by the innovations within photographic reproduction and extended this as a competitive influence on the daily newspaper which itself had to become increasingly adept at including pictures into its layout. They included competitions and prizes as with the daily popular press of the time and provided a more domestic focus to appeal to women readers. They were also not without a deal of concern in their coverage of one of the great social and political issues of the day – unemployment. But the advent of television and the consequent readjustments within daily newspapers, for instance the launch of the *Sunday Times* magazine as the first colour magazine distributed with a broadsheet newspaper in Britain, meant that periodical journalism began to concentrate more on what was commercially appealing and on its readers as consumers rather than as political or social actors. The 1960s marked the decline of generalist magazines and the start of a narrowcasting in magazines which sought out particular niche markets and focused more intensively on them. Magazines emerged which targeted hobbies and lifestyles and special interest groups as never before and this trend was accelerated by the growing affluence of the readers and the emergence of an identifiable youth culture. Part of that same social configuration was the declining deference towards authority within British society which nurtured the development of one of the most significant reinventions of tradition of the time, the satirical review in printed form, *Private Eye* of 1961. The entertainment and culture guide *Time Out*, from 1968, provided an example of how anti-establishment political perspectives could be grafted, not unproblematically, onto London's entertainment culture. This was an experiment which was pushed further by the breakaway, co-operative version of the magazine, *City Limits* from 1981. Both of these trends, satirical political commentary and contemporary cultural review, were increasingly adopted by the wider newspaper press.

The contemporary trend within periodical publication is for a range of narrowcast magazines which target very specific readerships whether they are based on lifestyle, hobby or gender. Readers are encouraged more and more to see themselves and their self-fulfilment as being channelled through identity and individual activity. The same trend which has seen the expansion of this market has had, as always with magazine developments, a crossover effect on the content of newspapers, and all forms of broadcast journalism. They are all seeking their own specific ways to combat this fragmentation of media markets by providing a diversity of content and appeal to a breadth of readership and, in doing so, they are all taking on aspects of magazine culture. As magazines become more specialized, news formats become more formalized and general.

The ability of magazines to influence the mainstream of journalism within daily newspapers has been evident even in this newly narrowcast market. *The Face* from 1980, the self-proclaimed 'style bible', was hugely influential not only on the magazine market for young and affluent readers but also on the broadsheet newspapers as they sought to develop a model for magazine supplements in the 1990s which could guarantee an appeal to a readership younger than the traditional profiles of the serious press. In its combination of youth culture and serious political journalism on related issues, it single-handedly launched the lifestyle magazine boom of the 1980s.

Men's Magazines

The most interesting extension of such narrowcasting has been to develop the niche magazine for men as a general audience with all the paradoxes that this implies. Most men's magazines before the 1990s in Britain had been reserved for specific hobbies or DIY. The magazine market for hobbies and specialist interests for men had expanded in the twentieth century as growing affluence permitted men to indulge hobbies which had become commodified for the first time. Titles launched in the aftermath of the Second World War are characteristic of a growing affluence among male niche markets and their attractiveness for advertisers, for example, *Practical Houseworker* (1955), *Practical Photography* (1959) and *World Soccer* (1960). However, specialist magazines aimed at men, as men, are a relatively recent phenomenon, particularly in the UK. One of the reasons why magazines for men, in general, were latecomers to the media market was that to all intents and purposes the newspaper, with its sports pages, business and political news was a medium aimed at men for general interest. There was simply not the cultural space available for the development of a parallel to the woman's magazine. The new generation was launched with *Arena* in 1986 but by the mid-1990s *FHM* (1994), *Loaded* (1994), and *Maxim* (1995) were the market leaders. They were influenced as much by the market-orientated lifestyle journalism of the 1990s as by the gonzo journalism of the likes of Hunter S. Thompson and the continuing trend of irony in contemporary journalism. They have been interpreted as providing a reaction to feminism, a bastion of newly acceptable sexism or part of an increasing crisis in masculinity (Jackson et al., 2001). *FHM*'s peak was 775,000 in 1999 and is now down to 570,000 (2002).

The magazines continue in their proliferation and energy to form a very important contribution to contemporary journalism as print media become increasingly cross-pollinated. As broadcasting technology intensifies the flow of journalism, newspapers have moved to more magazine-style features, such as consumer supplements or lifestyle commentary and even political commentary on contemporary affairs, which would previously have all been found predominantly in magazines or periodicals. Newspapers become more general, general magazines become more fragmented into different and more specialized markets.

Magazines, in all their variety, produce a range of social and cultural knowledge which is not specifically, but implicitly political. They demonstrate in their commodification the social aspirations of their readerships in terms of identity politics, not in terms of broader party politics. Magazines have been heralds of social and cultural change in contrast to the way that newspapers at their very best have been the main prompts for political change. They continue to act as contributors to a public sphere and in ways that are sometimes similar to the early eighteenth-century writing of Steele and Addison as they sought to educate their target readerships into tastes and views which were appropriate to the times. Now, as then, magazines are reluctant to engage with politics of a narrow sort and leave this by and large to newspapers. However, as then, they continue to be politically very significant in terms of their journalism. This is not because they contribute to a bourgeois public sphere through what Eagleton has called the 'occlusion' of property, but rather that for an intensely commodified contemporary society they appear to be inducting consumers of a post-bourgeois public sphere in ways that foreground property and commodity as the most important contributors to the politics of lifestyle. Narrowcasting within periodical journalism has led to a post-bourgeois public sphere of commodity display. This kind of journalism has moved the focus of the public sphere from a broad and even depersonalized concentration on political communication to a narrower integration of cultural and economic experiences among specialized sections of consumer society. It is the periodical/magazine which performs this task, particularly in the close association between the idealized reader, lifestyle and periodical identity which brings a set of micro-identifications in terms of niche markets, rather than macro-identifications based on general social issues. This sort of journalism has a powerful normative influence in reinforcing the individual consumer within a fragmented social world as the dominant political actor of the post-bourgeois public sphere.

9

From New Journalism to the Web

Commerce Becomes the Dominant Voice

Newspaper journalism moves in a complex and sometimes surprising fashion, from its liberalization after the lifting of taxes from 1855 to the twenty-first century, but certain patterns have persisted. The economics of the market have combined with technology to produce significant changes in its organization, distribution and content. Yet this is no straightforward narrative of either triumph or decline as these changes set profound challenges for print journalism in the twenty-first century. The continuity across this era has been remarked upon by Negrine who has observed how in the writing of the great historian of political journalism, Koss, there are concerns in the Victorian era about issues which have a very contemporary ring to them: 'the commercialism of the press, the effect of advertising, the trend to sensationalism, concentration of ownership, and the reduction of political coverage' (Negrine, 1994: 39).

While some characterize the changes which followed 1855 as a decline from a golden age of journalism, others argue that the discourse of public dialogue from that point was replaced with a commodified and commercialized discourse within journalism (Chalaby, 1998: 66) which was targeted at the public only insofar as the public constituted a market which could be exploited commercially. There are even dissident voices which invert the conventional trajectories and claim provocatively that journalism experienced a rejuvenation in this period: 'in the early sixties ... Journalism was at a turning point. A poor order of things was passing away; a better order of things ... by the attraction of many fresh, bright, strong, and scholarly minds to journalism as a power – was coming in, and coming in on well prepared ground' (Greenwood, 1897: 708).

Driven by an improved climate for commercial newspapers after 1855, the penny press of the middle Victorian era was beginning to experiment with a lighter style and more human interest, perhaps best characterized by the 'Telegraphese' of George Augustus Sala and the influential gossip column 'The Flaneur' by Edmund Yates, in Samuel Lucas's penny *Morning Star*, founded in 1856 (Wiener, 1988: 61). At the same time the respectable, upmarket papers such as the *Times* and the *Morning Post* maintained a sober and anonymous gravitas in their journalism bringing 'a heavy overdose of politics' (Herd, 1952: 222) with verbatim accounts of Parliament and politics, composed in blocks of solid and unbroken type without the sort of banner headlines with which we are familiar today. The tradition of authorial anonymity in journalism was being eroded by the magazine and by the 1870s correspondence columns, signed articles and personal detail were being used at the cheaper end of the newspaper market as well. This had the effect of substituting an apparent pluralism of many authors and spokes-people in place of the single authority and voice of the newspaper which had been the implicit norm in Victorian journalism up to this point (Jackson, 2001: 145).

Transatlantic cable was laid in 1866 and telegraphed dispatches became an accepted part of a more internationalized news-gathering operation meaning that: 'henceforth daily journalism operated within a new tense ... of the instantaneous present' (Smith, 1978: 167). In fact, it was the increas-ingly efficient exploitation of the telegraph in combination with the new cat-egory of the sub-editor that signalled the only substantive improvement of these years in the extinction of the old 'penny-a-liner', 'a very inferior race of reporters' (Lee, 1976: 112). By the 1880s a combination of stylistic experi-ments, technological innovations, political advances and economic condi-tions were to transform the ambition and content of journalism and orientate it irrevocably to mass audiences via the New Journalism. The introduction of the telegraph, the telephone, the typewriter, the high-speed rotary press and the half-tone photographic block began to transform the look of printed material as journalism became a more visualized practice. After 1875 there was a reconstruction of the newspaper industry on a more economically coordinated pattern, which enabled a more integrated capital investment in technology, circulation, and advertising. The technological advances which promised a more attractive and profitable product for a wider audience attracted more commercial entrepreneurs into an industry which offered increasing returns on their investment through wider distribution and a more astute harnessing of advertising. Above all else, it was the broadening of the franchise through the Third Reform Act in 1884 which meant that this New Journalism was able to address the people as having a stake in public affairs like never before: 'the New Journalism acquired a political resonance which had been largely lacking in press discourse during the previous 50 years' (Jones, 1996: 132).

The Innovators: Newnes and Stead

The first of the pioneers to draw together these strands preceded the term 'New Journalism' but it was George Newnes who drew on American styles and adapted them to a British market, testing and creating new boundaries for English journalism in a wide range of journals such as *Tit-Bits* (1881), *The Strand Magazine* (1891), *The Million* (1892), *The Westminster Gazette* (1893), *The World Wide Magazine* (1898), *The Ladies' Field* (1898) and *The Captain* (1899).

Tit-Bits from all the interesting Books, Periodicals, and Newspapers of the World was launched as a penny weekly on 22 October 1881 with competitions, statistics, history, bits of news, editorials, correspondence columns, fiction, anecdotes, jokes, legal and general knowledge and adverts. Celebrity portraits and interviews were also a prominent inclusion in each edition. It was a triumph of promotion, formatting and editorial flair and soon boasted 400,000 to 600,000 weekly sales, leading Jackson to claim that: 'far from lowering the standards of popular journalism, it [*Tit-Bits*] undoubtedly raised them' (2001: 55). It was widely imitated because of its success, most notably by *Answers* and *Pearson's Weekly* which were aimed at the same market and, in securing similar sales figures, demonstrated the potential market for this type of journal. Most importantly, Newnes developed a popular community within his paper through a 'sympathetic intimacy' (Jackson, 2001: 13) with his readers which anticipates much of popular journalism's subsequent appeal. He even found ways of extending that projection of community into other areas of his readers' lives and embarked upon an astute commercial branding of his product that went beyond simply selling papers. In May 1885 he launched its life insurance scheme for anyone found dead in a railway accident with a copy of the paper on them and in 1889 at the Paris Exhibition he set up a pavilion and inquiry office as an extension of the textual space of his paper. There have also been those less appreciative of Newnes' achievements:

> Newnes became aware that the new schooling was creating a class of potential readers – people who had been taught to decipher print without learning much else, and for whom the existing newspapers, with their long articles, long paragraphs, and all-round demands on the intelligence and imagination, were quite unsuited. To give them what he felt they wanted, he started *Tit-Bits*. (Ensor, 1968: 311)

The potential of the New Journalism was to be further explored and the term itself coined in response to the work of W.T. Stead on the *Pall Mall Gazette*. The genius of the *Pall Mall Gazette*, launched in 1865 by Greenwood, was to bring the scope and variety of the periodical reviews into daily journalism. It has been observed that: 'Greenwood brought lightness, polish and intellectual alertness into daily journalism at a time when the morning papers had become heavy and tradition-bound' (Herd, 1952: 226). It was an 8-page, large folio, 2d evening paper which contained politics and arts coverage plus controversy and articles on social questions of the hour.

As economic forces were taking a determining role in the development of journalism, it was no coincidence that the New Journalism became crystallized in the practices of the evening London papers whose search for new readers drove the innovations in journalism which were to lead to the New

Journalism of the 1880s. This competition intensified as cheaper evening newspapers such as the *Pall Mall Gazette* and the *St James' Gazette* reduced their prices from twopence to a penny in 1882 and it was in these papers, most notably the *Pall Mall Gazette*, that the newer styles of journalism were introduced as a further commercial ploy to distinguish them from their more sedate morning relations.

The driving force behind a journalism which sought social commitment through wider readership and influence was the non-conformist and politically radical W.T. Stead. Even in 1880, writing on the Liberal political programme, he had stressed both the 'political education' of the electorate and the 'prophetic character of the journalists' vocation' (Baylen, 1979: 373), and in this he demonstrated a link to the women's prophetic tradition within the print culture of the seventeenth century (see MacDowell, 1998). He was a pioneer of investigative journalism pursued for moral ends and saw the journalist as 'the uncrowned king of an educated democracy'. For him journalism should aim to change the world. Some commentators have located him within a longer tradition of radical journalism: 'Stead's mercurial, hell-fire temperament was that of the great pamphleteers. In his boldness and versatility, in his passionate belief in the constructive power of the pen, in so many of his opinions, even in his championship of women, he resembled Daniel Defoe and Jonathan Swift' (Boston, 1990: 101).

He was editor of the *Pall Mall Gazette* from 1883 to 1889 and brought to the paper cross-headings, illustrations, popular developments such as scoops, a flair for self-publicity which drew attention to his newspaper, the development of investigative, campaigning journalism in the pursuit of socially progressive causes, and the use of emotive and colourful writing. The cross-head was a development which he copied from American newspaper practice. In contrast to the dense columns of the morning newspapers, the *Pall Mall Gazette* could be scanned at speed. He included illustrations and line drawings which further broke the monotony of the traditional printed page. He employed specialist commentators to popularize knowledge of contemporary affairs and in his 'Character Sketch' he blended the interview, word picture, and personality analysis. The implications of these changes were clear, making 'the page accessible to less resolute reading at the end of the day and possibly by the family at home' (Brake, 1988: 19).

The development of the interview was again an American import but Stead deployed it with aplomb in broadening the popular reach of his journalism. One major coup was his interview with General Gordon in January 1884 before he embarked for the Sudan. As if to underline the growing importance of women in this era of journalism, Stead's chief interviewer was Hulda Friedrichs. From 15 September 1884 he started a campaign entitled 'The Truth About the Navy', during which he exploited all of the techniques of the New Journalism to publicize inadequacies in naval provision and to agitate for the modernization of the British Navy. This was clearly preparatory for his most famous exposé, the 'Maiden Tribute of Modern Babylon' story of 6 July 1885. This synthesized all the ambition of Stead's journalism and campaigning fervour. He had discovered that the government were about to reject the Criminal Law Amendment Bill and that therefore the age of sexual consent would not be raised. To highlight the problems of prostitution among young girls he bought a girl, Liza Armstrong, for £5 to demonstrate how widespread this practice had become and used sensational reporting, eye-witness accounts and interviews to launch his campaign to have the Bill approved and shame Victorian London. It was a sensation, boosting sales to 100,000, although he was eventually imprisoned for three months for procuring the girl but not before he had conducted a nationwide defence of his position and drawn support for his cause from all sections of society. Beyond the technical and organizational details of what was shortly to be christened the New Journalism, Stead's goal was more a moral and political one. His passionate opposition to the wrongs of society was in keeping with much of the tradition of the 'old corruption' but grafted onto a moral purpose and a well-developed commercial pragmatism. He was a forerunner of a journalism of attachment from a deeply religious perspective. Yet there are those who are more cautious about his sensationalizing of sexual mores and its implications for journalism: '"Sex" had long been a journalistic staple. Stead not only brought it into a "respectable" middle-class paper. He made it central to journalism as political intervention' (Beetham, 1996: 125).

In a journal article in 1887 Arnold called the new phenomenon which was becoming such a prominent issue in public debate, the 'new journalism': 'We have had opportunities of observing a new journalism which a clever and energetic man has lately invented. It has much to recommend it; it is full of ability, novelty, variety, sensation, sympathy, generous instincts; its one great fault is that it is feather-brained' (Arnold, 1887: 638–9).

The success of Stead's paper generated a proliferation of penny newspapers in London, all attempting to exploit the market for the sort of journalism he had provided and their success undermined the circulation of the *Pall Mall Gazette*. It suffered a further blow when much of his revenue was lost because advertisers were not keen to be associated with the scandalous reputation it had acquired. His importance for journalism goes beyond the technical details of the changes and the moral mission which informed his work. The New Journalism's 'government by journalism' meant that the civic responsibilities of the journalist, and increasingly the editor, were forced to the forefront of the agenda. Stead was particularly prominent in this through his imprisonment and his national campaigning to get the issues raised by the 'Maiden Tribute' story aired in public meetings up and down the country and by bringing well-known figures to contribute to the debate he had started. The editor, in the most melodramatic way, had become the news. C.P. Scott, J.L. Garvin, H.W. Massingham and A.G. Gardiner continued this trend as editors became public figures of note. Such men viewed:

> their function essentially as a political one, with newspapers as a means
> of exercising political influence and power. And influence and power were

achieved, not by their newspapers acting as a check or restraint on politicians, but, on the contrary, by their papers gaining for them access to the political élite whose decisions they intended to shape. Journalists like this aspired to be part of the political system: more – they were part of it. (Boyce, 1978: 29)

The Continuing Discursive Formation

The New Journalism, by the time the term was coined retrospectively by Arnold, was a new combination of already existing features but made more commercially attractive for a wider readership. In vehement opposition to the crusading conviction of Stead, Arnold believed that Stead's New Journalism was the very antithesis of a medium which stimulated and elevated the masses (Baylen, 1979: 367). In the way that the moment of its definition provided a fresh impetus to the self-rationalization and critique of journalism, it could be argued that the New Journalism was predominantly a discursive moment in the history of journalism. The clearest expression of its motivations came from Stead himself, championing his own cause spectacularly from prison and claiming the function of government by journalism. 'Anybody paying a penny could cast a "vote" for a particular paper' (Stead, 1886: 655). Some saw the New Journalism as the natural extension of the traditions of the Fourth Estate: '... the newspaper press is the only strong means of keeping in check that prodigious evil, the decomposition of political probity ... its natural position of complete independency' (Greenwood, 1890: 118).

The debate extended throughout the clubs and societies of London and has been recorded in the reflective journals of the time. Much of it subjected the language of the new journals to ridicule: 'Garniston. What, Warnford! corrupting your style by studying a newspaper?' (Traill, 1884: 436). Even Greenwood was moved to comment on the language of the newer variant of journalism as it approached the new century: 'But of the general mass of journalism it would have to be said that it has dropped into a looseness of speech that does not improve anything and must even diminish the writer's own sense of self-respect ... it lowers the importance of whatever it is employed upon – brings it down' (Greenwood, 1897: 718).

Much of the concern encapsulated in Arnold's article represented a middle-class moral panic that this sort of populist writing would incite the newly extended electorate and it continued to reverberate into the new century. Adams claimed a shift in emphasis in the newspapers had meant that 'Instead of being the instructors of the people, many of our newspapers have become mere ministers to the passions of the people' (1903: 584).

Perkin has commented on the New Journalism: 'A knack of clever writing, great enterprise in bringing together the kind of information which amuses or interests the public, tact in catching and following the first symptoms of changes of opinion, a skilful pandering to popular prejudice' (1991: 51). Critics of the *Times* earlier in the nineteenth century might have recognized the editorial pragmatism even in this new commercialized format.

The Widening Scope of the New Journalism

Stead was the champion of what Wiener sees as the Americanization of the British press between 1830 and 1914 (Wiener, 1996: 61). Gossip, display advertising, sports news, human interest, fast stories transmitted by tele-graph, cheap and increasingly visual newspapers, summary leads and front page news were all introduced in England in the 1890s. Many cheaper weekly publications had introduced some of these features from the 1840s in England but Stead had brought them to a daily readership. Stead, as well as being an innovator associated with the New Journalism, was an exception within the growing trend of the commercialized discourse of journalism as it widened its scope to broader and more profitable markets to the exclusion of social aims. The polarities within popular journalism are well captured in a communication from one style of editor to another when Newnes wrote to Stead in 1890 on their parting as collaborators on the *Review of Reviews*:

> There is one kind of journalism which directs the affairs of nations; it makes and unmakes cabinets; it upsets governments, builds up Navies and does many other great things. It is magnificent. This is your journal-ism. There is another kind of journalism which has no such great ambi-tions. It is content to plod on, year after year, giving wholesome and harmless entertainment to crowds of hardworking people, craving for a little fun and amusement. It is quite humble and unpretentious. This is my journalism. (Friederichs, 1911: 116–17)

Stead had been the journalistic conduit between these two extremes but was redundant once he had served his purpose. Passion had been ousted by the more pragmatic requirements of a commercialized industry. The dividing point at which he stood is well captured in the following:

> The duty of journalism in the first half of the nineteenth century ... was not to discover the truth. The emphasis was on the polemical power of the writer's pen. Opinion and commentary were the essence of good journalism – except in the recording of parliamentary activity where accuracy was con-sidered vital ... By the end of the century technology and commercial need had elevated accuracy and reliability, as well as the ability to meet the daily news deadlines, to the heart of [the] profession of journalism. (Williams, 1998: 54–5)

It was this tension between the altruistic and populist ambitions of journal-ism which was to shape the continuity of discourses around journalism to the present day. What had started as a consolidation of journalistic trends was developed by the daily press in the form of the *Star* and others and by the end of the 1880s, Stead's 'New Journalism' was being rendered obsolete. His missionary zeal was not in keeping with the more commercially successful miscellanies of his rivals. The business acumen of Newnes, Harmsworth and Pearson allowed them to generate huge financial resources from a broad-based magazine and periodical publishing which they then deployed in the development of daily newspapers which integrated technological and stylistic innovation with the staples of popular print culture in order to make a widely popular daily possible. Competition meant that success in the popular market began to converge around one commercialized and dominant form of newspaper.

The *Star* developed this trend. Edited by T.P. O'Connor from 1888 to 1890, it was a halfpenny evening paper which was radical in both its politics and its layout and a continuation of the accelerating trends of the New Journalism but more commercially acceptable. O'Connor espoused a brighter method of writing, speed and human interest and his political aim was to demonstrate that 'the journal is a weapon in the conflict of ideas'. He was also aware of the need for journalism to gain attention from the reader in an accelerating world:

> We live in an age of hurry and of multitudinous newspapers ... To get your ideas across through the hurried eyes into the whirling brains that are employed in the reading of a newspaper there must be no mistake about your meaning: to use a somewhat familiar phrase, you must strike your reader right between the eyes. (O'Connor, 1889: 434)

The *Star* was politically radical, with human interest on a daily basis and a fresh layout, breaking information up much in the style of the *Answers* and *Tit-Bits* but with a different, news-orientated content which distinguished it from these papers. It introduced the Stop Press and lower case type for its crossheads and lesser headlines. Its essential novelty, according to Williams, was that the 'New Journalism' began to look like what it was (1961: 221).

The style of the New Journalism encapsulated the changing relationship between reader and newspaper. There was more sport, crime, entertainment and less politics, all in a livelier style with more emphasis on human interest and laid out more clearly in an attempt to be more broadly accessible and therefore more profitable. There was also a commercial imperative to cultivate a consistent voice within these papers. Familarity bred profit. Salmon interprets the way in which the 'discourse of journalism should so insistently declare its personalized character' (2000: 29), as inevitable at this point in the commercialization of journalism as a simulacrum standing in for its lack of a relationship with its readers, which was in a way as authentic as some of the Radical or Chartist experiments had been, or even of the *Times* at the height of its influence with its mid-Victorian readership. A political irony with implications which continue to resonate within popular journalism today is that as readers were increasingly addressed in a more personal tone about matters which touched the everyday, they were increasingly marginalized from politics in these newspapers (Hampton, 2001: 227). Above all, journalism in the daily press began to accommodate a more complete range of human experience in a form which increasingly allowed a selective reading of it: 'it is the sound principle to which we shall all come at last in literature and journalism, that everything that can be talked about can also be written about' (O'Connor, 1889: 430).

The Next Stage in the Commercialization of Journalism

The *Daily Mail* was launched on 4 May 1896 as THE BUSY MAN'S DAILY JOURNAL and was an immediate commercial success, backed by the fortune Harmsworth had amassed in periodical publication and the appreciation of the importance of the link between advertising, capital investment and circulation. It was presented not as a cheap newspaper but a bargain, well worth the small outlay; 'A Penny Newspaper for One Halfpenny'. It was traditional in that it carried no news on its front page, but advertisements instead. It laid the emphasis on the lighter side of life while remaining respectable in tone. It had a breadth of appeal in its articles, fashion pieces, personalities, and increased background on politicians in the news. Its style was more conversationally based. Above all, however, it had more news than its rivals. In terms of its layout, its headings and subheadings allowed the gist of a piece to be taken in at speed. It contained no long articles as all pieces were broken down into short sections with a great variety of coverage and lots for an idealized woman reader who was hitherto a neglected part of the newspaper audience. The daily women's column soon became a whole page and then ladies were targeted specifically in the Daily Magazine section.

With Northcliffe, 'newspaper ownership had become a crucial element in the development of journalism' (Chalaby, 2000: 29), and whereas the content had always been of central importance, Northcliffe now orientated the appeal of his paper predominantly towards the advertisers through its mass circulation and charged them rates based on each 1,000 copies sold. Northcliffe's genius lay in his ability to harness consumption, circulation and profit, rather than in any journalistic experimentation. 'Whereas the "New Journalism" had been a radical alternative to the more conservative newspapers, Northcliffe created a popular journalism which was less interested in political and social action per se than as the means to increase circulation' (Goodbody, 1985: 23). His *Daily Mail* did not sensationalize and moved to positions it was confident would gain the support of his lower middle-class readership, such as the jingoism of his coverage of the Boer

War. It had reached the first million daily sales by 1900 'partly stimulated by a rabid jingoism that was a common feature of the New Journalism' (Wiener, 1988: 56). Above all, he concentrated on increasing the range and quality of news coverage in all his newspapers. This included overseas, especially imperial news. Wiener identifies 'a seismic shift' (1996: 65) in the broadening definition of news as journalists increasingly go out and find news and gossip to differentiate their newspapers from the dull routine of the news agencies. Harmsworth brought exciting writing about contemporary events. This has always been able to find a readership; his trick was to market it to the maximum. Just as the commercialized radical weeklies such as *Reynolds'* and *Lloyd's* had incorporated descriptions of the lives of the wealthy and famous as both implicit criticism of abuse of social status and prurient fodder for a wide readership, and O'Connor had included this as part of a daily diet of news in the *Star*, Harmsworth included celebrity news too but his was more assimilationist and aspirational in tone, appealing to the upwardly mobile lower middle classes who bought his penny paper for a halfpenny. Harmsworth's approach, hugely successful as it was, had an effect on the shape and content of journalism across the twentieth century, forcing other proprietors to adapt the content of their newspapers to match or improve upon the pattern he had set. Northcliffe was able to demonstrate an anticipation of the condensation of information flow later in the twentieth century when on 1 January 1901, in his experimental edition of Pulitzer's *Daily World*, he showed his appreciation of the commercial appeal of instant news digest when his slogan boasted: 'All the news in sixty seconds'.

On 26 April 1900 the *Daily Express* was launched to rival the *Daily Mail* and to exploit the new market for popular daily journalism which Harmsworth had opened. It innovated itself with news on the first page from 1901. Both Harmsworth and Pearson, the owner of the *Daily Express*, had developed an appreciation of the reading tastes of the public and to a large extent fashioned it by their successful experimentation in the mass-periodical market of the 1880s and 1890s. The popular dailies were successful in that they were able to integrate the tone and content of the magazines into their own pages, while maintaining a distinctiveness from the magazines themselves in their news coverage and political columns. The changes in typography, make-up and content made newspapers more attractive to both readers and advertisers throughout the period 1880 to 1914 and quadrupled the number of purchasers of daily newspapers (Wiener, 1988: 56). This was the culmination of steady growth over a longer period of time (1856 to 1914), since the abolition of taxation on papers, during which the numbers of newspapers in the UK and Ireland had increased from 274 to 2,205 and in London from 151 to 478 (Lee, 1976: 80).

Some commentators such as Q.D. Leavis, in *Fiction and the Reading Public* (1932) have argued that the popularization of a mass journalism had a negative cultural effect. She claimed that the papers of Newnes, Harmsworth and Pearson created a cultural division that had not existed before. There had certainly been no evidence of mass lower-class readerships in the fare of the newspapers before them but this readership had remained marginalized within a lower public sphere of alternative print media. All the New Journalism achieved was to make this reading public more tangible and, in commercially targeting the lower classes for the first time in daily newspaper form, it indicated the growing reality of the economic attractiveness of the lower classes as both a mass readership and a mass market for advertising. Certainly it brought a further de-politicization of the working person's journalism as it sought out beneficial advertising connections unlikely to be associated with any form of radicalism. The cost of starting a newspaper in London had by this point made the launch of anything resembling a popular radical paper impossible without considerable financial and advertising support. The cost of bringing out a new paper has been estimated as increasing from £25,000 in 1850, to £100,000 in 1870, and to £500,000 by 1900 (Lee, 1976: 76–103). This long-term trend was also less than fully appreciated with Escott complaining that, 'journalism has sunk, or is at least in danger of sinking, from a liberal professional to a branch of business' (1917: 368).

The political and generic implications of mass journalism have been well articulated by Tulloch:

> To assemble mass readerships, the new press had to adopt the formula of the popular Sunday press and the burgeoning magazines. Mass readerships are essentially a coalition of different tastes, interests and political positions. Newspapers had to be created that had 'something for everyone'. The process pushed newpapers towards a consensus politics that aimed to maximize the audience. (2000: 142)

Changes ushered in by the New Journalism began to make their presence felt across the whole field of journalism. The version of headlines which Stead had introduced from American journalism in the *Pall Mall Gazette* from 1881 had become integrated into the layout of the *Times* by 1887, along with extensive use of sub-headings, and soon this integration of many of the features which had begun with Newnes and Stead had become the subject of commentary across the press such as in this example from *The Queen* of 1900:

> This is an inquisitive age: all daily papers from the august *Times* downwards have now their daily column of personal news, and few are the magazines which do not publish monthly some report of an interview with this or that celebrity. So keen is the general thirst for information touching the private life of every individual. The telegraph wire and the penny post, the periodical press and the special reporter have, during the last half-century provided the curious with new and extraordinary means of gratifying their relish for personal detail. (White, 1970: 78)

The language of this journalism was as important a site for the changes within journalism as its visual appeal and organizational practices. Matheson has identified one of the most important shifts of the era in the way a totally new and modern version of journalistic discourse came into being and was shared to a large extent across the range from quality to popular newspaper. This involved much more editorial intervention to make copy fit the format and style of the paper and saw the development of house styles. The role of the sub-editor was pivotal in the creation of this new discourse in fitting the copy into a format which allowed a newspaper to be read on the move and tailoring it to fit the space available within the pictorial and advertising space (Matheson, 2000: 565). Smith also considers the language of this period's journalism as having undergone a fundamental change. The 'story' became the basic molecular element of journalistic reality and the distinctions of categories of news into hard and soft became reconfigured as part of its discourse (Smith, 1978: 168). By 1900 daily journalism had become an area of increasing specialization and professionalization with sub-editors and managers of departments plus an increasing role for the political ambitions of powerful owners. Some journalists, particularly on large national newspapers, were becoming well paid, increasing the status if not the reputation of journalism. The journalism of this period enabled a textual inscribing of many of the major characteristics of this era into a radically restructured journalism: 'The entrepreneurial component of editing and publishing, the professionalization of journalists and journalism, and the transition from the wealthy, educated, leisured reader to the working, literate reader of the middle classes are inscribed in the changing cultural formations of the periodical and newspaper press throughout the period' (Brake, 1988: 10).

Along with these changes in its discourse, there was an increasing professionalization of journalism caused by the increasing specificity of many of its activities. This was signalled by the formation of bodies associated with a profession. In 1879 the first School of Journalism was opened in Crewe. The National Association of Journalists was set up by owners of newspapers in 1886 and in 1890 it became the Institute of Journalists by charter. In 1895 a Society of Women Journalists was formed and in 1907 the National Union of Journalists was created.

The Intensification of Press Competition

By the twentieth century, journalism had become identifiably big business. The leading proprietors, referred to as 'press barons', notably Northcliffe, Beaverbrook and Rothmere, presided over a period which continued the trends towards concentration, competition and entertainment in print media. Curran argues that instead of personifying a radical interlude in the history of print journalism they, in fact, continued to develop the medium in precisely the same ways as had preceded it and were to follow it (Curran and Seaton, 1993). He observes though that one function of representing them as a breakdown in normal service is that this allows a golden age to precede and a liberalized era of professionalized independence to follow. All the press barons attempted to use their publishing power to propagandize to large readerships and assumed an absolute measure of power over the opinions of both ordinary readers and leading politicians, but Boyce concludes that this was a major reason for their ultimate failure to achieve lasting influence: 'Northcliffe failed in his supreme ambition because he sought to mould rather than exploit, the world of high politics' (1987: 103). This confirmed the discursive logic of the processes at work within journalism since 1855 that journalism was less the predominantly political activity of previous generations and increasingly a commercial proposition at heart, a consummation of the process Lee summarizes as one in which 'economic forces would gradually dominate political ones' (1978, 117). This did not prevent Rothmere and Beaverbrook from attempting to reinforce their political ambitions through their business. A late example of their intervention was the Empire Crusade of the early 1930s which pitched the *Express* and the *Mail* against the Conservative government of Stanley Baldwin. Such aggressive attempts at political intervention by proprietors in the pages of their newspapers was one of the decisive factors in the government decision in the 1920s to set up the BBC according to the character delineated by Reith, as a public service without a hectoring proprietor or the commercial demands of advertisers.

In addition to technology and style, the understanding of the place of advertising was becoming a more precise and sophisticated activity within journalism. Attempts to make circulation calculations and readership profiles more accurate led to the foundation from 1931 of the Audit Bureau of Circulation which was the end product of the growth of the American import of market research in the 1920s.

Even with the success of the *Daily Mail*, daily journalism had only just begun to appreciate its social and commercial potential. It was merely the start of a trend towards massification in newspaper and other news media formats, and with it a consequent movement to consolidate the popularity of journalism among the lower classes. This had two driving imperatives. First, there was a need for an extended electorate to be politically informed in a broadening democracy and, second, a need for an increasingly expensive journalism industry to be run as profitably and efficiently as possible. To ensure the second, newspapers increasingly used more entertaining features to lighten the diet of politics. As this eventually involved both broadsheets and popular newspapers, it saw a certain convergence of what for many years had been located in different areas of journalism practice. Therefore the history of twentieth-century newspaper journalism is the process of popularization and the attendant resistance of the quality press to retain an element of specialized commentary and in-depth coverage.

The circulation wars triggered in the popular market in the 1920s and 1930s saw 30 newspapers close between 1921 and 1936, although the total sales of newspapers doubled (Curran and Seaton, 1993). This competition led, among other things, to a concentration of the market and a narrowing of political range. Sensationalism, special offers, campaigns, layout and aspects of writing style of the 1930s all contributed to the further development of the dynamics of New Journalism which continued to define the pattern of popular journalism. Free insurance had been offered before, in daily newspapers from 1914, but the 1930s saw the competition reach new heights with an array of competitions, complete sets of Charles Dickens' works, encyclopaedias and even pianos as enticements to new subscribers. To keep up with this frenetic pace, relaunches became a necessary strategy to revive market interest in particular papers and keep them in the public eye. The *Daily Herald*, launched as a trade union supporting newspaper in 1912, was relaunched in 1930 to rival the *Daily Mail* and *Daily Express* and while remaining the official voice of trade unions, reached a circulation of 2 million before the *Express.*

Yet beyond competition and marketing, it was the incorporation of visual elements into popular journalism which determined the most significant changes of the period. On 7 August 1933 Cristiansen on the *Daily Express* produced a cleaner, better spaced newspaper with more and bigger headlines and more crossheads to break up the page. It was followed by all its rivals including the relaunched *Daily Mirror* which from 1934, under the editorial direction of Bartholomew, triggered the tabloid revolution with its signature heavy black bold type for its headlines, pin-ups, young style, simplified language and a prominent use of pictures to reach a new readership. It redrew the map of popular journalism in print by integrating all the visual appeal of popular culture and consumerism for the first time. After the war, the *Daily Mirror* soon began to climb to a pinnacle of influence in popular journalism (Engel, 1996), ousting the *Daily Express* with a populist, proletarian and youthful appeal encapsulated in the slogan which ran from 11 May 1945 'Forward with the People'.

Post-war Developments

After paper rationing and the decline in advertising which had hampered the press in the years of the Second World War, newspaper journalism needed to cope with a very changed commercial landscape. It was one which was increasingly affected by the financial damage of the commercial rivalries of the pre-war years and by the rise of radio and television broadcasting as rivals first, to its audience and, from the mid-1950s, its advertisers. The continuing intensification of competition for circulation, advertising and profit was creating a certain sort of journalism with clear political implications. This is what McManus (1994) has criticized as 'market-driven journalism'. It saw newspapers of the left of centre and liberal tradition forced out and an increasing leveling of journalism towards a market-orientated consensus which appealed to the advertisers and economic interests of owners. Consequently, this consensus was very much to the right of the political spectrum. As Curran has explained:

The market was not a mechanism which impartially represented consumer demand, and harmonized editorial and public opinion. On the contrary, it gave added impetus to the right-wing drift of the post-war press in a way that exceeded the rightward shift of public opinion because the market mechanism was itself skewed to the right. (Curran and Seaton, 1993: 106)

These trends were exacerbated in the 1960s by the continuing process of commercial rationalization which saw more newspapers taken into the owner-ship of larger cross-media conglomerations. During this surge of concentra-tion, the Left liberal tradition of the newspaper journalism was further eroded with the loss of the *News Chronicle* in 1960, the *Daily Herald* in 1964 and the *Sunday Citizen* (previously *Reynolds' News*) in 1967.

Under the influence of more intrusive television reporting of politics, the 1960s became the great decade for investigative journalism. The *Sunday Times* Insight Team set the pace along with the 'Shock Issues' of the *Daily Mirror* at the popular end of the market. Broader developments within the regular coverage of politics, however, saw a widening of the gap between popular newspapers and the quality newspapers which were targeted at elite sections of society. The demands of advertisers for specific target groups meant that newspapers increasingly restricted their appeal to particular groups based on income as well as social class. Advertisers in quality news-papers did not want to extend their appeal to a readership which could not afford (or aspire to identify) with their products. This market rationalization has been categorized in these terms: 'what happened in the 20th century was that newspapers came to look upon their potential readers as segments of consumerdom' (Smith, 1979: 147). The example of the investigative work of the *Daily Mirror* notwithstanding, public affairs news in the popular newspapers began a steep decline and in the *Daily Herald/Sun*, for example, public affairs as a proportion of editorial space declined by almost two-thirds in 1976 compared with 30 years earlier (Curran and Seaton, 1993: 116). Popularizing tendencies within journalism which downplay the importance of general newspapers in the provision of contextual political and social material and in-depth debate on issues of public concern, and shift such matters to a specialist or elite readership, have profound impli-cations for the breadth of democratic involvement. The specific attributes of print journalism are not considered expendable by many critics who insist upon its special place even within a multi-media news environment. Some years ago, Bairstow pointed out that it is the written form of journalism which allows for the greatest degree of engagement with the contemporary world:

with its unlimited capacity for comprehensive investigation of a situation and the detailed unravelling of complex issues beyond the scope of the oral bulletin, its unrivalled quality as a forum in which ideas can be exchanged and pros and cons set out and argued ... must be the most important safeguard of the democratic process. (Baistow, 1985, *i*)

One consequence of the restriction of political debate to a narrow range of elite broadsheets and specialized journals is that analytical, contextualized journalism becomes a source accessed only by the political and economic elites who continue to value print media for their analytical information (Dahlgren, 1995: 58–9).

While divergence between broadsheet and popular newspapers characterized their political coverage, a tendency to converge has been in evidence with regard to other parts of their content. In 1962, the *Sunday Times* first colour supplement heralded the start of a process of commercialization within the qualities which sought to broaden their coverage while at the same time enhancing their appeal to advertisers trying to attract readers from higher-income groups. More specialist correspondents grew up on both sorts of newspapers as they sought to redefine the substance of their journalism under pressure from television as the primary provider of news of the moment. Anonymity declined still further as a consequence of these developments: 'Its disappearance fitted an era in which electronic media were taking over the "hot" news role and papers were selling the personal expertise of their staff at interpretation, comment, analysis, more than for traditional hard news' (Seymour-Ure, 1991: 135–6). Newspapers also exploited the new technological environment for their own purposes and developed an interesting co-dependence on television as it provided opportunities for previews and reviews of television programmes and also, particularly but not exclusively, in the tabloids, a host of stories on the stars and storylines of popular television programmes. All newspapers have media correspondents who maintain close links with this fertile territory for entertaining, profitable and easy news sources.

The post-war period witnessed much official concern with various aspects of print journalism and there were three Royal Commissions set up to investigate it. The Royal Commission of 1947–49 explored proprietorial control and press standards. From this came recommendations on the education of journalists which, it was hoped, would raise standards in the profession. In 1961–62 the financial state of the press and concentration of ownership were its chief remits. In 1974–77 the structure and performance of the press were debated as well as the privacy of individuals, balanced against press freedoms, which was to become the most contentious of all issues for print journalism for the rest of the century.

Concern may have been limited at this governmental level to structural and ethical issues but for newspapers themselves, the burning question that remains is of their ultimate survival. Newspaper circulation, under intense competitive pressure, is in a long and downward spiral. There are slightly more readers of quality titles (in 1986, the *Independent*, the first new broadsheet daily for over a hunded years was launched to respond to this) but overall circulations are down. The *Mirror*, which claimed 5 million daily sales in the late 1960s, has now been overtaken by the middle market *Daily Mail*. The latest ABC figures show that the only titles to buck this trend in a noticeable way are the *Daily Star*, 16 per cent up on the year, and to a lesser extent the middle market *Daily Express,* 5 per cent up on the year, (ABC January 2003), although in historical terms this is a minor readjustment of its overall decline. The *Star* concentrates on following an agenda very much based on a young readership which eschews political and foreign reporting and is focused almost exclusively on youth culture, with a strong, television-orientated agenda. In this strategy, it exemplifies an extreme of how popular newspapers have adapted to survive in an intensely competitive environment.

Tabloidization

The most sustained and widespread set of debates on contemporary journalism emanate from the tabloid newspaper. The label of tabloidization is given to the trend which has seen what critics perceive to be the chief characteristics of the tabloids transfer, infecting other forms of journalism, both print and broadcast. Despite popular views which consider tabloidization to be the Armageddon of journalism, change and even crisis are intrinsically woven within the narratives of journalism's historical narratives:

> In the course of four hundred years the newspaper press has not finally dealt with the issues into which it was born. Its methods of production and distribution are always inadequate to the ideals and purposes which appear to rise from the activities of collecting news. Every century or so they undergo a major alteration. (Smith, 1979: 183)

We may consider that the list of trends associated with tabloidization constitutes journalism's major contemporary alteration. Tabloidization may refer to an increase in news about celebrities, entertainment, lifestyle features, personal issues, an increase in sensationalism, in the use of pictures and sloganized headlines, vulgar language and a decrease in international news, public affairs news including politics, the reduction in the length of words in a story and the reduction of the complexity of language, and also a convergence with agendas of popular and in particular television culture. Tabloids are characterized as being primarily to do with a combination of format and language: 'editorial matter is presented in emotive language in easy-to-consume formats' (Rooney, 2000: 91). It is clearly, if nothing else, a composite growl-list of elements, some of which have haunted the minds of commentators on journalism over centuries. It is because of this lack of specificity that Sparks (2000) questions whether tabloidization is a useful diagnostic tool at all, but he does concede that the debate itself is an indication of a specifically contemporary set of worries over the nature of journalism across media. Tabloidization may be the extended working out of the process of commercial logic within journalism as it enters its next discursive phase. News media are all trying to keep their market share in the face of increased competition driven by technological innovation and market fragmentation.

It may be the contemporary reformulation of the discourse of journalism as it engages with the politics, commerce and social configuration of a new era (Sparks, 2000: 35–6). It may be the crystallization of longer processes in this contemporary crisis: a different mix of entertainment and information to attract large enough audiences to maintain an essential commercial credibility. This does not mean that it does not have implications both for journalism itself, in the alleged 'decline in standards', for example (Bromley, 1998: 25), or for the political functions of journalism in a democratic system.

Although tabloidization is a problematic label which includes more than just format in its terms of debate (Esser, 1999), the tabloid popular papers have been the pioneers of the trend. The key moments in the tabloiding of British newspapers are defined initially and literally by the reformatting into tabloids of the *Sun* in 1969 and the *Daily Mail* in 1971. The *Sun* is widely acknowledged as having triggered a war of attrition over the dominant popular newspaper paradigm for the late twentieth century. The *Daily Mirror*, already a tabloid in format but identified with a previous era (Smith, 1975), was drawn into a competition for the blue-collar readership on terms dictated by the political and commercial ambition of Rupert Murdoch (Chippendale and Horrie, 1992). The rise of the tabloid as the dominant contemporary format within journalism was forged in the 1970s and the competition between the *Sun* and the *Daily Mirror* for the position of leading articulator of the popular (Conboy, 2002). This shifted popular journalism definitively away from public affairs (Rooney, 2000: 102) and the *Mirror*'s blend of campaigning populism on political causes – the champion of the underdog, notably its 'Shock Issues' looking at, for instance, social class and old age in Britain which had characterized the paper under Cudlipp – became consigned to the past (Engel, 1996). The 1980s saw the *Sun* establish its ascendancy in the market, sexualizing popular culture as a central strategy in its success (Holland, 1998) and other popular papers such as the *Mirror* and the *Star* followed suit, illustrating how this sort of competition always skews the market away from public issue journalism. The era of the *Sun* was presided over by the dominant and defining editor of the era, Kelvin MacKenzie, described by one of his leading journalists as simply a 'brilliant editor' (Littlejohn, 1994: 9–11). His instincts chimed with the aggressive ambition of the owner to deliver not just the dominant newspaper of the age but the dominant journalism paradigm – the one the field had to identify itself against.

In confirming one aspect of the generic transformation involved in tabloidization, Rooney has noted how popular newspapers now resemble 'leisure magazines' (2000: 107) rather than newspapers. This is an ongoing process contributed to by a huge increase in pages in the tabloids as well as the broadsheets with the 1990s' increase in consumer supplements. The success of the tabloid within journalism has divided commentators. Sparks has claimed that the structure of 'the popular' in modern journalism is one which is massively and systematically "depoliticized"' (1992: 38). From a slightly less dogmatic perspective, Connell is as harsh on the critics as on the tabloids themselves. He points out that a major criticism levelled at the tabloids is that they are incapable of presenting alternative sociocultural arrangements but responds by asking what convincing alternatives their critics have been able to present themselves (1992: 83)? His commentary exposes the market orientation of most journalism and its alignment with conservative consensus as it moves to incorporate aspects of the popular.

The 1980s saw the popular press retreat from political journalism towards an increasing dependence on sex, sensation and symbiosis with television's brand of mass popular culture. They were more dependent on circulation than advertising because of the advertisers' assessment of the income of their projected readership and this circulation was boosted by more reliance on celebrity, popular intertextuality with other media and selective and extremely vicious partisan politics. When the popular press chooses to articulate political opinion, it retains the potential for enormous social impact.

Competition among the tabloids in the 1980s drove newspapers to ever more desperate bids to attract readers by sensational and intrusive reporting. Concern about this had by the late 1980s reached such a point that the Calcutt Committee into Privacy and Related Matters was set up as a last attempt to encourage some sort of responsibility from newspapers, short of imposing legislation which would encroach upon the freedom of the press. The Calcutt inquiries of 1989 and 1992 into press ethics and professionalism did not lead to legislation to formally supervise newspapers but replaced the ineffectual Press Council with the Press Complaints Commission which continues to act with the voluntary co-operation of the newspaper industry. Nevertheless, the behaviour of the tabloids in the contemporary world, for instance, in the publication of nude photographs of Radio 1 DJ Sarah Cox, against PCC guidelines, have led to the increasing probability that self-regulation will need to be added to by legislation with all the consequent curtailment of freedom of the press that that would entail to prevent their excesses. Snoddy has indicated the importance of this form of self-regulation working to safeguard the future of newspaper journalism in this country:

> In the end, talking about and encouraging high standards and ethics in newspapers – tabloids as well as broadsheets – is not some sort of self-indulgence for amateur moral philosophers or journalists with sensitive psyches: it is a very practical matter, involving customer relations, product improvement and profit ... Unless such issues are taken more seriously, future generations could be reading about many of today's newspapers in the history books, rather than actually reading the papers themselves. (1992: 203)

The transfer of Murdoch's production to Wapping was a symbolic clustering of the technology, politics and ownership at the heart of much of tabloidization's imperatives and indicated provocatively one of the major shifts within newspaper journalism which has defined many subsequent debates and developments. The aquisition by Rupert Murdoch in 1981 of *The Times* and the *Sunday Times*, to add to his market-leading popular titles, had indicated the increasing conglomeratization of British journalism. One consequence of his determination to dominate the market and secure a safe position for his media investments came in the circulation wars of the 1980s, which were reminiscent of the 1930s in the way that they reshaped newspaper ecology. It may have been Eddie Shah with his *Today*, who first used new technologies including computerized typesetting and colour, in combination with non-union labour, but it was Murdoch whose provocative move to Wapping in 1986 showed the way forward for newspapers if they wished to remain competitive with his operations. Strategically exploiting the favourable political climate of Thatcher's anti-union, pro-free market administration, Murdoch employed new technologies, non-union labour and cutthroat competition to make journalism, as defined in his vision, even bigger business and an important contribution to his considerable political influence on party politics and the electorate. For both broadsheets and tabloids the consequences of Murdoch's move from Fleet Street to Wapping were to further emphasize the business and political imperatives of newspaper production as big business. The Wapping Revolution encouraged owners who had ditched the trade unions associated with the old print workers, to propose individual contracts for journalists, and many news organizations came to depend more and more on freelancers, trends which led to an increasing derecognition of the NUJ. Wapping and the technological revolution were rigged in favour of the wealthy entrepreneurs who already dominated the field. It may have reduced costs for the major players and arrested their dependence on the whims of the printers and the closed shop practices of the NUJ, but it did not significantly extend the political diversity of the press or enrich popular journalism through a growth of new papers aimed at minorities in the mass market (Curran and Seaton, 1993: 123). It might have been heralded as a brave new technological era but it was structured by the old political economy. It reinforced a news media led by commercialized consumer choice rather than one led by an altruistic vision of a contribution within a public sphere which defines the range of journalism. The move to Wapping was a decisive political and technological step in that former direction.

Broadsheet newpapers have also been enmeshed in the clustering of trends characterized as tabloidization. The late twentieth century has seen a further narrowing of ownership and the incorporation of newspapers into more broadly defined media conglomerates which have eroded the boundaries between journalism and media entertainment. In order to survive the intensification of competition, broadsheets have become heavier and have more lifestyle and consumer coverage. They have increased the numbers of specialist supplements and size and quantity of high profile advertisements. An increasing number of their journalists are given the media star treatment with their photograph accompanying their byline and freer rein to write from a more personalized perspective. Tunstall argues that even objectivity on newspapers has shifted considerably towards more of a house-style orientation than anything absolute and interprets this as part of their need to differentiate themselves within the media market: 'Newspapers, in any case, need to "take it further" than T.V. and radio. They need to go beyond the neutral and objective rituals of balance' (1996: 197–8). Such convergences within media entertainment have paradoxical consequences. Statistics show a mistrust of journalists' veracity (Worcester, 1998: 47) at the same time as the increasing domestication of certain household news anchors, the star journalists and rock 'n' roll documentarists. They have come a long way since Cassandra became perhaps the first celebrity political columnist on the *Daily Mirror* between 1935 and 1967, with a break from duty between 1942 and 1946. In the expanding tide of newsprint, the broadsheets' relative coverage of foreign news has decreased, yet they are providing a very different service than their predecessors in that, freed from the necessity to be first with breaking news, they can concentrate much more on the opinion, commentary and selective in-depth reporting. As the broadsheets retain an historical claim to the status of newspapers of record, they still are concerned with their reputation of prestige, influence and quality through their connections to the narrative of the Fourth Estate, yet Golding (1999) has identified a significant drift in even these papers towards a more entertainment-based diet. Bromley sees the convergence of tabloid and broadsheets from the late 1980s onwards as an extension of the blurring of boundaries between popular culture, consumerism and lifestyle journalism into other parts of the journalistic environment including TV news:

> In market terms, 'quality' and 'popular' newspapers began to overlap, and to compete directly, in the 'middle market' which once seemed to lie like a chasm between them. Although this is often presented as a disjunction, it was more properly part of the continuing development of the press in the twentieth century. (1998: 26–7)

Even in their serious journalism, political pressures leave the broadsheets often reluctant to do much in the way of investigative work which might ultimately challenge the rationale of their capitalist function. One of the consequences of the accelerating market orientation of journalism has been the decline in the reputation of investigative journalism because it is expensive, potentially politically and economically damaging, and not as easily popular as other staples of news. In a corporatized media world, there is pressure on journalism to conform to the beliefs and standards of corporate ideology. One aspect of mainstream journalism's repertoire has thus been been curtailed:

> The ability of the media and journalism to act as a 'watchdog' in the 1990s has been challenged by technological change, the new structure of broadcasting which works against serious and challenging journalism and programming, the concentration of ownership in Fleet Street and other parts of the British media, the increasing competition between media and the decline of resources, manpower and time available for campaigning journalism. (Williams, 1998: 249)

On the positive side, broadsheets have benefited from their ability to provide what is missing in instantaneous reporting, a reflective and analytical mode of commentary unavailable in most other news media, although one increasingly framed by the values of the status quo. Furthermore, they have been able to offer spin-offs in the form of exhaustive web portals from their own archives to enable readers to pursue interests with increasing depth. Thus, broadsheets become enablers, opening up from their own output into a range of parallel sources, albeit for a social range of readers as narrow as that of their hard copy circulation.

The websites of national and local newspapers and interactive e-mail addresses of prominent columnists allow a more in-depth view of contemporary journalism, while on-line archiving of stories and their links to related news sites are a boon for the engaged reader/participant in the twenty-first-century public sphere. This service is now open to more than the specialist researcher with huge potential for a broader and deeper perception of how events in the world are interlinked. The regular posting of web logs on the Internet brings another radical and personalized slant to the news as the diarist/journalist of the twenty-first century is generically related to the observational journalistic tradition of Pepys and Dickens, yet privileging individual accounts for sub-sections of audiences in another example of a very contemporary fragmentation. On occasions, such as the recent output of the Baghdad Blogger, one individual was able to provide for his audience an insider's view of life during the battles for control of Iraq in 2003. Newspapers are at the hub of a hybrid operation which makes the whole newspaper package more akin to an extended magazine with specializations ranged around the core of a more general news function. Broadsheet newspapers, in particular, at the start of the twenty-first century give a glimpse of a radically altered, more open-ended journalism under the influence of the Internet and its archival potential.

10

====== ======

Broadcast Technology
and Journalism

Technology and the Popular

As previous chapters have made clear, journalism in all its forms has been
defined and indeed judged in a variety of ways: by its relationship to democracy, through its publication of information of contemporary importance, by
its ability through critical intervention to monitor the activities of the rich
and influential, and through these activities by the extent to which it has
acted as a stimulus to the constitution of an interrelating series of public
spheres. It has always incorporated an element of entertainment either in its
content, such as human interest or witty writing style, or by its juxtaposition
with more distracting pieces alongside the serious. Technologies such as
radio and television enabled this entertainment to be more fully integrated
alongside and sometimes within the formats of informational journalism.
Twentieth-century technologies have led inexorably to an acceleration in the
popularization of journalism and this becomes the dominant theme within
the discourse of journalism, from papers for the millions and broadcast news
bulletins for the millions, to debates on tabloidization throughout the
twentieth and into the twenty-first century.

    The popularization of journalism, inevitably within a capitalist econ-
omy, means its commercialization (Garnham, 1990). This trait has always
met with critical resistance from cultural elites and from sections of a more
radically oriented citizenship. After the popularization of print journalism
from the middle of the nineteenth century had culminated in the New
Journalism and its advertising-driven descendants, the *Daily Mail* and the
Daily Express, the next popular convulsion was to be propelled by a series of
technological revolutions leading to a reconfiguration of journalism so dramatic that some have gone so far as to brand it 'postjournalism' (Altheide
and Snow, 1991). This chapter will outline the development of the technologies of radio, television and computer and explore the continuing negotiation of journalism through these media with the political and economic
changes of the century, as it adapted to both match and shape the contours
of an increasingly capitalized journalistic landscape. It will also assess the

extent to which the discourse of journalism has changed under pressure from a media-saturated society. This discourse already faces a shift from the Victorian preoccupation with facts to the very contemporary anxiety about relativism and a consequent uncertainty about fixed truths. Smith comments, for example, on the differential in institutional values between science and the communication industry: 'The training of journalists is shielded against the extreme doubts about the nature of factuality inherent in modern science ... The activity of journalism takes place in a world with two quite different value systems – perhaps more' (1978: 171).

Breaking Print's Monopoly on Journalism

The first new technology of the twentieth century to have an impact on journalism was radio. It was to add a completely new reach and status to journalism's repertoire and it was to do this, in the first instance in Britain at least, protected from the economic pressures for profitability that defined the activities of most other areas of journalism. Its reach was to encompass the whole nation in an imagined community and its status would take it beyond the financial concerns of newspaper businesses and into an attempt at politically independent public service broadcasting. The changes were to have consequences for the more established forms of print journalism and would be influential in the later development of a distinct British television journalism tradition.

   Broadcast journalism began in Britain with an explicit set of links with specific social and political frameworks. The Telegraphy Acts of 1869 and 1904 had put control of the emerging technology of radio in the hands of the Post Office which effectively meant the government. On 14 November 1922 the first live radio broadcasts were heard in Britain. The vital decisions which were to mark the social and economic identity of broadcast journalism as a public service for most of the twentieth century were taken in a few short steps. In 1923 the Sykes Committee rejected advertising as a possible form of revenue, fearing that it would lead to what was perceived as the anarchy of American broadcasting. This decision was reinforced in 1925 as the Crawford Committee secured the status of the BBC as a public company free from commercial and direct government or party political interference. Broadcasting in Britain, unlike its counterpart in the USA and its print rivals at home, was released from the pressure to make a profit and was enabled to engage in a prolonged struggle with government to produce a definition in practice of a public service medium, run on behalf of a public and free from sectional political or financial influence but one which had an additional pressure – to negotiate an independence from its state sponsors. These decisions culminated in the founding by Royal Charter of the British Broadcasting Corporation in 1927 with John Reith as its head. From the start, Reith had an extremely moral view of the role that radio broadcasting in general, and not simply its news service, could play in developing a broader sense of the national community as an enlightened and informed public. Reith's approach to radio and to radio journalism as part of this has been described as: 'Victorian ideals of service laced with Arnoldian notions of culture' (Scannell and Cardiff, 1991: 9). It represented a generational lag from a previous era in its ambition to provide a service to the public in informing, instructing and entertaining the nation. The introduction of radio journalism, particularly in its British variant, was designed to produce a strong normative influence on society as a whole (Williams, 1990). Radio became the first major technological shaper of a new national public in the twentieth century, a public which could begin to imagine itself as truly synchronous and immediately bound in time, more than the communities of print media could ever claim. Radio journalism was created gradually around an understanding that it needed to communicate in different ways to this new public because of its immediacy. For a start, the medium allowed the once inscribed and virtual voice of the journalist to become an aural and immediate reality.

Although not construed as a predominantly journalistic medium, the triple goals of the BBC in general were entirely suitable for the vision of British journalism in its broadcast form. However, broadcast journalism was severely curtailed in its early years. The newspapers immediately identified radio as a threat to their monopoly and attempted to restrict the amount of news and its format on BBC broadcasts. The Newspaper Proprietors' Association pre-emptively pressured the government into restricting radio news broadcasts to one 30-minute bulletin per day, supplied by Reuters without features or interviews, as they feared that radio news would prove 'more fleet than Fleet Street' (Crisell, 1997: 15) and compromise the circulations of their own products. It was dry stuff indeed, much more medium than message. Yet despite the primitive nature of the early radio offerings, particularly in its journalism, newspapers refused to carry listings of radio programmes, including news programmes, for fear they might detract from their own fare. This led to the early appearance of the *Radio Times* in 1923 to counter this stance.

While the anxieties of the newspaper owners were predominantly economic, those of politicians were more grounded in cultural concerns over the nature and impact of the more immediate transmission of political reporting. The content and style of broadcasting were determined to a large extent by a fear of the potential of radio to brainwash listeners. Such fears were to appear justified throughout the 1920s and 1930s as totalitarian governments employed broadcasting to shape the politics of the era and fears of the negative cultural effects of mass communication became commonplace among cultural commentators. Despite an agreement not to editorialize and a commitment to political balance in its reporting, the BBC was also required to broadcast government messages in a national emergency: it would maintain a new and journalistically unique form of editorial independence based on a concept of public service. For many years, it was not allowed to involve itself in the reporting of politically controversial views or political speeches. Radio

190   Journalism: A Critical History

journalism was constructed around a set of anxieties reminiscent of those which had accompanied the development of political reporting in print in previous centuries. What public service broadcast journalism needed to achieve was a balance between these anxieties and the scope of the new technology, between the economic implications of public ownership and the weight of government expectations that it should retain a balance often lacking in the newspaper press. In his struggles with the Post Office and the newspaper owners, Reith enabled radio to develop its own path as he demonstrated consistently to the satisfaction of the government that broadcast journalism under his tutelage was able to maintain that balance.

Reith's ability to juggle these competing demands on the new medium as a transmitter of news were tested during the General Strike of 3 to 12 May 1926 when most national newspapers were closed by industrial action. With restrictions on its broadcasting of news on the national strike lifted, the British Broadcasting Company was the sole national forum for the dissemination of news. It broadcast five daily bulletins and attempted to provide an authoritative and balanced range of reports as well as attempting to demonstrate to its listeners and government that it could remain independent. The success of radio broadcasting in demonstrating how it could balance the expectations of government and public satisfied neither trades unions nor government absolutely, but persuaded the listening public of its ability to provide news in what would otherwise have been an information blackout during a national crisis. Reith, as the mastermind of an approach which sought to inform and to create an impression of consensus in the midst of a national emergency, used the BBC strategically to develop an approach to broadcast journalism during this brief period which was to claim a distinct operational style and to encroach significantly on newpapers as the, hitherto, sole suppliers of current information.

Radio journalism from this point could claim to provide a position around which a consensus of national opinion could form, thus playing a part in the construction of a reinvigorated sense of mediated national community. It has been pointed out, however, that this construction of consensus was far less impartial than it claimed to be, in that it filtered out the social causes of the massive gulf between government and working people which had triggered the general strike (Scannell and Cardiff, 1991: 33). The political and cultural consequences of this approach to balance are still evident in the traditions and practices of today's broadcast journalism, as they still address a national-specific audience and underplay analysis of social issues in so far as they remain driven by events not processes and remain prohibited from editorializing.

The Royal Charter of 1927, coming so soon after the strike, provided proof that Reith had achieved his goal for broadcasting to the extent that the government had been persuaded that radio journalism could be trusted to develop its own news, albeit still heavily dependent on the same sources which provided the newspapers with their material. The development of alternative networks for newsgathering was slow. Radio tentatively started to develop its own independent network of reporters and sources, yet did not founded a dedicated News Department until 1934. One of the most important indicators of the increasing autonomy of radio journalism was its ability to report live on national sports events from 1927 onwards. One only has to recall the words of T.S. Elliot in his list of contributory factors to a sense of national culture to grasp the centrality of the live sports coverage to a growing sense of national community: 'all the characteristic activities and interests of a people. Derby Day, Henley Regatta, Cowes, a Cup Final' (Elliot, 1948: 31). To the vast majority of people these events would have gained most relevance to their contemporary lives because of their coverage nationally on radio. This was really news as it happened and newspapers were correct to interpret it as a technological threat which would compromise their claims to be the first to provide the news. The development of radio journalism became significant to the shape of newspapers as they responded to this intrusion upon what had been until now their territory. Radio's immediacy as a technology threatened the greater claims to factual objectivity which had been gathering credibility as a professional discourse in newspaper journalism since the invention of the telegraph (Schiller, 1981; Schudson, 1978). It was to capture for itself the 'strategic ritual of objectivity' (Tuchman, 1978) as an integral part of its own claims to a professionalized discourse as newspapers turned elsewhere to justify their continued existence. In Britain, this apparent merging of technology and objectivity was amplified by the potency of the BBC myth of neutral information in the service of the public and without the pressure to make a profit which was in formation during this early phase of the development of radio as a journalistic medium, fostered to a large extent by the radio journalists themselves (Smith, 1973).

The Representation of the People Act of 1918 had given universal voting rights based on residence to those aged over 21 and over 30 in the case of women. The government needed from this point to pay much more attention to the widest possible public opinion. What Reith managed to construct in negotiations with newspaper owners, Post Office officials and politicians and through trial and error in an evolving medium was a politically acceptable role for radio journalism in making a distinctive contribution to this democracy. Radio journalism increased its credibility after the General Strike because the carefully constructed tone of sobriety of Reith's project could be contrasted against the extremes of opinionated newspapers with which both public and politicians were familiar. Radio journalism offered a fresh and optimistic novelty at a time when the excesses of both newspaper barons and the interference of politicians were becoming more glaring. Its location outside the direct influence of advertising and the financial imperative to make a profit, combined with the subscription via a licence fee from the general public as consumers and together with its commitment to provide a balanced approach to political issues, created an impression of a medium of consensus which could serve as a guide to citizens in their decision-making. The increasingly profit-driven, commercial press was more transparently a business than a balanced reporter on important current affairs and was not, after Lloyd George's purchase of the *Daily Chronicle* in 1918 and the political machinations of Beaverbrook and Harmsworth, above the suspicion that it could be bought and programmed by those with money and influence. The hopes for radio journalism as it arrived on the political scene of the 1920s could not have been higher:

> A sense of civic responsibility and a wider knowledge of public affairs might be encouraged through common access to the discourses of public life, through the balanced presentation of the facts and the issues at stake in current political debates and policies. These interlocking processes were to be the desired effects of a conception of broadcasting as an instrument of democratic enlightenment, as a means of promoting social unity through the creation of a broader range of shared interests, tastes and social knowledge than had previously been the portion of the vast majority of the population. (Scannell and Cardiff, 1991: 13)

In 1930 the BBC won an important victory in its move towards autonomy by constructing a specifically aural approach to the reporting of news. It gained the right to alter Reuters' material so that it could be rewritten in a way which was better suited to a voice reading than to an internal ear reading. But fears about radio's influence and hopes for its rapid success were often confounded by the early shortcomings of a restricted network and a technology which appeared to be developing very slowly. On Good Friday 1930, for example, there was a brief announcement that 'there is no news tonight' and the next programme was introduced (Scannell and Cardiff, 1991: 118). The impediments to the development of radio broadcasting were further illustrated by the fate of the *Weekly Newsreel* experiment over six months in 1933 which sought to exploit the movie/visual metaphor of its title in providing a more popular approach, similar to that on offer in the cinemas. It was well received but too costly as it ran for half an hour and had no practical recording facilities. It did not survive.

To counter the growing sensationalism of the newspaper press in the 1930s and its increasing dependence on circulation-boosting stunts and competitions, the version of radio journalism which was being slowly nurtured at the BBC was one which, mindful of the domestic and family setting in which it was received, by and large, and of the contemporary view of its huge potential to influence people's beliefs, set out to adhere to its own notions of taste, tact and propriety. One consequence of this was to present a voice on air in the accent of Home Counties upper-middle class which sat at odds with its remit to provide an inclusive public service but in contrast transferred much from the Arnoldian perspective of the best that has been thought and written into the most elite of spoken discourse! If radio had made the hitherto metaphorical voice of journalism literally audible, it was now doing the same for social class.

Newspapers were beginning to react more creatively to the perceived threat posed by radio news to their circulations. As the immediacy of their news was becoming less of an issue, they were free to concentrate more on layout, commentary and opinion. This was accompanied, particularly in the popular newspapers, by a more visual approach to layout triggered by the revolutionary redesign of the *Daily Express* in 1933 with its better use of space, integration of illustration, bolder headlines and reader-friendly print (Conboy, 2002: 114–26).

The 1930s also saw radio becoming the dominant medium for royal stories, particularly those of a dramatic nature which could be enhanced by the live reporting of events. Reith himself announcing the death of George V on air in 1936 brought a new intensity and intimacy to such news. This was followed up with the live broadcast of the funeral which again invited a nation to join in a simultaneous and extended demonstration of communal mourning hitherto only possible for a relatively small number of spectators or, vicariously and with a time-lag, in newspapers and magazines. Another royal story which gained in resonance by its immediacy through radio was that of the abdication of Edward VIII, speaking live to the nation. The reception of such stories in a domestic setting also enabled the royal family to be more fully integrated in the everyday life of the nation than ever before.

Although handicapped to an extent by its inability to cover matters of political controversy because of agreements based on interpretations of the Charter, there is evidence that Reith was able to use the notion of 'balance' as a strategy to enable the BBC to find ways of covering contested issues. There was also evidence in its experiments with documentaries that the BBC was taking a much broader view of its responsibilities to extend the social reach of its current affairs programming during the 1930s. Programmes such as A.E. Harding's *Crisis in Spain* (1931), which was based on real events but employed actors and scripted dialogue, provided an early example of drama documentary, blurring generic boundaries to provide a livelier account. These were complemented by actuality programmes which sought to focus on ordinary people's domestic lives and leisure. On the burning social question of the day, unemployment, the BBC's attempts at balanced documentaries, in 1933 with *S.O.S* and in 1934 with *Time To Spare*, produced a polarization of opinion similar to radio journalism's earlier attempts to chart a middle course during the General Strike:

> The two series on unemployment, fundamentally similar in conception, created almost diametrically opposite political problems for the broadcasters. *S.O.S.* was regarded by a section of the Left as evidence of a ruling-class conspiracy, while *Time To Spare* was so effectively appropriated by the Labour Party in the House of Commons as a stick with which to beat the National Government that the Prime Minister, Ramsay MacDonald, attempted to stop the series. (Scannell and Cardiff, 1991: 58–9)

Questions of access and accountability became extended to the audience in ways which had hitherto been only implicit through circulation figures and profitablity in print journalism. In establishing its credentials as a public service broadcaster, keen to include the opinions of an audience who were consumers only through the compulsory licence fee, the BBC introduced the Listener Research Unit from 1936. In the same year, the Ullswater Committee recommended the ground rules for proportional broadcasting time for the major parties during election campaigns, again indicating the politically inclusive and balanced role which radio journalism was playing in allowing a fuller access to politics to a wider electorate.

One significant radio journalist is regarded in accounts of the evolution of broadcast journalism as instrumental in single-handedly creating new criteria for authenticity. Richard Dimbleby's enthusiasm for radio journalism was fired by his experience of American radio and he pioneered many of the features of radio broadcasting which we now take for granted, such as live interviews and pacy reports from foreign locations. Two examples will suffice to demonstrate his innovative contributions. In 1936 Dimbleby sent a live report on the fire raging at Crystal Palace from a telephone box outside and scooped the newspapers as they had already finished printing the next day's news. Early in 1939, Dimbleby from the radio car broadcast unscripted from the Franco-Spanish border, quite literally straddling it, on the 10 o'clock news with gunfire in the background.

It was the lack of independent source material and over-reliance on Reuters as their only source around the time of Munich 1938 which led the BBC into an over-optimistic reception to Chamberlain's return from Germany with his promise of 'Peace in our time'. This highlighted the BBC's journalistic weakness and its need to build its own network of correspondents as on *The Times* and the *Manchester Guardian* who themselves used Reuters and other agency material as checks on their own sources. It also indicated how the BBC needed to develop more reliable strategies to ensure its independence from government and therefore enhance its credibility with listeners in times of national crisis. The Second World War was the defining moment in the prestige of the BBC both nationally and internationally and, more importantly, of radio journalism as a medium which could deliver a quality and speed of information which were to become admired as a model of democratic discourse to counter the flow of broadcast totalitarianism. The newspapers were handicapped during the war by a lack of paper and, in a period of severe shortages and rationing, the advertising budgets they had become so dependent on were severely diminished. Yet radio journalism did more than simply fill the spaces left by print journalism, it evolved into something much more assured and confident in its mission to inform and, just as importantly, it became much more competent in using the technology available and in adapting to innovations. Before the war, largely but not only because of the impositions of the vested interests of newspaper owners, bulletins had sounded very much like pieces intended for internal reading being read aloud – which is of course what they were, having been derived from Reuters' reports written for newspapers. During the war this changed rapidly and the news was constructed in a way which was much more directed towards the spoken word. Attempts were also made to be more inclusive of the social varieties of English and to dispel the impression than a Received Pronunciation accent was either more authoritative or acceptable than regional variants. The speed of information flowing through radio bulletins and the ability of this new medium to deal with events as they happened meant that newspapers could not compete in the same way with broadcasting immediacy ever again. It also meant that radio journalism had to fashion ways to create a fully rounded version of events than the format of the bulletin could allow. The most successful of these innovations was *Radio Newsreel* (1940), broadcast on the General Overseas Service, which borrowed and adapted techniques from film 'newsreels' to blend newsreading with a wider range of actuality techniques such as interviews, correspondents' reports and, most importantly, the live sounds of a world at war that no newspaper could bring. The insistence on accurate and balanced reporting of the war for radio listeners was underlined by R.T. Clark of the News Department as the only sensible and viable strategy: 'It seems to me that the only way to strengthen the morale of the people whose morale is worth strengthening is to tell them the truth, and nothing but the truth, even if the truth is horrible' (Briggs, 1961: 656). The experiment with radio newsreels indicated a narrowing gap within radio between entertainment and news in its journalism given that Movietone's newsreels from the 1920s, the media they emulated, were shown in the cinema, the site for the most popular entertainment medium of the era. Another indicator of how the generic boundaries were being crossed in the pursuit of a more popular and representative form of radio journalism was the series of talks from 1940 by famous author J.B. Priestly, entitled *Postscript*. The growing maturity and variety within radio journalism from its bulletins to its actuality began to gain for it a level of credibility which it had not enjoyed before the war. Furthermore, as it was the provider of news to half of the population at 9 o'clock each evening: 'it gave the individual an unprecedented sense of herself as part of the larger community' (Crisell, 1997: 62).

Yet for all its progress in the war years, there was at the BBC still a 'suspicion and unpopularity of journalists' (Briggs, Vol. V, 1995: 64). Indeed, in 1944 Director General Haley underlined the subordinate place of journalism within the corporation to the Radio Industries Club, when he announced: 'It is no part of the BBC's function to become another newspaper. News is only a small fraction of the BBC's activities and output' (ibid.).

Developments in radio journalism were integrated into the BBC's peacetime routines. After the war, most news was still sourced from agency material although there was a growing trend towards foreign and specialist correspondents who were a legacy of the war years. The BBC expanded its own network of foreign correspondents which it had started to appoint as late as 1944 and it continued to develop the most progressive of its wartime experimentations within news and current affairs broadcasting, such as *Radio Newsreel* which was broadcast on the Light Programme from 1947 although, according to Briggs, it was a disappointingly 'brighter', 'less demanding' version of its wartime fare (Briggs, Vol. IV, 1979: 528). Its coverage of politics also progressed into a more sustained format with *Today in Parliament* which ran on radio from 1949.

Despite some concerns about the popularization of debate in BBC journalism 'borrowing some of the technique of the bogus wrestling arena' (*The Observer*, 4 March 1951, in Briggs, Vol. IV, 1979: 603), Briggs also identifies a restrictive conservatism within the BBC's attitudes to radio news when he recalls that, despite the moves towards a more vernacular style of reporting, there were self-imposed limits, as in the warning reported in *BBC Quarterly* 1: 3 October 1946: 'He who wants to read while he runs must expect to have his reading matter limited to the trivial and must expect to leave high themes alone' (Briggs, Vol. IV, 1979: 522).

This is an early rehearsal of the arguments that broadcast journalism by its nature, particularly after the introduction of television because it draws on predominantly entertainment genres, militates against a certain level of complexity and understanding. The introduction of vernacular and popular approaches to news and current affairs on radio went some way to satisfying the BBC's claim to be talking to all levels of society, but they were going to be further strained by the intervention of television into the area of journalism and its subsequent commercialization.

The Radical Impact of Television News

By the 1950s, the bold experiment to create a form of journalism as a conduit for an informed citizenship, independently located between the public and government, shielded from the imperative to make money and immune from the sway of one individual or interest group, had to all intents and purposes failed. Despite its heroic efforts to combat totalitarianism abroad, the BBC variant of radio journalism had proved unable to successfully negotiate its position with regard to the government. Scannell and Cardiff have observed the BBC's dilemma over loyalties to its twin audiences, the public and the government, stemming from the 1938 Munich crisis:

> what compounded its difficulties and prevented it from breaking the deafening silence was its own absorption within the state domain. The continuous routine contact that had built up over the years between senior personnel in Broadcasting House, Whitehall and Westminster meant that they all abided by the same rules and code of conduct. The Corporation had become the shadow of a state bureaucracy; closed, self-protective and secretive. No one in the BBC spoke out publicly at the time of Munich about the extent to which broadcasting was being gagged. (1991: 101)

Anxieties emanating from this time had been delayed rather than resolved despite the enhanced reputation of the BBC emerging from the Second World War. The next technologically led shift in the content and style of journalism was one that began with television journalism but whose implications immediately started to have an effect on all news media. It is this discursive shift whose content and aesthetic appeal continue to pose the most challenging questions to contemporary journalism. Movietone had provided newsreels to cinema from the 1920s before the advent of television in an example of the continuing tradition of miscegenation of news and entertainment in journalism. Although there had been television before the war, one of the pre-war successes having been the coronation procession of George VI in May 1937, it was only after 1946 that the BBC began to make wider use of the medium for journalism. Despite the head start which the BBC had had in terms of broadcast journalism experience and the speed of technological developments in the war, the conservatism of the BBC's version of journalism had much to do with its isolation from any competitor within broadcasting and its adherence to a particularly narrow view of the potential role of broadcast journalism. These were severe impediments for the BBC as it experimented with television.

Grace Wyndeham Goldie described the predicament of the BBC with regard to television thus:

> their speciality was the use of words; they had no knowledge of how to present either entertainment or information in vision, nor any experience of handling visual material. Moreover, most of them mistrusted the visual; they associated vision with the movies and the music hall and were afraid that the high purposes of the Corporation would be trivialised by the influence of those concerned with what could be transmitted in visual terms. (Crisell, 1997: 74)

The poor track record of the BBC in instigating change within the formats and presentational styles of television journalism indicated that nothing had been learned from the painfully tentative development of radio journalism from the 1920s to the 1940s. Radio journalism had moved itself away from a text-based approach to news, an approach largely imposed upon it by newspaper owners and government, yet the BBC was unable to fully grasp the imperative for television news to develop a visual approach appropriate to its material. From 1946 to 1954, television news was narrowly focused on words and suspicious of any personalization of news, particularly through presenters on screen. In a bizarre re-enactment of the first radio news as simply an aural version of the Reuters' reports written for newspapers, the evening television news was simply the radio news announced by an anonymous voice, the reader off-camera, with a photograph of Big Ben, the only visual element. Anonymity was inherited, almost as a reflex, from the radio broadcasting of news and was a short-lived attempt to make a new medium conform to the traditions which had emerged out of an older one. It was an attempt which was destined to fail. There was a short 10-minute newsreel five times a week but this merely copied the cinema format of footage with a voiceover, displaying both a lack of imagination toward the possibilities of the new medium as a purveyor of journalism and at the same time acknowledging the necessity of borrowing from other entertainment genres in its search for a suitable approach to visual news. Even in the late 1940s, it was becoming clear that television news would have to be as much about entertainment as it was about information. The question was whether the BBC was going to be able to provide it. The coronation of 1952 is widely considered to have been the watershed in TV's fortunes. It certainly enabled the medium to bring to television broadcasting some of the immediacy and communal involvement which radio had been able to generate around events of contemporary importance. As if to confirm the direction of this trend, in 1954 a new daily bulletin was launched, combining bulletin and newsreel format.

Belatedly, BBC journalism attempted to broaden its appeal and enliven its television offering. *In the News* from 26 May 1950 was based on an entertainment model and was broadcast first as a weekly programme. It was the only regular political programme on TV and featured politicians among its panel of guests discussing issues in the news. In July 1954, *News and Newsreel* was launched after a long and fractious debate among policy-makers at the BBC. It was the first concerted effort at 'news in vision' and drew widespread criticism. The nature of the debate indicated the inward-looking nature of television journalism at this point at the BBC. ITV news changed the terms of the debate entirely after 1955. It took the arrival of commercial television to generate the innovations which lifted television news into its own as a journalistic medium. The BBC's news was simply not as good, as exciting or as well presented as the new commercial variant. In particular, the introduction of television which was independent from government by reason of its commercial funding was to restructure the awkward collaboration between journalism and the state in the form of the BBC in its public service role.

In contrast to radio which had emerged in Britain predicated on a fear of a repetition of the American commercial model of broadcast journalism, commercial television moved with something approaching undue haste to incorporate the best of transatlantic practice. The ITV was moulded very much by American popular and commercial strategies, illustrating once again the intra-media influences which had flowed between the USA and Britain, facilitated by their anglophone cultures, since the mutual influences of print journalism in the eighteenth and nineteenth centuries. The ITN provided news for the independent stations from February 1955. Some of the differences in approach were immediate. As ITN was dedicated solely to the gathering and presentation of news, it made a formidable rival to the BBC as a journalism outlet. ITN's mission was 'to make significant news more interesting, more comprehensive and more acceptable' (Crisell, 1997: 92). ITN news included informal vox pops and was quicker to exploit a scoop than its more cautious competitor. From the first, broadcasters wrote their own news to project their personality and input. The 'due accuracy and impartiality' of news on ITV, required by statute and modelled on the obligations imposed on the BBC, had to be judged by the ITA but the ITN interpreted this obligation with less deference to the establishment and more stylistic flair. It marked the beginning of a popularization of broadcast journalism in terms of its content and the audience it was aimed at.

It was not only in terms of its news that ITN was to create a new generation of broadcast journalism. It brought a style of enquiry which was to reconfigure the relationship between the State and broadcast journalism in ways which Reith could never have imagined. Culturally, the ITN forced the changes onto the BBC as it was free of the latter's austere baggage and close association with the State. This discursive shift ushered in a new era, making politicians more accountable to the public via journalism and making politics more entertaining for the viewer: 'The struggle to make politicians answerable and accountable to the electorate through broadcasting was not joined until the establishment of commercial television and the new forms of broadcast journalism inaugurated by Independent Television News in the late fifties' (Scannell and Cardiff, 1991: 102). In its political coverage, ITN used fresh and articulate interviewers like Robin Day and Chris Chataway who rejected deference to politicians and took a professional pride in asking probing and sometimes blunt questions. Day himself recalls: 'ITN set new standards of rigour, enterprise and pace for television news, making the BBC version look stiff and stuffy, which it was. Ludicrous taboos were swept away by the post-1955 wind of change' (Day, 1989: 82). By 1956–57 the influence of this style of critical interviewing of politicians had become the norm (Seymour-Ure, 1991: 168). This was building the momentum for broadcast journalism which would lead within a few years to the detailed coverage of general elections.

The new journalism medium and its popularity with viewers also had an impact on politicians, particularly backbenchers, who saw the advantages of a brief TV or radio appearance over a Commons speech that got no coverage (Seymour-Ure, 1991: 170). It is, however, a tendency which is double-edged. This televisualization of politics tends towards a media spectacle in which power becomes more display than the rationalization of argument. You appear on TV because of who you are, not because of what you have to say. It is part of the shift which Habermas refers to as the 'refeudalization of society' (1992: 231). It is a change which concurs with one of the major themes of this book that there has been an absence of continuous enlightened progress in journalism as a rational public sphere, more a series of discursive realignments within a set of practices defined as journalism over time. This discursive realignment becomes particularly intense with the advent of the technology of broadcast journalism, especially in its televisual form.

The BBC was forced to respond to this new aesthetic of television journalism to retain its credibility as a public service in a newly competitive and therefore populist environment. Yet it is important not to forget the real gains which the BBC had brought to the range of journalism through its limited experiments with radio and their effect on forcing print journalism to begin to take on a markedly different role. Perhaps on the arrival of ITN, it would be best to measure the success of BBC journalism more modestly as in the backhanded compliment in 1956 from journalist Tom Driberg, who argued that the main role of the BBC had been to teach people to stop believing newspapers – 'newspapers at any rate of the more garish sort' (Briggs, Vol. V, 1995: 69).

Discursively, television, because of its visual nature and its immediacy, seemed to be a closer approximation to the truth while the partisanship and rhetoric of newspapers were exposed by this bright new form of journalism. The broadcast media have also played their part in nurturing this belief. Elliott claims that they have developed 'a peculiar fascination for the creed of factual objectivity' (1978: 184).

In response to the changes wrought by ITN in television journalism, from 1959 Hugh Greene, as head of news at BBC, precipitated a move to a more personalized, lively style. In order to effect this, old programmes were analysed. Reporters began to write their own commentary and speak it over the pictures broadcast. More drive and enthusiasm and above all a greater respect for the medium of television in all its visual aspects were to be insisted upon. In fact, the popularization project within BBC journalism had developed such momentum that Briggs claims that editor-in-chief of BBC Television News from 1959, Stuart Hood, was of the view that its News Division should be, 'as good as the *Daily Mirror*', which was at that time a serious popular paper with a circulation of over 4.5 million, larger than the audience for BBC television news (Briggs, Vol. V, 1995: 156).

ITN's influence was not only being felt through its impact on television journalism at the BBC. Its targeting of a mass and general audience also triggered widespread change in other parts of the journalism environment. In the pre-war years, half the population listened to the evening 9 o'clock news. Newspapers in 1945 contained mainly news rather than features. All this was changed rapidly by the sudden maturing of television journalism under the influence of ITN's populist strategies. It has been claimed that: 'TV's main effect was to change the way in which people used their papers, more than to reduce their use' (Seymour-Ure, 1991: 148).

General interest illustrated weekly magazines like *Picture Post* were forced out of business in the late 1950s and were joined by daily newspapers early in the 1960s with the closure of the *News Chronicle* and the *Daily Herald*. Such publications could simply not attract the amount of suitable advertising to fend off competition from highly popular television journalism nor could they resist the advance of the generalist medium *par excellence*. However, as always in technological changes within journalism, the picture is more integrative within the general news media environment rather than a straightforward case of a monopoly of influence with television driving all rivals for cover. Those who survived were able to adapt and integrate the lessons of television journalism's dynamism and popularity. Something of the subtlety of this interaction is caught by Murdock and Golding when they write on the post-war contraction of newspaper sales:

> Television is only a limited part of the explanation for this contraction. In its initial phase, commercial television generated much of its own revenue

rather than stealing it from the newspapers, and early research into audiences showed that viewing actually stimulated readership of the populars, though it did have negative effects on the purchase of the qualities. In the longer term, however, television clearly did provide an alternative and increasingly attractive source of popular journalism and general entertainment. (1978: 133)

TV journalism forced cinema out of the news business by the 1960s as it was better at providing the latest news. This was part of a more general realignment within journalism across media markets. By the early 1960s television journalism had become the dominant popular medium and the news/features balance in the press as a whole had shifted to accommodate television's demonstrable superiority in dealing with the news of the moment. Newspapers not driven out because of changing patterns of consumption began to specialize in more background and lifestyle material, away from a concentration on a hard news agenda. In 1957, 30 per cent of people chose newspapers as their main news, 46 per cent radio and 24 per cent television. By 1962, 52 per cent were treating television as their main news source, with only 31 per cent opting for newspapers and 17 per cent for radio (Crisell, 1997: 94).

The success of commercial television journalism required a strategic response to remain competitive. Broadsheet Sunday newspapers brought in free colour magazines and expanded feature coverage, starting with the *Sunday Times* in 1962. Other newspapers responded accordingly with an increase in lighter features, concentration on personality, contexts to the news and stories about television and its stars. The BBC began to respond within the area of current affairs programmes, extending its specific claim to public service broadcasting. Grace Wydham Goldie took *Panorama* in 1955 and changed it into a heavyweight contributor to political debate. It marked the beginning of current affairs as a highly respected contributor to the journalistic agenda of television. Briggs underlines its contribution in the following terms: 'During the years after Suez, it became a major weekly event in itself, whatever might be happening on any continent. People stayed at home to see it: public figures, British and foreign, sought to appear on it' (Vol. V, 1995: 164).

Radio journalism responded to the challenge of providing lively current affairs programmes on television by launching what was to become its flagship of quality political journalism. The *Today* programme was launched on 28 October 1957 as the earliest successful example of the current affairs magazine at breakfast time. It began as a general interest programme but soon became the hard news-dominated format which still characterizes it today. It created a blend of current affairs, live interviews with politicians on issues of the moment, and in-depth political reporting. Its success provided a pattern for subsequent political reporting on the BBC.

On television, *Tonight* was introduced by the BBC on 18 February 1957 at 6.05 p.m. as a 40-minute news magazine with a much more varied mix of entertainment, politics and even music. It was to provide an extremely influential model for the early evening current affairs magazine. Whereas news bulletins remained short on both channels, varying over the early years between 12 and 15 minutes until the arrival of the 30-minute *News at Ten* in 1967, real experimentation and change were introduced in the mixed format current affairs programmes *Tonight* and *Panorama* on the BBC and matched from 1963 by Granada's hard-hitting special reports and documentary *World in Action*. As these changes began to make their way into the public consciousness, so too the status of news and indeed television journalism improved through the 1950s and 1960s. The combination of innovation and commitment, in particular, to investigative journalism as part of its public service remit gave investigative journalism a new status (de Burgh, 2000: 26), defining it for a generation. Both stations became respected in dealing with current affairs and acting as a critical gaze for the public into politics and even politicians' pronouncements in more open ways than ever before.

It is generally accepted that for complex social reasons there was a decline in deference in British society from the 1960s onwards. From November 1962 on BBC, *That Was The Week That Was* provided television with its first topical satire, presented by David Frost. Irreverent and popular, it was watched by a regular audience of 10 million. This was accompanied and some claim accelerated by the advances in television journalism's iconoclastic tendencies (Crisell, 1997: 118). The satirical magazine *Private Eye* was launched in 1961 and provides a vital and successful link with a form of journalism whose roots are as old as periodicity and printed political comment themselves. Crisell argues that 'television showed people in close-up, 'warts and all'. It revealed every mannerism, uncertainty and hesitation. Mystique evaporated. The great and the good – aristocrats, statesmen, 'authorities' and experts – turned out to be people like the rest of us, their average physical blemishes and peculiarities implying average fallibility' (1997: 118).

Yet an historical approach to journalism which recalls Nedham's accusations of Charles I's cowardice, *The Times*' revelation of the testimony of a maid concerning Queen Caroline's bedsheets, not to mention Wilkes' allegations of Bute's relationship with the King's mother or the politically motivated, personal attacks of Carlile and Hetherington would generally conclude that television may have brought such irreverence to a greater number than any individual newspaper had ever done and in a more direct and immediate way, but it certainly could not claim to have initiated this. Its power was in the massification and simultaneity of this exposure and therefore its links to the broader democratic imperatives of the medium in its early stages not least, as mentioned above, because of its cumulative effect on other news media as they reacted to keep pace with the competition. The BBC's adherence to such narrow deference had been an exceptional case. Print journalism had never been burdened by such niceties. Television and broadcasting in general were simply coming of age journalistically, taking on the full potential of journalism's range of tradition. ITN was again to provide the initiative when it changed its successful format of main late evening news. After much internal debate within ITN because of concerns that it was risking the success of its short populist news format, *News at Ten* was launched on 3 July 1967. Drawing again on an American model, it employed two newscasters to develop pace and variety within the bulletin with the newscasters increasingly playing off each other journalistically and stylistically. Interviews were used more frequently to develop and contextualize stories and there was more reliance on visual presentation techniques and footage hitherto associated with documentary. The 30-minute slot enabled the ITN news to be more populist and more detailed at the same time.

According to Seymour-Ure:

> For TV news it was a symbolic moment. The BBC extended its own 9.00 pm bulletin. News was no longer an illustrated supplement to radio and newspapers. Newscasters worked as journalists and interviewers, not just announcers. Satellite transmission soon added immediacy and a much extended range of sources and material. 'The news' became less of a bulletin and more an integrated programme of 'reporter packages', capable of delivering large audiences in peak time. In due course, colour, electronic news gathering (an ITV innovation) and computer graphics would also add to the service. (1991: 141)

Beyond questions of format and content, one significant contribution of television news was its ability to further legitimate the traditional claims of broadcasting to provide a version of neutral information encouraging audiences to believe in the mimetic fallacy that what you see is how it is. For all the perceived innovation and iconoclasm of the broadcast news media of the 1960s in comparison with the previous BBC radio model, the broadcasters' belief in neutral information seemed intact. This tendency was reinforced by some of the common generic distinctions within the broadcasting organizations themselves, leading to divisions between journalism which seemed to constitute ontological observations rather than stylistic preferences. Briggs has observed that this perception was shared across news organizations in Britain: 'there was a division inside the BBC between news, which should be objective and unadulterated, and current affairs, which could be explanatory and speculative, a distinction that was not drawn in the United States but that was drawn inside ITN' (Briggs, Vol. V, 1995: 69).

Technology and the Market: Fragmentation and Convergence

For all its demonstrable contribution to the reshaping of the news media, broadcast journalism, as it was influenced by the changes emerging from the commercial sector, moved increasingly towards formats which prioritized market appeal just as most print journalism from 1855 had been shaped by commercial pragmatism. It is a paradox of technological developments in twentieth-century journalism that the very forces which enabled broadcast journalism to provide a genuinely popular version of public knowledge in a form which was lively and accessible to more viewers than ever should end the century accused by many of contributing a great deal to the destabilization of the concept of good journalism. The very technological and popular gains which appeared at one point capable of delivering more information more speedily to a larger group of viewers have engendered styles of presentation which are criticized as unable to deliver high quality journalism. The entertainment values which had done so much initially to contribute to the development of television journalism continued to encroach even in the sphere of its current affairs. It has been alleged that the most notable early victim of this tendency was *This Week*:

> *This Week* was taken off the air in 1978 because, in the words of Mike Towson, the editor of its replacement *TV Eye*, it was too journalist centred and had become boring. Townson was one of the first to be credited with 'grafting tabloid style and values on to broadsheet journalism'. (Holland, 1998: 85)

Technology has developed a multiplication of news delivery systems which have made the need to control and limit the amount of news available impossible to maintain. Digital, satellite and computer technologies have ushered in an era of news media surfeit in contrast to the previous scarcity of wavelengths. At this moment restrictions on space to fill with news are no longer a consideration. In practice there is no longer a need for limiting the hours of output or the number of outlets for broadcast journalism. As with print, the limitations came to be set simply according to the patterns of market demand. As well as commercial providers, the BBC was drawn into this market reflex because its audience share is plotted against commercial competitors to test its own position in terms of value-for-money and competitiveness. As we move through the twentieth century, increasingly efficient and capitalized technology creates more competition among news providers who are under pressure to deliver news more profitably. Technological change has led to a proliferation in the amount of broadcast journalism as well as consequent changes in content. The demands of the market have always been paramount in the structuring of the formats and technologies of journalism as it is shaped and reshaped as a site of informational activity. Bourdieu interprets the 'journalistic field' as inextricably linked to the economic field: 'like the political and economic fields, and much more than the scientific, artistic, literary, or juridical fields, the journalistic field is permanently subject to trial by market, whether directly, through advertisers, or indirectly, through audience ratings (even if government subsidies offer a certain independence from immediate market pressures)' (1998: 71).

Other writers, rather than stressing the inevitability of journalism's location within the sphere of capitalism, have chosen to critique the increasing convergence between profitability and provision in broadcast journalism as detrimental to the fundamental public service ethos of British broadcasting in an attempt to provide radical alternatives (Curran and Seaton, 1993; O'Malley, 2001). Dramatic changes in technology combined with the liberalization of the market for broadcast journalism came at a time of almost total credulity, from the end of the 1970s, about the benefits of free market approaches to the delivery of all sorts of public information, including journalism, on both sides of the Atlantic, meaning that there was little mainstream political or commercial opposition. Broadcast journalism's priorities have been dictated through a political push towards deregulation from the early 1990s. This trend is being continued in current discussions in 2003 about further media deregulation and ownership liberalization in the United States and Britain. This increasing ideological push towards the deregulation of news media ownership and control has become established as natural and inevitable within political and economic circles with only peripheral resistance. Control has been handed increasingly to major media conglomerates which have been trusted to act as allies of neo-liberal political groupings in power in Western Europe and the United States. This new, more lightly regulated market approach has become the new consensus between politics, commerce and journalism. It is a replaying by different rules of the nineteenth-century liberalization of the print journalism market which has a similar effect in reducing real choice, as the market narrows to concentrate on profitable and predictable formats and content for its broadcast news and current affairs, illustrating what Williams has observed: 'Serving democracy, encouraging diversity or expanding citizenship are very much in the back seat as entrepreneurs have to confront the increasingly competitive marketplace for global information' (1998: 240).

Yet in spite of deregulation, broadcast journalism in Britain continues to be judged discursively in terms of its role as provider of a public service, showing the resilience of the ethos of public service journalism even within a period of technological change and neo-liberal political hegemony. A critic such as O'Malley (2001: 33) points out that although notions of public service broadcasting have shifted over time, they still provide a benchmark which in his view illustrates that there has been a decline in its provision. He sees this decline as a direct consequence of the commercial pressures which have been brought to bear on PBS by the competitive expansion of broadcasting. Yet the opposite viewpoint, and certainly one prevalent within the news media itself, is that market forces enable people to be entrusted with making their own choices about the broadcast journalism they consume rather than having a restricted choice imposed upon them. In this version, the market is the ultimate arbiter of journalistic standards. Whichever version one subscribes to, it is clear that market demands in both commercial and state sectors, broadcast and print, have led to a significant reconfiguration of the 'journalistic field'.

Technological changes have had an impact above all on the immediacy and availability of journalism as it has proliferated as a mode of communication. Even before the satellites of the 1970s and the digital and computer technologies of the 1990s, the development of the transistor in the 1960s provided the technological impetus which was to profoudly alter the way that journalism was delivered to its target audience. It meant a complete reconsideration of the reach and content of radio. Portability and the installation of radios in cars meant that the concept of background listening was extended. Journalism was developing a culture of news reception which would lead to the contemporary format of drive time news and once the restrictions on commercial radio were removed, this became the cheapest and most popular form of news for millions. Radio journalism also developed an experiment in audience participation using the phone-in, from 1968 on BBC Radio Nottingham. The fact that it was pioneered on local radio was significant in the way that unlike letters from readers, a highly edited and slow form of communication with a newspaper, this interactive format was ideally suited to local issues and added a sense of immediacy to reporting and commentary on current affairs. It was to be developed as an additional support to national radio and television. These developments were a form of journalism which was increasingly designed to engage with the lives of people on the move, in need of more concise and varied pattern of information. Patterns of expectation in the consumption of news were to be extended through other technological innovations such as teletext, updates on mobile phones and digital news menus, while rolling TV news and breakfast TV news were further acknowledgements of the continually fragmenting and diversifying viewing patterns of audiences.

From the 1970s, one technology emerged which was to force the break-up of older patterns of control over television broadcasting. The use of satellite technology on ITN to bring pictures of the 1973 Yom Kippur War to television viewers on the day of action demonstrated the increasing obsolescence of newspapers as the best providers of overseas news. This process of increased speed of news delivery was accelerated by the introduction towards the end of the 1970s of electronic newsgathering. On the one hand, we have witnessed a proliferation of delivery systems for journalism and on the other hand there has been an increasing internationalization of television journalism in terms of conventions and formats. This has led to a reduction in variety as television journalism converges to chase fragmenting audiences to justify income or the legitimacy of the provider to claim the right to broadcast. The introduction of satellite television from CNN onwards accelerated the tendency towards convergence in television journalism of a more popular and formulaic range of presentational styles to attempt to maintain their share of viewers.

Technological change has also led to convergence within the genres and formats of journalism. Sky News from 1990 was the first UK-based rolling news channel and began to erode the barriers between news and current affairs as the scheduled slots became more blurred in a rolling format. BBC News 24 which started in November 1997 and other subsequent satellite, cable and digital services have all affected the output and pace of terrestrial, scheduled news, especially in the ways in which breaking news is broadcast. Nevertheless, the trends of convergence are not absolute. There is still room for generic demarcation. Despite round-the-clock availability via satellite, terrestrial news at scheduled points on TV and radio is still extremely popular and therefore viable and despite the reach of technology to provide a form of global news, cultural preferences are still for a content which reflects local audiences' needs and tastes, not a global staple.

Satellite and video technology have combined to give us truly live reporting from overseas in areas where traditional cameras are unsuitable. The reporting by videophone from Afghanistan in 2001 and Iraq in 2003 brought instant news from anywhere in the world within reach. Some commentators have expressed doubts that the semi-edited nature of some 'real-time' coverage does not necessarily enhance our understanding and that this is compounded by the ways in which this technology reinforces the myth of immediacy while at the same time masking the constructed nature of reports on screen (Dahlgren, 1995: 56). The proliferation of information which the technology allows and the speed and density of that flow now mean that there is more access to information which has had less editorial intervention. Web-based gossip, videphones and rolling news channels all intensify the provision of such raw material. The industries best equipped to follow that trend continue to produce ever quicker coverage with less time for the journalist or editor to reflect on content. This was demonstrated during the recent Iraqi conflict when the role of war correspondent was often reduced to that of uninformed speculator because of the immediacy of events. 24-hour news brought to the screen poorly sourced, insignificant reports which were often based on rumour. Reporters fronted speculation on-camera as unprocessed information, from smoke in the background and air-raid sirens in Bagdhad to on-screen contradictions as to whether defections of Iraqi troops had taken place or not, all were paraded as evidence of the profoundly disturbing mis-match between technology and reliable television journalism. Kittler (1997) has gone so far as to suggest provocatively that in such cases the war is in fact not primarily between military parties with their inevitable impact upon civilians but between the media technologies themselves. In the face of some coverage from Iraq, this thesis lost some of its extremity and moved closer to a plausible explanation of what was unfolding. Speed is in danger of becoming the ultimate aim of journalism. The post-telegraph compulsion to beat competitors to a story, accelerated by new technologies, can mean it becomes more important to be first than to provide an adequate assessment of context. The pace of breaking news drives the possiblity of in-depth analysis further down the line, adding to the fears of a commentator like Bourdieu that: 'Competition on the [journalistic] field creates a "sort of permanent amnesia"' (1998: 72). Technology extends journalism's tendency, under pressure of time and a perception that audiences need sense made for them, to frame new occurrences in terms of familiar and already constituted sense-making strategies (Schlesinger, 1992). Speed also necessitates an increasing efficiency in locating the probable sites for news and this means a growing concentration on predetermined locations and sources. Television news becomes confined to highly competent repetitions of news agenda, enlivened by the familiar interplay between anchorperson and reporter on the spot. The proximity of the commentator brings nothing particular to the quality of the story but an expectation that news organizations have their reporters placed around the globe and can have them reporting live from the privileged sites for news production. Sources of news are culturally and politically selected for their ease of access to large news-gathering organizations therefore improving their cost effectiveness, their predictability and their closeness to the fulcrum of the political status quo. All of this compromises the incredible speed and technological sophistication of the journalism produced as it is often lacking in analytical depth or political variety.

The overall development of media technology within a capitalist economic framework has determined much of the discourse of journalism in the late twentieth century. It forms part of a process of globalization, defined as a series of intensifications in flows of people, goods and most importantly for this study, information, around the world (Featherstone, 1993). It is inherent within the development of capitalism – technology is its vector. Journalism in the earliest form of newsletters was a contributory factor in both the spread of information about current affairs and the commodification of information. There are further consequences of globalization for journalism. Globalization leads the major stakeholders in the economics of the news media to employ technology to spread across media products, narrowing the gap between entertainment and information. The political economy of the news media in a capitalist system determines that the amount of investment required to provide increased profit should come from using the technology to extend concentration of ownership, bringing economies of scale. Such technological and economic convergence also encourages leading corporations to seek out the most popular and therefore profitable audiences for their products. For journalism, this means that technology becomes more complex and production of the sort of news viewers have come to expect becomes more expensive, so too the political economy of the news media is further restricted to those producers who are able to afford the increasing costs.

Technology and Content: Journalism and New Formats

Technological changes within the political economy of the news media market have brought in their wake a series of changes in content and format which seek to retain more of an audience which is fragmenting because of the variety of options open to it. Whereas in the early days of radio tens of millions of listeners would gather in their homes for the evening news bulletin from a monopoly provider, broadcast journalism in the early twenty-first century needs to attract people leading much more diverse lives and exposed to a teeming range of media output. The profit motive which had always formed an essential part of journalism in all its forms has now become the predominant partner and has turned journalism into something quite different from its previous incarnations (MacManus, 1994). This has led to a range of experimentation in the styles and formats of journalism in an attempt by broadcast journalism to maximize its competitiveness which has led to a 'deeply rooted professional tension between its "televisual" and "journalistic" dimensions' (Dahlgren, 1995: 47). The core of this debate lies in the fact that television is predominantly an entertainment genre and that as media markets converge, blurring the lines between information, education and entertainment, the tendency is to present television journalism as a complement to other entertainment on television in order to retain large viewing figures, but has the effect of compromising its journalism. Neil Postman concludes that entertainment has become 'the natural format for the representation of all experience' (1986: 87) and that television is the culprit. To confirm the show business appeal of the leading anchor persons in the news, their status as general media celebrities is so great that they have enormous cross-over potential in other broadcast formats. This indicates the progression of the status not of journalists *per se* but of journalists as media celebrities: Jeremy Paxman on *University Challenge*, Fiona Bruce on *Call My Bluff*, John Humphries on *Mastermind*, Alastair Stewart as host of *Police, Camera, Action* and Trevor MacDonald's news spin-off *Tonight with Trevor McDonald*.

A voice from within the industry expresses anxiety concerning the disturbing consequences of this set of convergences within television journalism:

> The technology enables us to package, graphicise and meld five minutes of old TV information into 60 seconds of new TV time – the whiz and bang of such presentation may be enticing but the content reduction is so acute that normal debate is in danger of being degraded to the absurd. (Snow, 1997: 3)

Baudrillard sees such tendencies as indicative of broader techno-cultural tendencies, a fascination with a technical sublime which is increasingly detatching people from wider social empathies and introducing the cocoon of individuated, consumer niches, collapsing our sense of the real through its expertise with the technologies of immediacy and simulation. Instead of objecting, Baudrillard seems to advise a campaign of apolitical resistance, going with the flow and refusing to take it seriously as the contemporary real has drifted out of view:

> private telematics, in a new technological moment, each individual sees himself promoted to the controls of a hypothetical machine, isolated in a

position of perfect sovereignty, at an infinite distance from his original universe; that is to say, in the same position as the astronaut in his bubble, existing in a state of weightlessness which compels the individual to remain in perpetual orbital flight and to maintain sufficient speed in zero gravity to avoid crashing into his planet of origin. (1983: 128)

This might seem an extreme and apathetic position to adopt, located somewhere between Major Tom and a couch potato, but it does force us to question the inevitability inscribed within certain narratives of journalism as a public sphere and some of the celebratory popular approaches to the changes in media technology as developed within journalism. Snow might perceive similar challenges to Baudrillard. The difference is, he would like to recuperate much of journalism's imperative to intervene.

Such pessimistic views should be tempered by what television has undoubtedly provided. It has contributed to a public sphere which is generally wider and better informed about events abroad and which can, at its best, trigger genuine social involvement across borders, as with international appeals which grow out of television news coverage. Television news has contributed to a more open and less deferential engagement with public figures and through its patterns of mass consumption it does add inexorably to a sense of social cohesion across a national context. If as in Crissell's polemic slogan: 'Television news is naive news' (1997: 154), it can still function usefully as a first port of call for audiences who can then go further in their search for information. However, because of its limitations, even experienced broadcasters such as Walter Cronkite are clear in their assessment: 'Those who get most of their news from television probably are not getting enough information to exercise intelligently their voting franchise in a democratic system' (1997: 2).

Television journalism has responded to technological and economic challenges by developing newer variations on generic patterns. Format itself in this context is not simply a stylistic variation. Within such a contested and complex medium it has hugely important political implications (Cottle, 2001). Questions of format are often central to the weighting of journalism between citizen access or commercial appeal. If journalism is not infinitely malleable and therefore a meaningless term, it must be located within a set of discourses which may shift or return over time, but which also carry certain core continuities in providing information and opinion about the world which are expected by its audience and without which it becomes simply a form of fictional entertainment. McNair considers these core continuities to be embedded within social expectations and to be intrinsically involved with questions of format (1998: 4).

The proliferation of information channels has led to an almost inevitable tendency for audiences to read and view more superficially. This has been assisted by parallel technologies such as remote-control devices and Internet search engines which allow for instant retrieval and channel hopping. The formats of twentieth-century journalism need to be able to establish new ways of defending their core practices in the face of political, technological and economic changes as they have had to throughout history but with the added complication that the changes are now more intense than ever before. The postmodern news seems to skim over the surface of things and is infected by a greater range of intertextual entertainment media at a faster rate than ever before.

In addition to the technological and economic changes of the late twentieth century, we are witnessing an epistemological shift referred to as postmodernity which thrives upon the increased speed and intensification of these flows of information. There is much evidence of postmodern trends within the technological changes within journalism. The acceleration and global reach of news are very much in line with Harvey's (1989) definition of postmodernity as a radical time–space compression. It is often identified as characterized by the cross-fertilization of formats between serious and popular, information and entertainment, and associated trends towards a concentration on the surface of things. Postmodernity is also characterized by a blurring of generic boundaries and a radical scepticism concerning definitions, fixities and teleologies, tendencies which have become heightened within the practice and reception of journalism. Furthermore, new technologies within broadcast journalism engender what Jameson has described as a 'fragmentation of time into a series of perpetual presents' (1985: 125). For all this, journalism may resist calls to feel included within postmodernity's scope because several of journalism's core functions as they have emerged over four centuries are deeply embedded within the epistemology of modernity. The political emancipation of journalism can be considered as one of the grand narratives of modernity and has in its myths of the Fourth Estate and objectivity the twin pillars of this tradition, and claims which underpin these narratives inform journalistic standards which continue to be given frequent rhetorical emphasis by broadcasters: '("eye-witness news", "live to air", "on-the-spot report", "the day's most comprehensive news round-up", "that's the way it is" and so on)' (Langer, 1998: 7).

One of the most problematic elements of postmodernity for journalism is the relativization of truth. This was explored recently, appropriately enough in the pages of the *Guardian,* by philosopher David Cooper:

> 'Comment is free, but facts are sacred'. When C.P. Scott, one of this newspaper's greatest editors, wrote his famous lines, he could count on general agreement – confident that intelligent readers were responsive to well-documented evidence and honoured a boundary between truth and interpretation, facts and their evaluation.
>
> Eighty years on, journalists no longer share that confidence. (2000: 14)

This theme is taken up once again in a leading article on the complexities of a world in which Al Jazeera and the Western news media provide their contrasting and potentially incompatible versions of the world: 'Truth may, indeed, be the first casualty, but there is usually more than one version of the truth' (the *Guardian*, 28 March 2003: 29).

Certainly the polysemy and multidimensionality of the truth in the general regime of postmodernity provoke critical questions about the nature and function of journalism as a truth-telling grand narrative. To a large extent we may consider the responses of journalism to this current configuration as less a fall from a 'golden age' and more an accommodation with shifts which enable it to maintain credibility in an intertextual media world of overlapping styles. This is why the examination of format is so important and one crucial question for this examination is how the discourses and formats of journalism manage to retain an identifiable coherence within its core continuities.

The building blocks of all journalism are the news bulletin, the feature article – whether in written form or a broadcast documentary current affairs format – commentary, the interview and the editorial, together with essential interactive features such as letters to the editor and more recent additions such as vox pop, phone-ins, live studio debate and e-mails to live news programmes. Within these basic configurations of contemporary journalism there are many combinations and cross-overs which challenge more traditionalist distinctions between hard news and soft news, fact and opinion, information and entertainment. Journalism has always enabled conflicting views of its functions to co-exist without closure around any one of them. Good journalism has always been able to incorporate textual, generic and epistemological variety, from Nedham to *Newsnight*. It therefore manages to draw them into a provisional stability and retains its coherence and legitimacy, as long as it is able to maintain that balance. There are still hierarchies of believability, from BBC News and the so-called 'newspapers of record' to the *Sunday Sport* and Kelvin MacKenzie's News Bunny. Even these hierarchies are problematized, however, by an 'informed scepticism about what is read, seen and heard in the journalistic media' which McNair assumes is a common feature of the contemporary reception environment (1998: 39) and which Billig (1992) has so astutely observed in his study of the reception of royal news.

It is the diversity and adaptability within its core functions which have certainly provided journalism with its longevity. We need here to be aware of the ways in which revisions of journalism's core begin to unravel when we extract them from their intertextual and discursive complexity. Generic variation within journalism is a cultural response to shifting technological and economic conditions as journalism continues to be negotiated between sources, laws and market demands. The commercial explosion mentioned in the previous section has had an impact on the format and content of journalism in its popularization as it seeks to establish broader strategies to engage with information and opinion about the contemporary world which are both culturally relevant and commercially viable.

We may see evidence for many of the developments discussed above in the way the format of television journalism is incorporating changes to maintain alignment with journalism's broader discursive constituents of technology, political-economy and culture. Format is defined by Dahlgren as: 'the manner in which material is defined, shaped, structured and presented, constituting a mediating link joining technology, subject matter, economics and audiences' (1995: 54). News, current affairs and documentaries are the three principal television forms of journalism. All three have demonstrated an increasing awareness of the values of entertainment in style, adroit exploitation of technology and the elevation of journalists to celebrity status. The main innovations and shifts within conventional genres of journalism on television have been identified as tabloid TV (Langer, 1998). Many of these developments are far from being restricted to the British market and form part of indigenous interpretations of (American) globalized formats which have travelled the world of broadcast journalism.

Documentary and Current Affairs
- -

De Burgh sees investigative journalism as a 'relic of Chalaby's and Habermas' nineteenth century', a mode of enquiry on behalf of citizens who demanded information beyond what the ruling elite of the day chose to tell them (2000: 45). It has a tradition which stretches from Russell through Stead to the *Sunday Times* Insight team in the 1960s, but it was in television that it reached new heights of popular impact up to the 1980s in the form of current affairs documentaries. The drawback of documentary investigative journalism is that in an era driven by the bottom line of profit, it is expensive, politically volatile for news corporations and not hugely popular unless it can be combined with some entertainment value. This has led to a range of recent hybrid experimentation as conventional cutting-edge documentary of the traditional style is marginalized or even transcended.

Holland cites Adam Holloway's *No Fixed Abode* produced by Granada in 1992 as a landmark:

> The role of the journalist has thus expanded. The introduction of the personality of the journalist and their own commitment to a story has added a different type of authority. The fascination generated by the emotional pull of these programmes means that they respond to the 'market' demand for bigger audiences, as well as to the demand for greater transparency in the journalist's role. (1998: 90)

Since then investigative television journalism has included the sensationalist and confrontational heavy-man investigative show with Roger Cook, the rise of alternative comedians as radical journalists as in the case of Mark Thomas, and the celebrity-driven Donal MacIntyre. All have contributed towards the trend of entertainer-journalists. The most famous contemporary who is both commercially successful yet radical at the same time is the American Michael Moore, demonstrating perhaps the potential for radical critique to come from this hybrid format. All of these share a foregrounding of the investigative journalist over the subject matter, the personality over the content and this has brought a more personalized approach to contemporary issues. Personalization of issues does not rule out quality journalism. Macdonald has vindicated its deployment, if it manages to 'to provoke the range of questions that need to be opened for debate if we are to have a vibrant democracy' and in doing so challenges 'unquestioning and complacent beliefs in the communicative success of rationality and abstraction' (2000: 264–5). We also recall the personal tone and commitment of early radical journalists from Cobbett to O'Connor as an established tradition within a much less commercialized brand of journalism. Donal MacIntyre's series of investigative reports *MacIntyre Undercover* (November 1999) could be taken as either an example of a new form of market-orientated, celebrity-driven journalism or a reinvigorated approach to establishing fresh channels of enquiry to reveal uncomfortable truths – or an astute blend of the two as some suspected of Stead a century before (Jones, 1988). MacIntyre's programmes dealt with issues such as football hooligans, the world of glamour modelling and the abuse of people in a care home and have brought arrests, resignations and closures. They were a wider media sensation because of his role as undercover reporter and *post facto* star. They reveal a great deal about the current configuration of journalism within the broader media landscape. Another remarkable recent example of this hybridity was the programme, *Living with Michael Jackson*, with Martin Bashir, which became in early 2003 one of the most talked about television events of the new millennium, dealing as it did with serious issues and exploring reflexively the nature of contemporary celebrity – a cross between celebrity interview, documentary and ultimately news-scoop. Bashir himself, his motivations and techniques, in the best contemporary fashion became a central part of the story.

Another phenomenon which is of related interest and also connected to the personality of the journalist in current affairs broadcasting is that of the 'journalism of attachment' which seeks to question the traditional neutrality of the journalist. Martin Bell coined this expression in 1997:

> that it is aware of its responsibilities; and will not stand neutrally between good and evil, right and wrong, the victim and the oppressor. This is not to back one side or the other; it is to make the point that we in the press, and especially in television which is its most powerful division, do not stand apart from the world. We are part of it. We exercise a certain influence and we have to know that. The influence may be for the better or for worse, and we have to know that too. (Bell, 1997)

Docu-soaps are further evidence of the popularization of the documentary/current affairs format but in this case they provide cheap and unchallenging primetime viewing. These bring us close to the everyday banality of the working lives of environmental health officers, airline employees and customs officers. Superficially they inform an audience about aspects of other people's working lives but never in a way which seeks to explore anything radical or controversial. On occasions, however, the lighter form of documentary can show as in the recent *Is Beckham Black?* that this apparently trivial format also can be put to interesting uses in chronicling changing opinions on life and values in Britain through fresh perspectives.

The Chris Morris satires have also radically reviewed the whole area of investigative journalism itself as the claims of television journalism are held up to sustained mockery from within the very conventions they employ. Morris had started with *On the Hour*, a spoof of the *Today* programme. With Armando Iannucci he produced and fronted *The Day Today*, which in 1994 ran parallel to the BBC's *Nine O'Clock News*, and boasted it 'knocks current affairs broadcasting off its axis, then blow a hole in its spluttering head'. One reviewer clearly appreciated the tendencies within television journalism which could provoke such a satirical onslaught: 'The editors of the Nine O'Clock News, News At Ten and Live At Five may find it uncomfortable viewing. And viewers who fear we are sliding towards a TV news agenda dominated by soundbites and trivia could find The Day Today too close for comfort' (Cuff, 1994: 9).

His television work on *Brass Eye* from 1997 on Channel 4 deliberately preys on the genres and conventions of television to satirize its truth-telling claims and especially its documentary and investigative journalism. Commenting on the success of the satire, a television reviewer, Will Self, knowingly locates it within the tradition of contemporary referential scepticism with regard to the media in general:

> So why did these people fall for such fakery? ... Because they aren't real people any more – they're hyperreal. They've made the Faustian pact of being that oxymoronic incarnation, 'television personalities' ...
>
> The other important point to be made about Morris's elision of 'real' and 'unreal' is that it's at the very core of his attack on television itself. What Morris realises is that television isn't a 'medium' in any meaningful sense at all. Rather it's a skein of different media imprisoned in a bogus proscenium. (1997: 8)

Overall, however, the changes in television investigative journalism are characteristic of investigative journalism in general. It has moved swiftly from systemic/political critique to more personality/populist entertainment. Contemporary journalism shows more interest in the private lives of politicians and their husbands and wives than in the implications of public policy which supports the Chomsky/Hermann thesis that it is concerned not to threaten the business interests of the dominant commercial and political players. Investigative journalism must occasionally be seen, for its own reputation, to be instrumental in exposing wrong-doing in high places but stretched resources in a competitive, commercial environment and rolling news agendas militate against sustained investigation. Successful investigative journalism, by which we mean sustained investigative journalism, within the mainstream, becomes less likely, the more that mainstream becomes commodified.

The 1980s saw the rise of the audience-based talk show, originating in the USA and popularized by Oprah Winfrey first on Channel 4. Since this they have become a familiar daytime format. They possess a problematic identity within journalism. Interviews and vox pops have long constituted part of journalism's repertoire but in these programmes the element of the popular voice, the non-expert, is foregrounded to the exclusion of every-thing else except the celebrity status of the presenter and his/her skill in weaving together the range of views on a particular aspect of the audience's collective experience. Holland suggests: 'In these newer, more open forms of journalism, the audience is no longer merely "imagined" and the pro-gramme is never completely finished. Authenticity is no longer to be found simply within the text itself' (1998: 92). In the words of Livingstone and Lunt, it was original because it challenged 'traditional oppositions of pro-grammes and audience, producer and subject, expert and laity' (1994: 36). It is an extension of the techniques first pioneered by the radio phone-in and yet it is doubtful whether its democratic and participative ambitions out-weigh the desire of networks to provide, as with docu-soaps, cheap and entertaining television. All of these types of programme offer a glimpse of what Dahlgren calls a 'postmodern condition' (1995: 66) in that they are self-referencing within the terms of the programme and detached from the con-ventional methods of reporting a reality external to the framework of the programme and the audience's experiences which the programme selects and edits. This self-referencing can be extended back into the real, external to the studio, by the development of an audience being ask to participate in real crime reconstructions with a view to solving them, on *Crimewatch UK* from 1984. It provides a vicarious pleasure of involvement in police investi-gations in an interactive update on the crime news periodical tradition of the Victorian era. The mysterious murder of one of its presenters, Jill Dando, turned the programme into a real-life case study and developed into an extraordinary intertextual media event, hovering between the vicariousness of the programme's conventions and the external reality of the loss of a media celebrity.

News: Style and Substance

The news format has expanded from set times to accommodate more differ-entiated viewing patterns and has created newer styles to address audiences at different times of the day. Within the proliferation of varieties the impera-tive is to popularize the format so as to best justify expenditure and retain market credibility. The first experiment in adopting television news to changing patterns of consumption and lifestyle was the regular breakfast television news in 1983 *Breakfast TV*. This saw a shift in the hitherto rather austere image of the newscaster. These journalists, easy on the eye and with tones suited to the new style of 'sofa journalism', were very different creatures to their counterparts in other broadcast news programmes. Breakfast television news introduced a softer range of human-interest angles on stories in the news and because of its man–woman double-act it was dubbed 'Ken and Barbie' journalism (van Zoonen, 1998: 40). After breakfast television news the presentational styles and formats of mainstream television news started a process of rapid transformation. Increased use of text on the screen, a sound-bite syntax which reduces the length of individual news items, the use of graphics to illustrate news, all newscasters on first name terms with each other, if not quite yet with the politicians they interview, are all indications of the popularization of the news format. As a summation of these trends, Channel 5 News was launched in April 1997: 'Presented by the photogenic Kirsty Young, and unapologetically targeted at an audience of "younger adults" … aggressively advertised its innovativeness in paying more attention to positive news stories, and incorporating more human interest and lifestyle coverage into its programming' (McNair, 1998: 117).

The BBC has not been immune from moves to introduce more visually appealing television newscasters and reporters. This has led to accusations that the Corporation, in line with commercial rivals, has been preparing to replace older faces such as Peter Sissons with more photogenic and younger replacements. The logic of more aesthetically-pleasing TV presenters seems to fit within a general movement of broadcast news towards entertainment values and may even represent part of a bid to regain some of a younger audience which is turning off from mainstream news and politics. Current affairs programmes such as *Tonight With Trevor McDonald*, drawing on the celebrity status of its anchorman despite its poor ratings, are symptomatic of an increased necessity for television journalism to appeal as widely as possible to maintain a popular appeal.

Another change within mainstream news has been in its content. There has been a shift to include more items of what Langer calls 'Tabloid Television': 'Items about fires, accidents, beauty contests, celebrities, peculiar occupations and hobbies, those "trivialities" which take audiences away from "intellectual activation" were all considered to be part of the "other news" ' (1998: 32–3). He argues that tabloid TV is less linked than popularly perceived to the generic features of print tabloids and has more to do with the generic characteristics of television and broadcast journalism in particular. This form of news can even be observed on CEEFAX which has, for example, recently featured Bootle Billy, the homing pigeon who took a detour via New York on his way from France to Liverpool and completed the final leg of his journey first class, by courtesy of British Airways, and a young holidaymaker whose tongue stud was hit by lightning, causing a couple of hours of speechlessness. In his 1992 article, Langer refers to the 'anarchic existentialism' of the disaster news at the heart of much tabloidization which implies that the world is a random place where such events occur

pparent reason. His perspective can be contrasted with the more
rientated melodramatic mode of Gripsrud (1992) who roots popu-
ormats in the tradition of a fixed universe of good versus evil. The
nplications of each of these views offer scant analytical potential
auses of events in the world and leave the viewer to occupy the
place of victim-observer rather than participant-citizen.

In response to the challenges of commercial competition and hostility
from conservative politicians towards the concept of the BBC as a public
broadcaster, Birt's 'Issue Journalism' was introduced in an attempt to create
a more in-depth variant of popular mainstream television news with a
Reithian-sounding mission to educate the viewer. It sought to provide less
stories but with more perspectives. This was to be counter-balanced by an
attempt to provide more accessibility in current affairs but has been interpreted as a drift towards more entertainment-driven values. Birt's contributions to the news and current affairs agenda were profoundly influenced
by the perceived necessity of providing the BBC with a distinctive brand of
journalism in an increasingly congested market and to legitimate its privileged position within public service broadcasting by offering a more popularized range of journalism. This has not been without its critics. Birt sought
to counter what he saw as the generic shortcomings of television journalism
in its 'bias against understanding' by expanding the time available to the
news issues of the day but was criticized for a style of reporting which was
more centrally managed and more overtly didactic in its 'mission to explain'.

Political Issues: Spin and Scepticism

Broadcast technology has forced a reconsideration of the relationship
between journalism and the state over the last century. As the narrative of
this book has shown, different eras can be defined by this relationship
(Siebert, 1965). The confluence of technological and commercial pressures on
journalism in the late twentieth century has produced a very contemporary
set of challenges with regard to the relationship between journalism and politics. Broadcast journalism, for instance, is even more sensitive within this
relationship because of its long-standing commitment to a model of a public
service ethos which is based on independence and impartiality. Whenever
broadcast journalism seems to be challenging the boundaries of these conventions, politicians have always been swift to accuse it of bias and of desert-
ing the principles which the public expects from it. The current dispute
between the BBC and government over the coverage of the Iraq war and the
contents of the intelligence dossier upon which the government went to war
is a striking contemporary illustration. The status of the independence of
television journalism has been strained at many points in recent years,
notably throughout the prolonged military intervention in Northern Ireland
(especially with the 1988–94 Sinn Fein broadcasting ban) and the war in the

Falklands. Since this point, Keeble (1997) has chronicled a general trend within the news media to self-censor genuine political criticism once hostilities have started as part of a process which, in negotiation with the state, allows a condition of crisis to be declared through the news media (Raboy and Dagenais, 1992).

Parliamentary reporting has become the dominant form of broadcast political journalism, moving initially from *The Week in Westminster* in 1929 to the daily radio reporting of Parliament in 1945. This trend has expanded from the first regular radio broadcasting of parliamentary debate in 1976, to the televising of the House of Lords in 1985 and finally the televising of the House of Commons in 1989. This constitutes a staged journey of increasing intrusion on behalf of the public into the processes of political debate and thus assists the credibility of broadcast journalism but generates, in response, an increasing sophistication from the political media machinery. Such a symbiotic relationship, though, is not without consequences for journalism. Politicians have become more aware of how they need to perform in the mediated public eye and are coached, groomed and styled for TV appearance and radio performance. More and more political reporting has become commentary upon the rhetoric of politicians as the main party political agendas have converged. Policy substance is consequently subordinated to policy rhetoric and journalism colludes in this by its rhetoricized reporting. Yet at the same time, in different parts of the broadcast news media there is a great deal of analysis of the processes involved and probing of the rhetoric of politics rather than a straightforward reporting of political events and policies as facts. It is unclear whether this contributes to the growing scepticism of the public about the political process or enables consumers of the news to be better placed to interpret and assess the reality of present-day politics. Both processes are interconnected and both tell of cultural shifts in politics and public reception via journalism rather than the latter's decline from a high point of public service. The two in combination are accused of ushering in an era of citizen apathy with consequences for public communication in general leading to a range of responses from the public, the politicians themselves and the broadcasters. The public is locked into a 'penumbra of cynicism' (Blumler and Gurevitch, 1995: 220) about media manipulation which may in part be responsible for a decline in interest in hard political reporting and involvement in politics itself, contributing to the decline in numbers voting in general and local elections. From the politicians, there are attempts to put the blame squarely on the broadcasters while attempting to increase the efficiency of their own media management. Much of the journalistic response has been an attempt to counter the strategy of political media presentation that has become known as spin. From the broadcasters, within political discussion programmes, there are increasingly forceful attempts to brow-beat politicians into submission on air which squares conveniently with an increasingly entertainment-led news media agenda masquerading as public-spirited enquiry.

The most vociferous complaints about radio journalism's political coverage have concerned the tenacity and intensity of interviews with politicians on Radio 4's flagship news programme *Today*, which still averages 6 million listeners a week and is a vital part of the setting of the daily news agenda. Television's high profile bear pit for politicians is *Newsnight* on late night BBC television. Channel 4 News, as an exemplar of good practice in the commercial sector, provided some particularly sustained questioning of political and military personnel early in the Iraq war. There is obviously a commercial as well as a public service motivation if such coverage can attract viewers/listeners within a provision which is often judged on its popularity. As well as interviewers probing in the time-honoured role as watchdogs for the public, they are aware of the gladiatorial spectacle of such interviews and the thrill of the event for the audience. There has been from the late twentieth century an increasing awareness of the commercial appeal of adversarial political journalism and the role the interviewer plays as part of this. The self-conscious role of the journalist as counterbalance to the PR and spin of politicians and public spokespeople adds as much to the entertainment value as it helps boost the credibility of his/her media organization. As politicians, in their turn, become more adept at playing the media's games, analytical attention and a corresponding increase in self-awareness and reflexivity among journalists themselves have given rise to a more partisan notion of objectivity and impartiality. One solution suggested to this current stand-off has been to follow the lead of newspapers and modify or even drop the rigorous requirements for impartiality and objectivity in broadcast journalism. Hargreaves suggests this may be one solution to political apathy among the public (Hargreaves and Thomas, 2003). Channel 5's *News on Five* is already experimenting with a mixture of news and debate with speakers from well-flagged political orientations giving their views of the topic under discussion.

The economic imperatives of broadcast journalism in particular have led news media organizations to concentrate on tried and tested routines and sources. In mainstream news programmes on television, we see increasingly formulaic representations of events. The sight of reporters standing in front of the important locations of public life relating the events of the day has become a familiar and dull part of television reporting routines. Such approaches converge on Westminster as the sole site of politics and have detrimental implications for the quality and range of discussion in a democracy. They generate in return an increase in the sound-bite presentation from political communicators which reduces the content of policy to the formats which broadcast news specializes in.

Journalism throughout the twentieth century has become more socially pervasive, providing the potential for more people to access a wider range of information and entertainment in the construction of citizens/consumers of a global public sphere. There continues to be a fair range of probing investigation but this tends to be broadcast outside the primetime band of mid-evening viewing reserved for guaranteed peak audiences. The century has also witnessed increasingly sophisticated attempts to harness journalists' disruptive potential as 'the agents of instability' (McNair, 1998: 165), through media management and manipulation and by bringing journalism ever closer to the sources which it seeks to retain a critical distance from. This has an additional consequence of bringing pressure on journalism to present source material favourably as the threat of withdrawal of such privileged access may threaten cooperation from essential news suppliers. This is a very different sort of pressure on the reporting of politics and public life than that faced by Cave, who simply sought to report the affairs of Parliament in the *Gentleman's Magazine*. The current complex relationship between politics and journalism certainly does not represent a permanent stalemate when viewed from an historical perspective. More likely, it is a momentary pause before one side or the other develops a new set of strategies to take the initiative in a struggle over information and control which is even older than either journalism or the print media. Perhaps the growing weariness towards the cynical manipulation of both journalists and politicians is the moment of rebirth rather than the endgame.

11

Conclusion

New Configurations for the Definition of Journalism

Negative criticism of the state of journalism today comes from a position which often identifies itself as traditionalist, a classic statement of which comes from Franklin:

> Journalism's editorial priorities have changed. Entertainment has super-seded the provision of information; human interest has supplanted the public interest; measured judgment has succumbed to sensationalism; the trivial has triumphed over the weighty; the intimate relationships of celebrities, from soap operas, the world of sport or the royal family are judged more 'newsworthy' than the reporting of significant issues and events of international consequence. Traditional news values have been undermined by new values; 'infotainment' is rampant. (1997: 4)

Other criticism with more profound epistemological scepticism concerning the identity and even the existence of journalism comes from Bardel who claims that, '"Journalism" – if it ever existed – is falling apart' (1996: 301). Michael Bromley also alludes to this possibility although from an organiza-tional perspective (1997). One problem with the traditionalist view from the discursive perspective of this study is that journalism has always sought to align itself within a broad range of economic, political and cultural impera-tives and the surviving discourse has been shaped by the selection of prior-ities in any particular era. Langer criticizes Franklin's reproach for its, 'desire for an idealized "information model" of news which, in order to exist in a "pure" form, requires overlooking news as cultural discourse, already con-stituted as more than just information delivery' (Langer, 1998: 155). In these terms, Bardel is right in his radical scepticism; journalism as a fixed practice has never existed but only ever as a discursive combination of a variety of practices negotiated within power relationships which have shifted over time. It continues to exist because of its very ability to adjust to a radical reconfiguration of many of these practices under pressure from contemporary influences. Perhaps Franklin confuses change with decline, although this study would be the first to acknowledge that change always has political implications, not all of which are necessarily politically progressive.

Certainly, an increase in lifestyle features and a general popularization and commercialization are common threads through the development of mainstream journalism over the twentieth century. They have impinged even upon the areas of public service broadcasting. But one cannot simply bemoan this situation. It seems more appropriate to attempt to assess it as part of cultural change rather than contrast it to the perspective of a 'golden age'. It could well be that these sorts of anxieties are cyclical as they do share overtones of all debate over the place of journalism in public life from the Civil War to the contemporary. Tulloch warns of the seductive pull of such cosy narratives:

> And each generation stages a version of the new journalism debate and projects into the past a tale of a more rational public sphere. Once upon a time, according to this recurring tale, arguments were expounded at length and listened to. Once upon a time the public meeting, the serious newspaper, the radio discussion, the television, news, the television documentary – take your pick – was a model for public discourse. But each has been destroyed or subverted by unthinking change. The golden age beckons tantalizingly. (2000: 134)

There are many more opportunities to engage with the contemporary world through the existing range of journalism than ever before. The increasing diversification and hybridity of news genres need to be considered within a broader view of how consumers and citizens (who are after all the same creatures in different modes) are addressed culturally by a whole range of interconnecting media and how they draw their choices and information from the totality of the media sphere, not just from those parts of their media experience labelled 'quality journalism'. Journalism has always contained elements of intertextuality; what we see now is a particularly heightened, accelerated and technologized form of it which draws journalism inexorably across previous boundaries and into new relationships.

In a postmodern era where representation often borders on the hyper-real because of the speed and clarity of visual information, journalism struggles to maintain a coherent space for public discussion of the social. The intensification of intertextual flows is not, in itself, a good thing or a bad thing but it is radically restructuring journalism in the same way as it radically overhauls other parts of the social world. Whether it produces results which are positive or negative depends as much on how journalism adapts to them as it does on how people as both citizens and consumers remain interested in shaping their own public and social understanding of their worlds. There is no guarantee that journalism will remain the privileged truth-telling public narrative which it has claimed to be in its various historical guises unless it is able to engage positively with the increased flows and generic variety unleashed by de-regulation and the multiplication of forms of public information. Corporate ownership has never encouraged genuine social involvement from the public within journalism. In such an intensified environment, it is less likely that such corporations will change their ways unless politicians and the public begin to exert their own influence. Perhaps it is naive to expect much more than stability from the mainstream and we should look outside the traditional networks of journalism for radical change. Atton (2002) illustrates how the strategic deployment of new technologies in online media and 'zines' have the potential to create counterpublics, drawing on the energies of autodidacts in public information who are anti-professional.

Journalism continues to have a range of competing and overlapping functions. These include giving information, political aims, entertainment, normative/integrationist creation of social identities, agenda-setting and consumerist motives, but maybe we should look within the contemporary for the spaces where these important functions are fulfilled within increasingly complex networks of a more integrated and wider mediasphere. Journalism is defined in each era by its particular engagement with politics, technology, economics and culture. Dahlgren is one leading commentator who appreciates this diversity and stresses that the 'cultural discourse' (1988: 51) of news is not simply informational but part of a broader set of symbolic representation. This multiplicity and generic variation have always formed part of journalism's resilience and vitality and explain much of its ability to realign within different historical and political settings. The 'cultural discourse' of contemporary journalism is to be observed in the media-saturated everyday life of its audience both as citizens and consumers. The intertextual merging of journalism with other formats and discourses is maybe its most pressing present challenge and its future will certainly be inscribed within our responses to it. Yet not everything can simply converge. If it is to survive, journalism must be able to assert a specific location within this media sphere, demonstrate that it can deliver a particular form of service to the public, however fragmented and commodified that public might become. The current situation, rather than a convergence, can be better described by Bakhtin's term of heteroglossia. Within the heteroglossia of cultural discourse, journalism remains determined ultimately by the voice of the political economy. This has always been the case for journalism despite its generic variety and political pragmatism. Bakhtin's heteroglossia does not imply egalitarian exchange, but rather conflict and instability as each voice seeks to gain provisional dominance. The contemporary discourse of journalism with its vitality and intertextual energy is composed by a set of voices which are informally licensed by the dominant economic paradigm. The increasing dominance of this current phase of the political economy of journalism risks jeopardizing the structural balance necessary for its long-term survival as a discourse which can provide something other than the voice of a commercially successful and ultimately political conservative set of formulae. Journalism must remain distinguishable from just another commercial media product. Almost as a manifesto for the populist, postmodern challenges which face contemporary journalism, Dahlgren outlines the combination which journalism must draw together if it is to survive in any coherent way as a set of practices entitled to claim the discursive heritage of journalism. It needs to combine 'popular pragmatics' in its appeal to the market to make it a viable form of communication and it needs to maintain an engagement with 'serious thematics' (Dahlgren, 1995: 52).

Part of the solution to a market-dominated form of journalism may lie in the anarchic influence of web technology on established journalism. New technologies such as the Internet are undermining conventional journalism traditions to such an extent that the Association for Journalism Education conference, the body which represents journalism educators in the UK, debated at City University in 2003 whether people can even now become better informed by going to Internet, rather than edited, journalistic sources. Some areas of journalism are attempting to incorporate much of the interactive/archival potential of the web. On-line services and digital technology illustrate the potential for public participation in the media of journalism, providing news formats which could arguably counteract the superficial tendencies of more traditional and mass-market journalism, if they were not limited to a smaller audience than general news programmes. The digital red button can generate a blended menu of self-selected news agendas. BBC online has a similar service together with the extensive archiving and multi-media links of most major news providers including broadsheet newspapers. The implications of the web for journalism are multiple. It holds out the potential for a proliferation of alternative sources of information and the cheap publication of alternative views. It opens up specialist information as never before and poses questions about the long-term viability of journalism as a professional practice if consumers are able to access what they need without editorial selectivity. It allows people to access archives in ways available only to professional researchers a few years ago. It is destablizing norms of journalism, expanding and challenging them. These developments do not necessarily mean the end of journalism but they certainly demand a dynamic set of responses from journalism which involve audiences in the social aspects of its core practices if it is to survive as something other than either a commercial staple or an esoteric hobby for an intellectual elite. The encouraging news for those who believe that journalism is necessary for a broadly informed public, able to engage critically and empathetically with the contemporary world, is that it always has survived and according to the same rules as today. It has always negotiated a path of compromise between politics, commerce and technology in pursuit of reliable information about the world we live in and opinion on that world. Journalism survives by its ability to develop popular and pragmatic ways of engaging with the broad variety of public life, thus vindicating a Foucauldian perspective of journalism as a discourse which manages to produce opportunities for pleasure and resistance within the constraints and disciplinary mechanisms which combine to shape its limitations and its potential.

This history has attempted to show how journalism has not degenerated from a 'golden age' but has always been dynamically formed and reformed as a discourse at a complex intersection of many competing voices claiming it for their own. Technology, economy, politics, society, power and knowledge have been those voices and provide the heteroglossia within journalism's discourse. Contemporary changes within journalism may well enable it to reinvigorate its function of providing a public form of knowledge as well as maintaining its profitablity. To allude to an early pamphleteer, John Milton, whose work has been quoted earlier in this book, in terms of journalism, paradise has never existed, so we need not trouble ourselves in trying to regain it. Maybe the best we could always hope for was that the discourse might be renegotiated. The present situation may be one of formative crisis but the story is far from over.

Bibliography

Adams, W. (1903) *Memoirs of a Social Atom*. Vol. 2. London: Hutchinson.

Adburgham, A. (1972) *Women in Print: Writing Women and Women's Magazines from the Restoration to the Accession of Victoria*. London: George Allen and Unwin.

Alison, A. (1834) 'The influence of the press', *Blackwood's Edinburgh Magazine*. September.

Allen, S. (1999) *News Culture*. Milton Keynes: Open University Press.

Altheide, D. and Snow, R. (1991) *Media Worlds in the Postjournalism Era*. New York: Aldine de Gruyter.

Anderson, B. (1986) *Imagined Communities*. London: Verso.

Anderson, P.J. (1992) 'Factory girl, apprentice and clerk: the readership of mass-market magazines, 1830–60', *Victorian Periodicals Review*, 25: 64–72.

Andrews, A. (2000 [1847]) *The History of British Journalism: From the Foundation of the Newspaper Press in England to the Repeal of the Stamp Act in 1855, with Sketches of Press Celebrities*. Vols 1 and 2. London: Routledge/Thoemmes.

Angell, N. (1922) *The Press and the Organisation of Society*. London: Labour Publishing Company.

Arnold, M. (1887) 'Up to Easter', *The Nineteenth Century*, CXXIII, May, 627–48.

Aspinall, A. (1945) *Politics and the Press c 1780 1850*. London: Home and Van Thal.

Asquith, I. (1978) 'The structure, ownership and control of the press 1780–1855', in G. Boyce, J. Curran and P. Wingate (eds), *Newspaper History from the Seventeenth Century to the Present Day*. London: Constable.

Atherton, I. (1999) 'The itch grown a disease: manuscript transmission of news in the seventeenth century' in J. Raymond (ed.), *News, Newspapers and Society in Early Modern Britain*. London: Frank Cass.

Atton, C. (2002) *Alternative Media*. London: Sage.

Bainbridge, C. and Stockdill, R. (1993) *The News of the World Story*. London: Harper Collins.

Baistow, T. (1985) *Fourth Rate Estate*. London: Comedia.

Bakhtin, M.M. (1996) *The Dialogic Imagination*, (ed.) M. Holquist, trans. C. Emerson and M. Holquist. Austin, TX: University of Texas Press.

Baldasty, G.J. (1992) *The Commercialization of News in the Nineteenth Century*. Madison: University of Wisconsin Press.

Ballaster, R., Beetham, M., Frazer, E. and Hebron, S. (1991) *Women's Worlds: Ideology, Femininity and the Women's Magazine*. Basingstoke: Macmillan.

Bardel, J. (1996) 'Beyond journalism: a profession between information society and civil society', *European Journal of Communication*, 11 (3): 283–302.

Barker, H. (1998) *Newspapers, Politics and Public Opinion in Late Eighteenth Century England*. Oxford: Oxford University Press.

Barker, H. (2000) *Newspapers, Politics and English Society 1695–1855*. Harlow: Longman.

Baron, S. (2001) 'The guises of dissemination in early seventeenth century England', in B. Dooley and S. Baron (eds), *The Politics of Information in Early Modern Europe*. London: Routledge.

Baudrillard, J. (1983) 'The ecstasy of communication', in H. Foster (ed.), *The Anti-Aesthetic: Essays on Post-Modern Culture*. Seattle: Bay Press.

Baylen, J.O. (1979) 'The press and public opinion: W.T. Stead and "The New Journalism"', in *Journalism Studies Review*, 4, July: 45–9.

Beetham, M. and Boardman, K. (eds) (2001) *Victorian Women's Magazines*. Manchester: Manchester University Press.

Beetham, M. (1996) *A Magazine of Her Own? Domesticity and Desire in the Women's Magazine 1800–1914*. London: Routledge.

Bell, D. (1979) *The Cultural Contradictions of Capitalism*. London: Heinemann.

Bell, M. (1997) 'TV News: How Far Should We Go?' in *British Journalism Review*, 8 (1): 7–16.

Behrendt, S.C. (1997) *Radicalism, Romanticism and the Press*. Detroit: Wayne State University Press.

Berridge, V. (1978) 'Popular Sunday papers and mid-Victorian society', in G. Boyce, J. Curran and P. Wingate (eds), *Newspaper History from the Seventeenth Century to the Present Day*. London: Constable.

Billig, M. (1992) *Talking of the Royal Family*. London: Routledge.

Black, J. (ed.) (1984) *Britain in the Age of Walpole*. Basingstoke: Palgrave.

Black, J. (1991) *The English Press in the Eighteenth Century*. Aldershot: Gregg Revivals.

Black, J. (2001) *The English Press 1621–1861*. Stroud: Sutton Publishing.

Blumler, J. and Gurevitch, M. (1995) *The Crisis in Public Communication*. London: Routledge.

Bond, D.F. (ed.) (1965) *The Spectator Vol. IV*. London: Oxford University Press.

Bourdieu, P. (1998) *On Television and Journalism*. London: Pluto.

Boston, R. (1990) *The Essential Fleet Street: Its History and Influence*. London: Blandford.

Boyce, G. (1978) 'The Fourth Estate: the reappraisal of a concept', in G. Boyce, J. Curran and P. Wingate (eds), *Newspaper History from the Seventeenth Century to the Present Day*. London: Constable.

Boyce, G. (1987) 'Crusaders without chains: power and the press barons 1896–1951', in J. Curran, A. Smith and P. Wingate (eds), *Impacts and Influences: Essays on Media Power in the Twentieth Century*. London: Methuen.

Boyce, G., Curran, J. and Wingate, P. (eds) (1978) *Newspaper History from the Seventeenth Century to the Present Day*. London: Constable.

Boyd, D.H. and MacLeod, W.R. (1977) *Newsletters to Newspapers*. West Virginia: West Virginia University Press.

Brake, L. (1988) 'The old journalism and the new: forms of cultural production in London in the 1880s', in J. Wiener (ed.), *Papers for the Millions: The New Journalism in Britain 1850–1914*, London: Greenwood Press.

Brake, L., Bell, B. and Finkelstein, D. (eds) (2000) *Nineteenth-Century Media and the Construction of Identities*. Basingstoke: Palgrave.

Bray, T.C. (1965) *A Newspaper's Role in Modern Society*. Queensland: University of Queensland Press.

Brewer, J. (1976) *Party Ideology and Popular Politics at the Accession of George III*. Cambridge: Cambridge Univeristy Press.

Briggs, A. (1961) *The Golden Age of the Wireless*. Oxford: Oxford University Press.

Briggs, A. (1979) *The History of Broadcasting in the United Kingdom*. Vol. IV. Oxford: Oxford University Press.

Briggs, A. (1995) *The History of Broadcasting in the United Kingdom*. Vol. V. Oxford: Oxford University Press.

Briggs, A. and Burke, P. (2002) *A Social History of the Media: From Gutenberg to the Internet*. Cambridge: Polity Press.

Bromley, M. (1997a) 'The end of journalism?: Changes in workplace practices in the press and broadcasting in the 1990s', in M. Bromley and T. O'Malley (eds), *A Journalism Reader*. London: Routledge.

Bromley, M. (1997b) 'From Fleet Street to cyberspace: the British "Popular" press in the late twentieth century', *European Journal of Communication Studies*, 22 (3): 365–78.

Bromley, M. (1998) 'The "Tabloiding" of Britain: quality newspapers in the 1990s', in H. Stephenson and M. Bromley (eds), *Sex, Lies and Democracy*. Harlow: Longman.

Bromley, M. (ed.) (2001) *No News is Bad News: Radio, Television and the Public*. Harlow: Pearson.

Brown, L. (1985) *Victorian News and Newspapers*. Oxford: Clarendon Press.

Burke, P. (1978) *Popular Culture in Early Modern Europe*. London: Temple Smith.

Burton, R. (1972) *The Anatomy of Melancholy*, (ed.), H. Jackson. London: J.M. Dent and Sons.

Campbell, K. (2000) 'Journalistic discourses and constructons of modern knowledge', in L. Brake, B. Bell and D. Finkelstein (eds), *Nineteenth Century Media and the Construction of Identities*. Basingstoke: Palgrave, 40–53.

Capp, B. (1979) *Astrology and the Popular Press: English Almanacs 1500–1800*. London: Faber and Faber.

Carter, C., Branston, G. and Allen S. (eds) (1998) *News, Gender and Power*. London: Routledge.

Chalaby, J.K. (2000) 'Northcliffe: Journalist as Proprietor', in P. Caterall, C. Seymour-Ure and A. Smith (eds), *Northcliffe's Legacy*. Basingstoke: Macmillan.

Chalaby, J.K. (1998) *The Invention of Journalism*. Basingstoke: Macmillan.

Chartier, R. (1988) *Cultural History: Between Practices and Representations*. trans. L.G. Cochrane. Cambridge: Cambridge University Press.

Chippendale, P. and Horrie, C. (1992) *Stick It Up Your Punter*. London: Mandarin.

Clark, S. (1983) *The Elizabethan Pamphleteers: Popular Moralistic Pamphlets, 1580–1640*. London.

Clegg, C.S. (1997) *Press Censorship in Elizabethan England*. Cambridge: Cambridge University Press.

Cleverley, G. (1976) *The Fleet Street Disaster*. London: Constable and Company Ltd.

Clyde, W.M. (1934) *The Struggle for the Freedom of the Press from Caxton to Cromwell*. University of St Andrews/Humphrey Milford.

Colley, L. (1992) *Britons: Forging the Nation 1707–1837*. London: Pimlico.

Conboy, M. (2002) *The Press and Popular Culture*. London: Sage.

Connell, I. (1992) 'Personalities in the popular media', in P. Dahlgren and C. Sparks (eds), *Journalism and Popular Culture*. London: Sage.

Cooper, D. (2000) 'Missing Manchester values', the *Guardian*. Friday 22 December.

Corner, J. (1991) 'Meaning, genre and context: the problematics of "public knowledge" in the new audience studies', in J. Curran and M. Gurevitch (eds), *Mass Media and Society*. London: Edward Arnold.

Cottle, S. (2001) 'Television news and citizenship: packaging the public sphere', in M. Bromley (ed.), *No News is Bad News*. Harlow: Pearson.

Cranfield, G.A. (1978) *The Press and Society: From Caxton to Northcliffe*. Harlow: Longman.

Creedon, P. (1989) (ed.) *Women in Mass Communication: Challenging Gender Views*. London: Sage.

Cressy, D. (1980) *Literacy and the Social Order: Reading and Writing in Tudor and Stuart England*. Cambridge: Cambridge University Press.

Crisell, A. (1997) *An Introductory History of British Broadcasting*. London: Routledge.

Cronkite, W. (1997) The *Guardian*, Media Supplement, 27 January, 2.

Cudlipp, H. (1953) *Publish and Be Damned*. London: Andrew Dakers.

Cuff, A. (1994) 'The mickey-take on news', The *Guardian*, Media Supplement, 10 January, 9.

Curran, J. (1978) 'The press as an agency of social control: an historical perspective', in G. Boyce, J. Curran and P. Wingate (eds), *Newspaper History from the Seventeenth Century to the Present Day*. London: Constable.

Curran, J. and Seaton, J. (1993) *Power Without Responsibility*. London: Routledge.

Cust, R. (1986) 'News and politics in seventeenth century England', *Past and Present*, 112: 60–90.

Dahlgren, P. (1988) 'What's the meaning of this? Viewers' plural sense-making of TV news', *Media, Culture and Society*, 10: 285–301.

Dahlgren, P. (1995) *Television and the Public Sphere*. London: Sage.

Dahlgren, P. and Sparks, C. (1992) *Journalism and Popular Culture*. London: Sage.

Dallas, E.S. (1859) 'Popular Literature – The Periodical Press', in *Blackwood's Edinburgh Magazine*: 96–112.

Dancyger, I. (1978) *A World of Women*. Dublin: Gill and Macmillan.

Darnton, R. (1996) *Forbidden Fruit*. London: HarperCollins.

Davis, L.J. (1983) *Factual Fictions: The Origins of the English Novel*. Philadelphia: University of Pennsylvania Press.

Day, R. (1989) *The Grand Inquisitor*. London: Weidenfeld and Nicholson.

de Burgh, H. (2000) *Investigative Journalism*. London: Routledge.

Defoe, D. (1704) 'An essay on the regulation of the press'.

Defoe, D. (1715) 'An appeal to honour and justice'.

Defoe, D. (1718) 'A vindication of the press'.

Dooley, B. and Baron, S. (eds) (2001) *The Politics of Information in Early Modern Europe*. London: Routledge.

Downie, J.A. (1979) *Robert Harley and the Press: Propaganda and Public Opinion in the Age of Swift and Defoe*. Cambridge: Cambridge University Press.

Eagleton, T. (1991) *The Function of Criticism: From The Spectator to Post-Structuralism*. London: Verso.

Easley, A. (2000) 'Authorship, gender and power in Victorian culture: Harriet Martineau and the periodical press', in L. Brake, B. Bell and D. Finkelstein (eds), *Nineteenth Century Media and the Construction of Identities*. Basingstoke: Palgrave.

Eisenstein, E.L. (1979) *The Printing Press as an Agent of Social Change*. Cambridge: Cambridge University Press.

Elliott, T.S. (1948) *Notes Towards a Definition of Culture*. London: Faber and Faber.

Elliott, P. (1978) 'Professional ideology and organisational change: the journalist since 1800', in G. Boyce, J. Curran and P. Wingate (eds), *Newspaper History from the Seventeenth Century to the Present Day*. London: Constable.

Epstein, J. (1976) 'Fergus O'Connor and the *Northern Star*', *International Review of Social History*, 21: 51–97.

Engel, M. (1996) *Tickle the Public: One Hundred Years of the Popular Press*. London: Gollanz and Prentice Hall.

Ensor, R. (1968) *The Oxford History of England: Vol. XIV: 1870–1914*. Oxford: Oxford University Press.

Escott, T.H.S. (1875) 'Old and new in the daily press', *Quarterly Review*, CCXXVII, 368.

Esser, F. (1999) 'Tabloidization of News: A Comparative Analysis of Anglo-American and German Press Journalism' in *European Journal of Communication*, 14 (3): 291–324.

Featherstone, M. (ed.) (1993) *Global Culture: Nationalism, Globalization and Modernity*. London: Sage.

Ferguson, M. (1983) *Forever Feminine*. London: Gower.

Finkelstein, D. (2002) *The House of Blackwood*. Philadelphia: Pennsylvania State University Press.

Foster, H. (1983) *The Anti-Aesthetic. Essays on Postmodern Culture*. Seattle: Bay Press.

Foucault, M. (1974) *The Archaeology of Knowledge*. Trans. A.M. Sheridan. London: Tavistock.

Foucault, M. (1980) 'The eye of power', in C. Gordon (ed.), *Power/Knowledge*. Brighton: Harvester Wheatsheaf.

Fox-Bourne, H.R. (1998) *English Newspapers*. Vols 1 and 2. London: Thommes/ Routledge.

Frank, J. (1961) *The Beginnings of the English Newspaper*. Cambridge Mass: Harvard University Press.

Franklin, B. (1997) *Newszack and News Media*. London: Arnold.

Fraser, P. (1956) *The Intelligence of the Secretaries of State and Their Monopolies of Licensed News, 1660–1688*. Cambridge: Cambridge University Press.

Friederichs, H. (1911) *The Life of Sir George Newnes*. London: Hodder and Stoughton.

Friedman, J. (1993) *Miracles and the Pulp Press during the English Revolution*. London: University College Press.

Garlick, B. and Harris, M. (eds) (1998) *Victorian Journalism Exotic and Domestic*. St. Lucia, Queensland: Queensland University Press.

Garnham, N. (1990) *Capitalism and Communication*. London: Sage.

Gilmartin, K. (1996) *Print Politics: The Press and Radical Opposition in Early Nineteenth Century England*. Cambridge: Cambridge University Press.

Golding, P. (1999) 'The political and the popular: getting the measure of tabloidization', in *Moving On: Changing Cultures, Changing Times*. Proceedings of the AMCCS Conference, Sheffield: Hallam University.

Goodbody, J. (1985) 'The *Star*: its role in the rise of popular newspapers 1888–1914', *Journal of Newspaper and Periodical History*, 1 (2): 20–9.

Gough, H. (1988) *The Newspaper Press in the French Revolution*. London: Routledge.

Graham, W. (1926) *The Beginnings of English Literary Periodicals*. Oxford: Oxford University Press.

Graham, W. (1930) *English Literary Periodicals*. New York: Thomas Nelson.

Greenwood, F. (1890) 'The press and government', *Nineteenth Century*, July: 109–118.

Greenwood, F. (1897) 'The newspaper press: half a century's survey', *Blackwood's*, May.

Grieve, M. (1964) *Millions Made My Story*. London: Gollancz.

Gripsrud, J. (1992) 'The aesthetics and politics of melodrama', in P. Dahlgren and C. Sparks (eds), *Journalism and Popular Culture*. London: Sage.

Habermas, J. (1992) *The Structural Transformation of the Public Sphere*. Cambridge: Polity Press.

Halasz, A. (1997) *The Marketplace of Print*. Cambridge: Cambridge University Press.

Hampton, M. (2001) '"Understanding media": theories of the press in Britain, 1850–1914', in *Media, Culture and Society*. 23 (2): 213–231.

Hanover, P.M. (1965) *History of the London Gazette 1665–1695*. London: HMSO.

Hargreaves, I. and Thomas, J. (2003) *New News, Old News*. London: I.T.C. Viewer Relations Unit.

Harris, M. and Lee, A.J. (1978) *The Press in English Society from the Seventeenth to the Nineteenth Century*. London and Toronto Associated University Presses.

Harris, B. (1993) *A Patriot Press: National Politics and the London Press in the 1740s*. Oxford: Oxford University Press.

Harris, B. (1996) *Politics and the Rise of the Press: Britain and France 1620–1800*. London: Routledge.

Harris, M. (1987) *London Newspapers in the Age of Walpole*. London and Toronto: Associated University Presses.

Harris, M. (1978) *The Structure, Ownership and Control of the Press, 1620–1780*, J. Curran and P. Wingate (eds) Oxford: Oxford University Press.

Harrison, S. (1974) *Poor Men's Guardians*. London: Lawrence and Wishart.

Hartley, J. (1996) *Popular Reality*. London: Arnold.

Harvey, D. (1989) *The Condition of Postmodernity*. Oxford: Blackwell.

Hazlitt, W. (1823) 'The Periodical Press', *Edinburgh Review*: 349–378.

Hazlitt, W. (1910) *Table-Talk: Essays on Men and Manners*. London: Bell, Bohn's.

Heath, R.B. (1975) *The Popular Press*. London: Thomas Nelson and Sons.

Hellmuth, E. (1990) *The Transformation of Political Culture: England and Germany in the Late Eighteenth Century*. Oxford: Oxford University Press.

Herd, H. (1952) *The March of Journalism: The Story of the British Press from 1622 to the Present Day*. London: George Allen and Unwin Ltd.

History of The Times (1935) Vol. 1. *The Thunderer in the Making: 1785–1841*. London: Times Publishing Company.

History of The Times (1939) Vol. 2. *The Tradition Established: 1841–1884*. London: Times Publishing Company.

Holland, P. (1998) 'The politics of the smile: 'soft news' and the sexualisation of the popular press', in C. Carter, G. Branston and S. Allen (eds), *News, Gender and Power*. London: Routledge.

Holland, P. (2001) 'Authority and authenticity: redefining television current affairs', in M. Bromley (ed.), *No News is Bad News*. Cambridge: Pearson.

Hollis, P. (1970) *The Pauper Press*. Oxford: Oxford University Press.

Holstun, J. (1992) *Pamphlet Wars: Prose in the English Revolution*. London: Frank Cass.

Houghton, W.E., Houghton, E.R. and Slingerland, J.H. (eds) (1987) *Wellesley Index to Victorian Periodicals* Vol. IV. Toronto: University of Toronto Press.

Hunter, J. (1977) 'The lady's magazine and the study of Englishwomen in the eighteenth century', in D.H. Bond and R. McLeod (eds), *Newsletters to Newspapers: Eighteenth Century Journalism*. West Virginia University.

Inglis, H.A. (1949) *The Press; A Neglected Factor in the Economic History of the Twentieth Century*. Oxford: Oxford University Press.

Jackson, K. (2000) 'George Newnes and the "loyal tit-bitites' – editorial identity and textual interaction in Tit-Bits', in L. Brake, B. Bell and D. Finkelstein (eds), *Nineteenth Century Media and the Construction of Identities*. Basingstoke: Palgrave.

Jackson, K. (2001) *George Newnes and the New Journalism in Britain 1880–1910*. Aldershot: Ashgate.

Jackson, P., Stevenson, N. and Brooks, K. (2001) *Making Sense of Men's Magazines*. Cambridge: Polity.

Jameson, F. (1985) 'Postmodernism and consumer society', in H. Foster (ed.), *Postmodern Culture*. London: Pluto Press.

Jonson, B. (1816) 'The Staple of News', in F. Cunningham. (ed.) *The Works of Ben Jonson*. Vol. 2. London: John Camden Hotton.

Jones, A. (1996) *Powers of the Press: Newspapers, Power and the Public in Nineteenth Century England*. Aldershot. Ashgate: Scolar Press.

Jones, V.P. (1988) *Saint or Sensationalist*. East Wittering, West Sussex: Gooday.

Jonson, B. (1816) *Collected works*, (ed.) F. Cunningham. London, Hotton.

Keeble, R. (1997) *Secret State, Silent Press*. Luton: University of Luton Press.

Kittler, F. (1997) 'Media wars: trenches, lightning, stars', in J. Johnson (ed.), *Literature Media Information Systems*. Amsterdam: G and B Arts International.

Langer, J. (1998) *Tabloid Television: Popular Journalism and the 'Other News'*. London: Routledge.

Leavis, Q.D. (1932) *Fiction and The Reading Public*. London: Chatto and Windus.

Lee, A. (1978) 'The structure, ownership and control of the press 1855–1914', in G. Boyce, J. Curran and P. Wingate (eds), *Newspaper History from the Seventeenth Century to the Present Day*. London: Constable.

Lee, A.J. (1976) *The Origins of the Popular Press 1855–1914*. London: Croom Helm.

Leveller petition of 1648 Thomason tract 669, f. 13, (75) listed as 74.

Levy, F.J. (1982) 'How information spread among the gentry, 1550–1640', *Journal of British Studies*, 21: 11–34.

Levy, F. (1999) 'The decorum of news', in J. Raymond (ed.), *News, Newspapers and Society in Early Modern Britain*. London: Frank Cass.

Littlejohn, R. (1994) 'Sun-set … at Wapping', *British Journalism Review*, 5 (1): 9–11.

Livingstone, S. and Lunt, P. (1994) *Talk on Television*. London: Routledge.

Love, H. (1993) *Scribal Publication in Seventeenth-Century England*. Oxford: Clarendon Press.

Lubasz, H.M. (1958) 'Public opinion comes of age: reform of the Libel Law in the eighteenth century', *History Today*, vii: 453–61.

MacDonald, M. (2000) 'Rethinking personalization in current affairs journalism', in C. Sparks and J. Tulloch (eds), *Tabloid Tales*. Oxford: Rowman and Littlefield.

MacGregor, S. (2002) *Woman of Today*. London: Headline.

MacManus, H.R. (1994) *Market Driven Journalism: Let the Citizen Beware*. London: Sage.

Martineau, H. (1859) 'Female Industry' in, *Edinburgh Review*, 109: 293–336.

Matheson, D. (2000) 'The birth of news discourse: changes in news language in British newspapers, 1880–1930', *Media, Culture and Society*, 22 (5): 557–573.

McCalman, I. (1988) *Radical Underworld: Prophets, Revolutionaries, and Pornographers in London*, 1795–1840. Cambridge: Cambridge University Press.

McCracken, E. (1993) *Decoding Women's Magazines: From Mademoiselle to Ms*. Basingstoke: Macmillan.

McDowell, P. (1998) *The Women of Grub Street*. Oxford: Oxford University Press.

McLuhan, M. (1995) *Understanding Media.* London: Routledge.

McNair, B. (1998) *The Sociology of Journalism.* London: Arnold.

Mendle, M. (2001) 'News and the pamphlet culture of mid-seventeenth century England', in B. Dooley and S. Baron (eds), *The Politics of Information in Early Modern Europe.* London: Routledge.

Milic, L. (1977) 'Tone in Steele's *Tatler'*, in D.H. Bond and R. McLeod (eds), *Newsletters to Newspapers: Eighteenth Century Journalism.* West Virginia University.

Miller, D.L. O'Dair, S. and Weber, H. (eds) (1994) *The Production of English Renaissance Culture.* Ithaca, NY: Cornell University Press.

Milton, J. (1979) *Collected Prose.* (ed.), C.A. Patrides. Harmondsworth: Penguin.

Mountjoy, P.R. (1978) 'The Working Class Press and Working Class Conservatism', in G. Boyce, J. Curran and P. Wingate (eds), *Newspaper History from the Seventeenth Century to the Present Day.* London: Constable.

Murdock, G. and Golding, P. (1978) 'The structure, ownership and control of the press 1914–76', in G. Boyce, J. Curran and P. Wingate (eds), *Newspaper History from the Seventeenth Century to the Present Day.* London: Constable.

Negrine, R. (1994) *Politics and the Mass Media in Britain.* London: Routledge.

Neubauer, H.-J. (1999) *The Rumour: A Cultural History.* London: Free Association Books.

Nevitt, M. (1999) 'Women in the business of revolutionary news: Elizabeth Alkin, "Parliament Joan," and the Commonwealth Newsbook', in J. Raymond (ed.), *News, Newspapers and Society in Early Modern Britain.* London: Frank Cass.

O'Connor, T.P. (1889) 'The New Journalism', *New Review*, I October: 423–34.

O'Malley, T. (2001) 'The decline of public service broadcasting in the U.K. 1979–2000', in M. Bromley (ed.), *No News is Bad News.* Harlow: Pearson.

O'Malley, T. (1994) *Closedown: The BBC and Government Broadcasting Policy 1979–1992.* London: Pluto.

Ong, W. (1982) *Orality and Literacy: The Technologizing of the Word.* London: Methuen.

Park, R.E. (1940) 'News as a form of knowledge', *American Journal of Sociology*, 45: 675–7.

Perkin, H. (1981) *The Structured Crowd.* Brighton: Harvester Press.

Pincus, S. (1995) 'Coffee politicians does create: coffeehouses and Restoration political culture', *Journal of Modern History*, 67: 822–7.

Postman, N. (1986) *Amusing Ourselves to Death: Public Discourse in the Age of Showbusiness.* London: Methuen.

Raboy, M. and Dagenais, B. (eds) (1992) *Media, Crisis and Democracy.* London: Sage.

Raymond, J. (1996) *The Invention of the Newspaper: English Newsbooks, 1641–1649.* Oxford: Oxford University Press.

Raymond, J. (ed.) (1999a) *News, Newspapers and Society in Early Modern Britain.* London: Frank Cass.

Raymond, J. (1999b) 'The newspaper, public opinion, and the public sphere in the seventeenth century', in J. Raymond (ed.), *News, Newspapers and Society in Early Modern Britain.* London: Frank Cass.

Reed, D. (1997) *The Popular Magazine in Britain and the United States 1880–1960.* London: The British Library.

Reeve, H. (1855) 'The newspaper press', *Edinburgh Review*. cii, October, 470–98.

Rhea R.R. (1961) '"The liberty of the press" as an Issue in English politics 1792–1793', *The Historian*. xxiv, i: 26–43.

Riley, S.G. (1993) *Consumer Magazines of the British Isles.* Westport, CT: Greenwood.

Robson, J.M. (1995) *Marriage or Celibacy? The Daily Telegraph on a Victorian Dilemma.* Toronto: University of Toronto Press.

Rooney, D. (2000) 'Thirty years of competition in the British tabloid press: The *Mirror* and the *Sun*', in C. Sparks and J. Tulloch (eds), *Tabloid Tales.* Oxford: Rowman and Littlefield.

Ross, A. (ed.) (1982) *Selections from the Tatler and the Spectator.* Harmondsworth: Penguin.

Rowbothom, S. (1996) *Hidden from History: 300 Years of Women's Oppression and the Fight Against It.* London: Pluto.

Sanders, K. (2002) *Journalism Ethics.* London: Sage.

Salmon, R. (2000) '"A simulacrum of power": intimacy and abstraction in the rhetoric of the New Journalism', in L. Brake, B. Bell and D. Finkelstein (eds), *Nineteenth Century Media and the Construction of Identities.* Basingstoke: Palgrave.

Scannell, P. and Cardiff, D. (1991) *A Social History of Broadcasting 1922–1939: Serving the Nation.* Vol. 1. Oxford: Blackwell.

Schlesinger, P. (1992) *Putting Reality Together.* London: Routledge.

Schwoerer, L.G. (1992) 'Liberty of the press and public opinion: 1660–1695' in J.R. Jones (ed.), *Liberty Secured? Britain Before and After 1688.* Stanford, CA: Stanford University Press.

Schiller, D. (1981) *Objectivity: The Public and the Rise of Commercial Journalism.* Philadelphia: University of Pennsylvania Press.

Schudson, M. (1978) *Discovering the News: A Social History of American Newspapers.* New York: Basic Books.

Sebba, A. (1994) *Battling for News.* London: Hodder and Stoughton.

Self, W. (1997) 'Chris the saviour', *Observer.* Review Section, 9 March, 9.

Seymour-Ure, C. (1991) *The British Press and Broadcasting since 1945.* Oxford: Blackwell.

Shephard, L. (1973) *The History of Street Literature.* London: David and Charles.

Shapiro, B.J. (1983) *Probability and Certainty in Seventeenth-Century England: A Study of the Relationships between Natural Science, Religion, History, Law and Literature.* Princeton, NJ: Princeton University Press.

Sharpe, K. (2000) *Reading Revolutions: The Politics of Reading in Early Modern England.* New Haven, CT: Yale University Press.

Sharpe, K. and Zwicker, S.N. (1987) *Politics of Discourse: The Literature and History of Seventeenth-Century England.* Berkeley, CA: University of California Press.

Shattock, J. (1989) *Politics and Reviewer: The Edinburgh and The Quarterly.* Leicester: Leicester University Press.

Shattock, J. (2000) 'Work for women: Margaret Oliphant's journalism', in L. Brake, B. Bell and D. Finkelstein (eds), *Nineteenth Century Media and the Construction of Identities.* Basingstoke: Palgrave.

Shattock, J. and Wolff, M. (1982) *The Victorian Periodical Press: Samplings and Soundings.* Leicester: Leicester University Press.

Sherman, S. (1996) *Telling Time: Clocks, Diaries and English Diurnal Form.* Chicago: University of Chicago Press.

Sherman, S. (1996) 'Eyes and ears, news and plays: the argument of Ben Jonson's staple', in B. Dooley and S. Baron (eds), *The Politics of Information in Early Modern Europe.* London: Routledge.

Shevelow, K. (1989) *Women and Print Culture.* London: Routledge.

Shibutani, T. (1966) *Improvised News: A Sociological Study of Rumour*. Indianapolis: Bobbs-Merril.

Siebert, F.S. (1965) *Freedom of the Press in England 1476–1776: The Rise and Fall of Government Control*. Urbana, IL: Urbana University Press.

Skerpan, E. (1992) *The Rhetoric of Politics in the English Revolution 1642–1660*. Columbia: University of Missouri Press.

Smith, A. (1973) *The Shadow in the Cave*. London: Allen and Unwin.

Smith, A. (1975) *Paper Voices*. London: Chatto and Windus.

Smith, A. (1976) *The British Press Since the War*. London: David and Charles.

Smith, A. (1978) 'The long road to objectivity and back again: the kinds of truth we get in journalism', in G. Boyce, J. Curran and P. Wingate (eds), *Newspaper History from the Seventeenth Century to the Present Day*. London: Constable.

Smith, A. (1979) *The Newspaper: An International History*. London: Thames and Hudson.

Snoddy, R. (1992) *The Good, the Bad and the Unacceptable*. London: Faber and Faber.

Snow, J. (1997) 'Is TV news telling the whole story?', *The Guardian*, Media Supplement, 27 January, 3.

Sommerville, J. (1996) *The News Revolution*. Oxford: Oxford University Press.

Sparks, C. (1992) 'Popular journalism: theories and practice', in P. Dahlgren and C. Sparks (eds), *Journalism and Popular Culture*. London: Sage.

Sparks, C. (2000) 'Introduction: the panic over tabloid news', in C. Sparks and J. Tulloch (eds), *Tabloid Tales*. Oxford: Rowman and Littlefield.

Sparks, C. and Tulloch, J. (eds) (2000) *Tabloid Tales*. Oxford: Rowman and Littlefield.

Stephenson, H. and Bromley, M. (1998) *Sex, Lies and Democracy*. Harlow: Longman.

Sutherland, J. (1986) *The Restoration Newspaper*. Cambridge: Cambridge University Press.

Stam, R. (1983) 'Television news and its spectator', in E.A. Kaplan (ed.), *Regarding Television*. Los Angeles: University Publications of America.

Stead, W.T. (1886) 'Government by journalism', *The Contemporary Review*, XLIX, May: 653–74.

Targett, S. (1991) 'Sir Robert Walpole's Newspapers 1722–42: Propaganda and Politics in the Age of Whig Supremacy'. PhD thesis: Cambridge University.

Terdiman, R. (1985) *Discourse/Counter-Discourse: The Theory and Practice of Symbolic Resistance in Nineteenth Century France*. Ithaca, NY: Cornell University Press.

Thomas, P.D.G. (1959) 'The beginning of parliamentary reporting in newspapers, 1768–1774', *English Historical Review*, LXXIV: 623–31.

Thomas, P.D.G. (1960) 'John Wilkes and the freedom of the press (1771)', *Bulletin of the Historical Institute of Historical Research*, 3: 86–98.

Thompson, D. (1935) 'A hundred years of the higher journalism', *Scrutiny*, 4 June, 25–34.

Thompson, E.P. (1979) *The Making of the English Working Class*. London: Harmondsworth Penguin.

Traill, H.D. (1884) 'Newspapers and English: a dialogue', *Macmillan's Magazine*, October.

Tuchman, G. (1973) 'Making news by doing work: routinizing the unexpected', *American Journal of Sociology*, 79: 110–131.

Tuchman, G. (1978) *Making News: A Study in the Construction of Reality*. New York: Free Press.

Tulloch, J. (2000) 'The eternal recurrence of new journalism', in C. Sparks and J. Tulloch (eds), *Tabloid Tales*. Oxford: Rowman and Littlefield.

Tunstall, J. (1996) *Newspaper Power*. Oxford: Clarendon.

Van Arsdel, R.T. (1994) *Victorian Periodicals and Victorian Society*. Aldershot: Scolar Press.

Van Zoonen, L. (1994) *Feminist Media Studies*. London: Sage.

Van Zoonen, L. (1998) 'One of the girls', in C. Carter, G. Branston and S. Allen (eds), *News, Gender and Power*. London: Routledge.

Vincent, D. (1993) *Literacy and Popular Culture*. Cambridge: Cambridge University Press.

Voss, P.J. (2001) *Elizabethan News Pamphlets*. Pittsburgh: Dusquesne University Press.

Watt, T. (1991) *Cheap Print and Popular Piety 1550–1640*. Cambridge: Cambridge University Press.

Whale, J. (1969) *The Half-Shut Eye*. Basingstoke: Macmillan.

Wheale, N. (1999) *Writing and Society: Literacy, Print and Politics in Britain 1590–1660*. London: Routledge.

White, C.L. (1970) *Women's Magazines 1693–1968*. London: Michael Joseph.

Wiener, J. (ed.) (1988) *Papers for the Millions: The New Journalism in Britain 1850–1914*, Westport, CT: Greenwood Press.

Wiles, R.M. (1965) *Freshest Advices*. Columbus: Ohio State University Press.

Williams, F. (1957) *Dangerous Estate*. Harlow: Longman Green.

Williams, K. (1998) *Get Me a Murder a Day*. London: Arnold.

Williams, R. (1961) *The Long Revolution*. Harmondsworth: Penguin.

Williams, R. (1978) 'The press and popular culture: an historical perspective', in G. Boyce, J. Curran and P. Wingate (eds), *Newspaper History from the Seventeenth Century to the Present Day*. London: Constable.

Williams, R. (1990) *Television, Technology and Cultural Form*. London: Routledge.

Winship, J. (1978) 'A woman's world: woman – an ideology of feminism', in CCCS Women's Group (eds), *Women Take Issue*. London: Hutchinson.

Winton, C. (1977) 'Richard Steele, journalist and journalism', in D.H. Bond and R. McLeod (eds), *Newsletters to Newspapers: Eighteenth Century Journalism*. West Virginia University.

Wiseman, S.J. (1999) 'Pamphlet plays in the Civil War news market: genre, politics, and "context"', in J. Raymond (ed.), *News, Newspapers and Society in Early Modern Britain*. London: Frank Cass.

Woolf, D. (2001) 'News, History and the Construction of the Present in Early Modern England' in B. Dooley and S. Baron (eds), *The Politics of Information in Early Modern Europe*. London: Routledge.

Worcester, R.M. (1998) 'Demographics and values: what the British public reads and what it thinks about its newspapers' in M. Bromley and H. Stephenson (eds), *Sex, Lies and Democracy*. Harlow: Addison, Wesley, Longman.

Zagorin, P. (1969) *Court and Country: The Beginning of the English Revolution*. London: Routledge.

Index